Assessing Risk in Sex Offenders

Assessing Risk in Sex Offenders

A Practitioner's Guide

Leam A. Craig

Forensic Psychology Practice Ltd, The Willows Clinic, Birmingham, and Centre for Forensic and Family Psychology, University of Birmingham, Edgbaston, Birmingham, UK

Kevin D. Browne

School of Psychology, University of Liverpool, Liverpool, UK, and World Health Organisation, Denmark

and

Anthony R. Beech

Centre for Forensic and Family Psychology, University of Birmingham, Edgbaston, Birmingham, UK

John Wiley & Sons, Ltd

Other Wiley Editorial Offices

John Wiley & Sons Inc., 111 River Street, Hoboken, NJ 07030, USA

Jossey-Bass, 989 Market Street, San Francisco, CA 94103-1741, USA

Wiley-VCH Verlag GmbH, Boschstr. 12, D-69469 Weinheim, Germany

John Wiley & Sons Australia Ltd, 42 McDougall Street, Milton, Queensland 4064, Australia

John Wiley & Sons (Asia) Pte Ltd, 2 Clementi Loop #02-01, Jin Xing Distripark, Singapore 129809

John Wiley & Sons Canada Ltd, 6045 Freemont Blvd, Mississauga, ONT, L5R 4J3, Canada

Wiley also publishes its books in a variety of electronic formats. Some content that appears in print may not be
available in electronic books.

Library of Congress Cataloging-in-Publication Data

Craig, Leam.
  Assessing risk in sex offenders : a practitioner's guide / Leam Craig, Kevin Browne, and
Anthony Beech.
     p. cm.
  Includes bibliographical references and index.
  ISBN 978-0-470-01897-2 (cloth) – ISBN 978-0-470-01898-9 (pbk.) 1. Sex offenders–United
States.   2. Criminal behavior, Prediction of–United States.   3. Risk assessment–United
States.   4. Recidivism–United States–Prevention.   5. Evidence, Expert–United States.
I. Browne, Kevin. II. Beech, Anthony R. III. Title.
  HV6592.C73 2008
  364.4'1–dc22   2008001320

British Library Cataloguing in Publication Data

A catalogue record for this book is available from the British Library

ISBN 978-0-470-01897-2 (hbk) 978-0-470-01898-9 (pbk)

Typeset in 11/13 Times by Thomson Digital, Noida, India

LAC: *For my parents, to whom I owe everything, and whose love and support have never waivered.*

KDB: *For the protection of my family, children and vulnerable people everywhere.*

ARB: *For Dawn and Jake, with all my love, who have to endure many hours without me to enable projects like this to see the light of day.*

Contents

PART V   POLICY AND PRACTICE

About the Authors

Leam A. Craig, PhD, MSc, BA (Hons), CSci, AFBPsS, EuroPsy, C.Psychol (Forensic) is a Consultant Forensic Psychologist and Partner of Forensic Psychology Practice Ltd. He is the holder of the European Certificate in Psychology. His current practice includes direct services to forensic NHS Adult Mental Health Trusts and consultancy to Prison and Probation Services. He acts as an expert witness to civil and criminal courts in the assessment of sexual and violent offenders. He coordinates community-based treatment programmes for sexual offenders with learning disabilities in NHS and probation settings and acts as a consultant to private forensic learning disability units. He has published numerous empirical articles and chapters in a range of research and professional journals. He has recently completed a book with Professors Anthony Beech and Kevin Browne entitled *Assessment and Treatment of Sex Offenders: A Handbook,* and is currently working on *Assessment and Treatment of Sexual Offenders with Intellectual Disabilities: A Handbook*, Wiley-Blackwell, with Professors Kevin Browne and William Lindsay. He is an honorary member of the teaching and research staff at the Centre for Forensic and Family Psychology, University of Birmingham, UK.

Kevin D. Browne, PhD, MSc, MEd, BSc, C.Biol, C.Psychol (Forensic) is both a Chartered Biologist and Chartered Psychologist employed by the University of Liverpool as Chair of Forensic and Child Psychology and Head of the World Health Organisation Collaboration Centre on Child Care and Protection in the UK. He has been researching family violence and child maltreatment for 30 years and has published extensively on the prevention of violence to children, acting as Co-Editor (with Prof. M. A. Lynch) of '*Child Abuse Review*' from 1992 to 1999. After 12 years as an Executive Councillor of the International Society for the Prevention of Child Abuse and Neglect (ISPCAN), he is now consultant to the European Commission, UNICEF, World Bank and the WHO. He has worked and presented in over 50 countries worldwide and is currently leading an EU/WHO investigation on the extent of early institutional care and its detrimental effects on child development. This involves training and capacity building to deinstitutionalise and transform children's services across Europe. Recently, he was a consultant and contributing author to the *UN Secretary General's World Report on Violence to Children* (published in October 2006). His other co-authored Wiley books include, *Preventing Family Violence(1997),* **Early Prediction and Prevention of Child Abuse: A Handbook** *(2002),* and most recently *Community Health Approach to the Assessment of Infants and their Parents (2006).*

Anthony R. Beech, D.Phil, BSc, FBPsS, C.Psychol (Forensic) is Professor of Criminological Psychology and Director of Centre for Forensic and Family Psychology, University of Birmingham. He has published widely on the assessment and treatment of sexual offenders and is the principal researcher on the Sex Offender Treatment Evaluation Project (STEP) team that has examined the effectiveness of treatment for sex offenders provided in UK prisons and probation services. His work is regarded as having a major influence on assessment and treatment in the UK. He has recently completed a book with Professor Tony Ward and Dr Devon Polaschek entitled *Theories of Sexual Offending,* J. Wiley & Sons, and with Dr Leam Craig and Professor Kevin Browne, *Assessment and Treatment of Sex Offenders: A Handbook,* Wiley-Blackwell.

Preface: The Extent of Sexual Violence and the Risk Approach

The more we can share our knowledge about the nature of sexual crimes and those who commit them, our experience with dealing with these offenders in custody and the community, our successes and our failures...the more we are likely to move towards our ultimate aim, which must be to protect the public from harm and to reduce the number of sexual crimes which can cause immense human suffering.

The Home Secretary (7 June, 1991)

Sexual assault is a worldwide phenomenon that has long lasting effects on the physical and mental health of individuals who are victimised in this way (Briere, 1992; Felitti et al., 1998). There are also complications for the sexual and reproductive health of victims following a sexual assault both in the short and long term, such as HIV infection (World Health Organisation, 2002). For the sex offender, forced or coerced sexual activities may result in sexual gratification, although it is considered more often to be an expression of power and dominance over the victim and therefore sexual assault is considered to be an act of violence (Groth, 1979). Sexual violence is directed at both men and women of all ages and may take many forms. It is not limited to acts of non-consensual sexual intercourse (rape or attempted rape of the vulva) but may involve penetration of other body parts, using the penis, fingers or any object. Other sexual assaults include fondling, kissing, sexual harassments, coercion, trafficking for sex, prostitution and sexual exploitation.

Sexual violence has been defined by the WHO (2002) as:

any sexual act, attempt to obtain a sexual act, unwanted sexual comments or advances, or acts to traffic women's sexuality using coercion, threats of harm or physical force, by any person regardless of relationship to the victim in any setting, including but not limited to home and work (p. 149).

Sexual violence is also evident in institutional settings with vulnerable adults or children, including those in secure environments. Sexual assault may also occur when the victim is unable to give consent, while under the influence of alcohol or drugs.

THE EXTENT OF SEXUAL OFFENCES AGAINST ADULTS

Sexual activity and behaviours that qualify as sexual offences have changed over time (see Sex Offences Act, 1956 & 2003). Therefore, it is difficult to determine whether there has been an increase or decrease in the number of sexual offences over the past 50 years. Reported rapes have doubled in the past 20 years but this may be related to changes in how the police deal with rape. Victims are now treated with a more caring manner by police officers, who are usually specially trained in how to interview sensitively and gain information from victims of rape and child sexual abuse. The environment for victim disclosure has also improved with the establishment of sexual assault referral centres, SARC (Cybulska, 2007; Matravers, 2003). Nevertheless, the majority of sexual offences still go unreported, which can be determined by the prevalence of sexual offending (as reported in the British Crime Survey) in comparison to reports to the police within the same time period. The British Crime Survey of households (2005/06) shows that approximately 3% of women and 1% of men self report experiencing a sexual assault in the previous 12 months, but only 62,081 were reported to the police in 2005/6, which represents approximately 1 in 10 victimisations.

The latest statistics, available from Jansson, Povey and Kaiza (2007), show that the police recorded 43,755 serious sexual offences for 2006/07 (1% of all recorded crime). This included rape, sexual assault and sexual activity with children. The police also recorded 13,787 other sexual offences which involved unlawful sex activity (between consenting partners), exploitation of prostitution and soliciting (but not prostitution itself), indecent exposure and sexual grooming. For 2006/07, in total, there were 57,542 recorded sexual offences in England and Wales compared to 62,081 for 2005/06. There were 13,780 rapes reported compared to 14,449 the previous year. Ninety-two per cent of reports involved female victims and 8% male victims of rape.

However, the conviction rate for adult rape is only a fraction of the number reported to the police. One third of reported cases failed to proceed past the investigation stage due to lack of evidence or victim credibility. Another third are lost as a result of victims not wishing to proceed due to fear of the emotional consequences and not being believed in court. Furthermore, many cases of sexual assault are associated with alcohol use in the victim as well as the offender and the majority of perpetrators are known to their victims. These facts complicate successful conviction of sexual offenders, with 9% regarded as false allegations and only 14% of reported cases leading to trial (Kelly, Lovett & Regan, 2005).

Prevalence studies of sexual violence by intimate partners or ex-partners reported in different countries (WHO, 2002) indicate that between 6% and 46% of women experience attempted or actual forced sex at some time in their lives. In London, it was estimated that 23% of women had had such experiences associated with domestic violence (Morley & Mullender, 1994). Female spouses are especially reluctant to disclose violence in the family as they recognise that this is one of the reasons why social services would intervene in family life and prioritise interventions to prevent emotional and psychological harm to children in the family. This may result in the children being taken into public care with the mother accused of 'failing to protect the child(ren)'. This social service response is not helpful to women who are victims of physical and sexual violence from their intimate partners. These women are not in a position to protect their children without help. Therefore, women in this position sometimes report the violence to the police and social services only to retract it later. An Australian study by Goddard and Hiller (1993) found that child sexual abuse was evident in 40% of families with intimate partner violence. Truesdell (1986) also claimed that domestic violence was more common than expected in North American incestuous families with nearly three quarters (73%) of mothers from incestuous families experiencing at least one incident of domestic violence, a third of who were threatened or injured with a knife or a gun.

THE EXTENT OF SEXUAL OFFENCES AGAINST CHILDREN

The World Health Organisation define child sexual abuse as 'the involvement of a child in sexual activity, by either adults or other children who are in a position of responsibility, trust of power over that child, that he or she does not fully comprehend, is unable to give informed consent to, or for which the child is not developmentally prepared, or else that violates the laws or social taboos of society' (Butchart et al., 2006: 10). This has been further extended by the Department of Education and Skills for England (HM Government, 2006) in their latest guide for inter-agency working to safeguard children as follows:

> *Sexual abuse involves forcing or enticing a child or young person to take part in sexual activities, including prostitution, whether or not the child is aware of what is happening. The activities may involve physical contact, including penetrative (e.g. rape, buggery or oral sex) or non penetrative acts. They may include non-contact activities such as involving children in looking at, or in the production of, sexual online images, watching sexual activities, or encouraging children to behave in sexually inappropriate ways. (p. 38)*

This broader definition incorporates internet offences and the coercion of children into sexual activities through 'grooming' which were introduced in the latest Sex Offences Act (2003).

According to statistical returns from English Local Government Authorities over the past five years (Department for Children, Schools and Families, 2007), there have been at least 100 less sexually abused children each year subject to a 'child protection plan'. Indeed, the percentage of children recognised as victims of sexual abuse, and placed on the child protection register, has dropped from 10% to 7% of all registrations for child maltreatment between 1 April 2002 and 31 March 2007. A similar decline has been observed for cases of sexual abuse that are identified to co-occur with other forms of maltreatment (that is, physical abuse, emotional abuse and neglect). These 'mixed cases', some of which include sexual abuse have decreased from 15% to 10% of all registrations over the same time period. Likewise, cases of physical abuse have reduced from 19% to 15% of all registrations. However, there has been a marked increase from 2002 to 2007 in the number of children identified as neglected (39% to 44% of all registered cases) and emotionally abused (18% to 23% of all registered cases).

Therefore, the number of children in England under 18 years who were registered under the category of sexual abuse has decreased from 3,000 a year to 2,500 a year while the overall number of registrations have increased from 30,200 (2002/3) to 33,400 (2006/7). There were 27,900 children subject to a child protection plan on 31 March 2007, representing 25 children per 10,000, 1 in 8 of these children (13%) had previously been on the Child Protection Register. Approximately 2 children in every 10,000 were identified as victims of sexual abuse. Research has shown that about 60% of sexual abuse registrations are girls and 40% were boys.

Over the past 15 years, similar declines in the incidence of child physical and sexual abuse has been observed in Canada (Trocme et al., 2005) and the USA (Finkelhor & Jones, 2006), together with increases in the rate of neglect. A greater professional commitment to safeguarding children and protecting them from all forms of child maltreatment in addition to violent and sexual offender programmes have been identified as partly responsible for the decline in physical and sexual abuse (Jones et al., 2001).

However, the British prevalence rates retrospectively reported by adults and teenagers reflecting on their childhood show little change over time. In the early 1980s, child sexual abuse in a British community sample was reported to be 12% of females and 8% of males (Baker & Duncan, 1985). A more recent NSPCC study (Cawson et al., 2000) of English young adults (18–24 years) found that 16% had reported sexual abuse (11% contact sexual abuse). However, the most recent US national survey measuring the prevalence of sexual victimisation of children at 8% did confirm a decline in comparison to previous surveys (Finkelhor et al., 2005). Fifteen years earlier, the US prevalence rate child sexual abuse was reported to be 27% of women and 16% of men (Finkelhor et al., 1990). An international comparison of 21 countries, around the same time, showed that the prevalence of child sexual abuse ranged from 7% to 36% for women and 3% to 29% for men (Finkelhor et al., 1994). According to these studies, girls were between 1.5 and

3 times more likely to be sexually abused than boys. Up to 56% of the girls and 25% of the boys were sexually abused within the family environment perpetrated by blood relatives, step parents, foster carers and adoptive parents.

The differences in prevalence rates can partly be explained by the variations in methods and samples used but all show that incidence figures only represent those few cases which are known to the authorities. Recent evidence from victim surveys and prevalence studies consistently indicates that the number of people reporting abuse in childhood at approximately ten times the incidence rate (Creighton, 2002). This demonstrates that, like adult rape, there is a significant 'dark figure' of unreported crime involving the sexual abuse of children and that there is a great deal of work to be done on the prevention and detection of such crimes.

Indeed, the sexual abuse of children fairs no better than adult victims in relation to the number of convicted offenders. Of those cases that come to the attention of the police, only 35% to 38% of the sex offenders are charged, 5% to 9% receive a caution and for 56% to 59%, there is no further action (Prior, Glaser & Lynch, 1997; Browne & Afzal, 1998). Nevertheless, 27% of children have previously been referred to child protection units in relation to child maltreatment in general and 30% of the alleged perpetrators are previously known to the police (Browne & Hamilton, 1999). Other research associated with child protection cases has reported that a third of all allegations involve a sexual abuse perpetrator aged 17 or younger (Glasgow, Horne, Calam & Cox, 1994). These figures indicate the need for greater resources for social work, probation and police services and more effective multi-agency strategies to detect perpetrators of sex crimes and prevent sexual assaults on adults and children. The figures also indicate the limitations of the UK Sex Offender Act (1997) which compelled by law all offenders who have been cautioned or convicted of a sexual offence to register their names and addresses with the police.

CHALLENGES FOR RISK ASSESSMENT AND INTERVENTION

The usual response to sexual abuse in the family and home environment is to take the children into public care and sometimes offer shelter to the mother (the non-abusive carer in the vast majority of cases). This is to prevent 'repeat victimisation' by the same offender. Nevertheless, without victim support and therapeutic help for these women and children, the victims remain at a higher risk of 'revictimisation' by a different offender (Coid et al., 2001; Hamilton & Browne, 1998, 1999).

The conviction and imprisonment of the sex offender only occurs in a minority of cases (6% to 10%), when there is sufficient evidence to prove a sex crime 'beyond all reasonable doubt'. More often the alleged perpetrator of sexual abuse is banned from contacting or approaching the victim by order of a family court (for example, exclusion and/or occupation orders) working with the principle 'on the balance of probability'. The alleged sex offender may only then be convicted and imprisoned for breech of the order and contempt of court. However, he is at liberty to 'befriend' other women and children. Indeed, single parent families are at considerable risk (Browne & Herbert, 1997).

'Risk' has been defined as '... a compound estimate of the likelihood and severity of an undesirable outcome' (Yates & Stone, 1992). The 'risk approach' can be seen as a management strategy for the flexible and rational distribution of limited resources to best effect (Browne & Herbert, 1997: 20) Therefore, 'risk assessments' are useful in the planning and management of sex offenders both in the community and in prison and are most applicable when a sex offender returns to a community. Resources and services that are required to monitor, manage and supervise the activities of convicted sex offenders in the community can then be targeted to those most dangerous who are highly likely to commit a violent and/or sexual offence, if left to their own devices. Thus, the maximal utilisation of resources by risk management ensures the safety of children and vulnerable adults.

In North America, Western Europe and Australasia, professionals concerned with the safety and protection of women, children and other vulnerable adults were the first to develop other initiatives beyond that of separating the offender from the victim. It was realised that responding to the needs of individuals who commit sex offences is a more effective way of protecting vulnerable individuals in the community. Therefore, comprehensive risk assessment and interventions are necessary to assess who can remain in the community for treatment and supervision and who cannot because of the danger they pose to individuals and families in the community. Sexual offenders who are assessed as low risk of re-offending may be treated and managed in the community, enhancing the chances of their rehabilitation. Individuals who are at high risk of violent and/or sexual offences require interventions while they are incarcerated in secure environments, such as young offender institutions, prisons and special hospitals. This dual track approach is likely to meet with more success in safeguarding children and vulnerable adults on a long-term basis.

Without treatment, *all* offenders are more likely to re-offend. Imprisoning sex offenders in isolation with other sex offenders (for their safety), means their fantasies and cognitive distortions are rarely challenged and indeed, may be shared with others which may reinforce cognitive distortions and make the chances of re-offending higher on release. By working with offenders, the number of victims may potentially be reduced and incidence studies are beginning to indicate that this may indeed be the case. However, further work is required to determine those who respond to the interventions available and reduce their risk of recidivism, as opposed to those who do not respond to interventions and remain at high risk of re-offending.

The first section of the book begins with the background, developmental frameworks and predictive accuracy of risk assessment methodologies. The first chapter describes the range of sexual offences and the characteristics associated with particular types of sex offender subgroups. In the second chapter we go on to describe the developmental pathways and offending behaviour trajectories from childhood and adolescence into adulthood and the approaches used to analyse significant factors, conditions and events in explaining offending behaviour. In the final chapter of this section we summarise the theoretical background on the development of actuarial risk instruments and consider the factors affecting the predictive accuracy of risk assessment systems. The second section of this book is concerned with the identification and assessment of static risk factors and the relationship to sexual recidivism. In the fourth chapter we review the different types of risk factors and pay particular attention to the effect of personality, psychopathy, sexual deviance and age on the assessment of risk. Following on from this, Chapter 5 provides a comprehensive review of the predictive accuracy of a number of actuarial and structured clinically-guided risk assessment scales currently available. The third section of the book considers the assessment of dynamic risk factors associated with sexual recidivism. In Chapter 6 we discuss the assessment of stable and acute dynamic risk factors as part of a stable dynamic framework and describe how assessments of sexual and psychological deviance can improve the predictive accuracy of actuarial frameworks. Chapter 7 draws on the current concepts in risk assessment and the general criminogenic principles of 'What Works' for offenders provides an overview of current treatment provisions in prisons and the community in the U.K. for sex offenders. The fourth section of the book is concerned with structuring risk assessment and Chapter 8 integrates some of the concepts outlined in previous chapters and discusses a conceptual aetiological framework to use in risk assessment and clinical formulation. The final section of this book is concerned with policy and practice and the implementation of risk assessment systems in managing sex offenders. In Chapter 9, discussion centres on the strategies used to manage sexual offenders in the community and the legal framework supporting community supervision and management. Chapter 10 considers the application of actuarial measures and whether the inclusion of dynamic factors integrated with existing actuarial scales can improve accuracy in predicting sexual recidivism. In an effort to improve risk assessment systems a Multiaxial Risk Appraisal (MARA) model is proposed. Finally, Chapter 11 considers the different approaches to risk assessment previously discussed and describes how ideas of strengths-based approaches and positive psychology more generally can impact on the assessment of risk.

Leam Craig
Kevin Browne
Anthony Beech

Autumn, 2007

Acknowledgements

Leam Craig – I am privileged to have the intellectual companionship of a number of world renowned practitioners and researchers in the field of violent and sex offender assessment, treatment and research both in the UK and overseas. In particular, I owe a debt of gratitude to Eugene Ostapiuk and Ian Stringer for their years of friendship, tutelage and guidance in refining my clinical practice. Apologies for those I have missed out, but special thanks goes to, Roger Hutchinson, Anthony Beech, Kevin Browne, David Thornton, Todd Hogue, and Doughlas Boer for their support and intellectual companionship.

Kevin Browne – I am grateful to the patience of my colleagues, wife and children. The boys may understand my study overtime when they reach adulthood and read this book, as the content of this book carries an 18 certificate. Children are best left to play and enjoy life without worry and concern. It is the parent's role (and the responsibility of all adults) to be worried and concerned for them, and on behalf of them.

Anthony Beech – I would like to thank all of those that helped shape my thinking over the years and have particularly shaped my thinking on risk assessment. Apologies for those I have missed out, but in no particular order: David Thornton, Tony Ward, Jackie Craissati, Karl Hanson, Andrew Harris, Richard Laws, Caroline Friendship, Bobbie Print, Dawn Fisher, Don Grubin, Richard Beckett, Ray Knight, Douglas Boer, Jenny Keeling, Leigh Harkins, and Rebecca Mandeville-Norden.

The authors are grateful to Leigh Harkins who contributed heavily to Chapter 7 on treatment and sexual recidivism, and to Ian Stringer and Todd Hogue for their contribution in constructing the Multiaxial Risk Appraisal (MARA) assessment framework discussed in Chapter 10. Thanks are also due to the support offered by Shihning Chou in the preparation of Chapters 1 and 9.

PART I

Background, developmental frameworks and predictive accuracy

personal computers and provide reinforcement for sexual fantasies involving children. Between 1988 and 2001, 3,022 individuals were cautioned or charged with downloading illegal child pornography from the internet (Carr, 2003).

Recent research has suggested three different types of internet offenders (Carnes, Delmonico & Griffin, 2001; Cooper, 2002):

1. The '*Discoverers*' with no evidence of a prior interest in sexual activities with children and adolescents but who now find these images interesting and stimulating.
2. The '*Pre-disposed*' who have previously fantasised about sex with children and/or adolescents and now use the images available on the internet to trigger and fuel these sexual fantasies.
3. The '*Sexually Compulsive*' who use images on the internet as another way of acting out their sexual fantasies and behaviours and who may heighten their arousal and lower their inhibitions by looking at these images prior to committing a sexual assault.

For all three groups, sexually violent material and sexual images of children and adolescents on the internet serve to 'normalise' a deviant sexual interest and reinforce the distorted view that sexual fantasies about children and young people, and non-consensual sex, are commonplace and not problematic. Furthermore, internet offenders create a market for the production and distribution of child sexual abuse and therefore are indirectly responsible for sexual offences against children and young people.

Investigating the possession of internet child pornography now accounts for one in ten child sexual abuse cases known to the police, but only 7% of these 'non-contact' offenders are also known to directly sexually assault others (Gallagher et al., 2006). It appears that only a small minority of internet offenders use images of children and adolescents in a sexually compulsive way and that even those predisposed to sexual fantasies about children and young people may not act out such fantasies, unless they become compulsive. Indeed, Foss (2003) showed that internet offenders have significantly less cognitive distortions and more emphatic concern for children (but similar low self esteem) compared to child molesters, which may partly explain why they are less likely to act out their deviant thoughts and fantasies.

Research into the preparatory effect of child pornography on paedophiles seeking to physically abuse children is contradictory, and there is no established research that indicates that child pornography either causes offending or even that it maintains molestation patterns (Howitt, 1997). However, paedophilic fantasy has been positively linked to offending behaviour and is unlikely to be effectively controlled by the exclusion of pornography.

Not surprisingly, the majority (86%) of child molesters have admitted under polygraph examination that they use pornography, in a compulsive way, as a precursor to offending. Earlier studies have found a smaller number of child molesters (21% and 33%) who use illicit pornography (Elliott, Browne & Kilcoyne, 1995; Marshall, 1998; respectively) but report how the men used thoughts and fantasies about their previous victims and sex assaults prior to committing another sex offence. Some men had their own 'scrap books' of cut out legal images of children taken from newspapers, magazines and shopping catalogues.

Seto, Cantor and Blanchard (2006) investigated whether being charged with a child pornography offence is a valid diagnostic indicator of paedophilia, as represented by an index of phallometrically assessed sexual arousal to children. In a sample of 685 male patients they found that child pornography offenders showed greater sexual arousal to children than to adults and differed from groups of sex offenders against children, sex offenders against adults and general sexology patients. Malamuth (2001) examined the effect of pornography on sexual aggression and found that pornography consumption is related to sexually coercive behaviour only among those who exhibit traits and attitudes (for example, hostile masculinity) that are well established correlates of sexual aggression. While the use of pornography itself has not been identified as a risk factor (Hanson & Bussière, 1998; Hanson & Morton-Bourgon, 2004), it is a potentially salient variable for those who are already at risk.

Indeed, Seto, Alexandra and Barbaree (2001) argue that the evidence for a causal link between pornography use and sexual offending remains equivocal. They suggest that individuals who are already predisposed to sexually offend are the most likely to show an effect of pornography exposure and are the most likely to show the strongest effects. Men who are not predisposed are unlikely to show an effect; if there actually is an effect, it is likely to be transient because these men would not normally seek violent pornography. More recently, Seto and Eke (2005) argue that the likelihood that child pornography offenders will later commit a contact sexual offence is unknown. In their study they examined 201 adult male child pornography offenders using police databases and examined their charges or convictions after the index child pornography offence(s). They found that 56% of the sample had a prior criminal record, 24% had prior contact sexual offences, and 15% had prior child pornography offences. One-third was concurrently charged with other crimes at the time they were charged for child pornography offences. The average time at risk was 2.5 years during which 17% committed other offences and 4% committed a new contact sexual offence. It was found that child pornography offenders with prior criminal records were significantly more likely to offend again in any way compared to those with no criminal histories.

RAPISTS

In line with the Sex Offences Act 2003 (see Chapter 9), rape is defined as an assault upon an individual with the intent to commit penetrative sexual acts without the victim's permission (Fisher & Beech, 2004). The British Crime Survey (1998; 2000), using a narrower definition of 'forced sexual intercourse (vaginal or anal penetration)', showed that one in twenty adult women, over the age of sexual consent of 16 years or more, claimed that they had been raped but only a minority (20% of rape victims) had reported it to the police. Twice as many (1 in 10) adult women claimed that they had suffered some form of sexual victimisation (Myhill & Allen, 2002).

Sexual assaults by strangers are those most often reported to the police and represent 36% of all reported rapes. This gives a distorted picture of the prevalence of rape by someone known to the victim. Date rape, acquaintance and marital rape are much less likely to be reported to the police, but according to prevalence studies, such as the British Crime Survey, appear to be more common (45% of rapes as opposed to 8% by strangers). In a recent review of marital rape, Martin, Taft and Resick (2007) estimated that 10% to 14% of married women have experienced forced sex by their intimate partner and as many as 40% to 50% of battered women are raped within their physically abusive relationship. In an earlier study, Russell (1991) interviewed 930 women in San Francisco, 644 of whom were married. It was found that 4% had experienced 'marital rape' but no other physical violence, 14% had been raped and battered, and 12% had been battered but not raped.

Likewise, Finkelhor and Yllo (1985) previously estimated that 1 in 10 women in Boston had experienced forced sex by their intimate partner. In 82% of the cases, this occurred after they had separated. They categorised 'marital rape' into three types, based on Groth's (1977, 1979) previous work:

- In 10% of the cases, the intimate partner was forced to engage in bizarre and perverse sexual activities without their consent (e.g. bondage). Such activities had an obsessive element and were likened to Groth's *'sadistic rapists'*.
- In 40% of the cases, violence was used only to obtain sex from the spouse and rarely occurred at other times. This control and authority over intimate partners was associated with Groth's *'power rapists'*.
- In 50% of cases, the forced sex is a part of the general domestic violence suffered by the woman and used as another way of humiliating and degrading her. This was associated with Groth's *'anger rapists'*.

The nature of sexual violence in intimate relationships, whether married or non-married, are not limited to heterosexual couples and occur to a similar extent between homosexual and lesbian relationships (Renzetti, 1992). Furthermore, the occurrence of physical and sexual violence is not restricted to co-habiting couples or those who previously lived together. Acquaintance and date rape is just as common and surveys of college students in the USA revealed that 15% reported having unwanted sexual advances (Levine & Kanin, 1987) and 7% to 9% reported being raped during a date (Pirog-Good, 1992; Mufson & Kranz, 1993).

CHARACTERISTICS OF RAPISTS

There are few significant differences between rapists and other men who commit serious crime (Brownmillar, 1975). All are likely to have low school achievement with a history of truancy, unstable family backgrounds, poor employment records and few social competences (Hudson & Ward, 1997). Furthermore, levels of psychosis, serious brain dysfunction or learning disabilities among adult rapists (5% to 8%) are similar to the general population (Marshall, 2000).

It has been claimed (Groth, 1979) that sexual activities are merely the medium used by adult rapists to express their feelings of anger and hostility towards women and sometimes men. There is a need to assert power and to control and dominate the victim to compensate for feelings of frustration, helplessness, anxiety and sexual inadequacy. Sometimes, these feelings are associated with cognitive distortions about masculinity, male identity and status. For example, the distorted belief that when women say 'no' to sex, they really mean 'yes' is a common myth, often portrayed on film and television. Where these 'myths' are held by a group of individuals, the chances of gang rapes are much higher. Indeed, US national data on rape and sexual assault estimates that 1 of out 10 cases involve multiple perpetrators (Greenfield, 1996).

The use of alcohol in some societies is used as an excuse for rape and sexual assault. It is used to explain a lack of responsibility both for the perpetrator's actions and for the victim's alleged compliance. Indeed, Grubin and Gunn (1990) observed a high prevalence of alcohol use among rapists in the UK; 58% of men convicted for rape had been drinking prior to the offence and 37% were considered to be dependent on alcohol.

Myths are often associated with socially and culturally accepted views, held by traditional societies (World Health Organisation, 2003). For example, the myth that only females of 'low moral character' get raped and that those who engage in prostitution and drug taking bring rape upon themselves. In fact, any individual can be a victim of rape regardless of their behaviour and the majority of sexual workers and drug abusers are vulnerable individuals, some of whom were abused in their childhood (Briere, 1992; Felitti et al., 1998). Therefore, anger, power and sexuality are the basic elements of any act of sexual violence, but the underlying motivations and methods of committing sexual assault vary dramatically from offender to offender, based on their beliefs and values.

PROFILES OF RAPISTS

As identified by Ainsworth (2000, 2002), the Federal Bureau of Investigation (FBI) have attempted a profile categorisation of rapists based on their behaviour at the time of the offence. Hazelwood and Burgess (1987) used a classification, based on sexuality, power and anger, developed by Groth (1977; 1979) for these profiles as follows:

- **Selfish/pseudo-unselfish:** the *selfish rapist* shows no regard for the victim and is often threatening and abusive. He is confident of dominating the victim and carrying out an assault to suit their own sexual fantasies and self gratification, regardless of the victim's suffering or protest. The victim's resistance has little effect on the behaviour of the offender. By contrast, the *pseudo-unselfish rapist* lacks the confidence to dominate and tries to reassure and compliment the victim and may even apologise for the assault. The behaviour of the pseudo-unselfish offender is related to the fantasy of victim compliance and is therefore affected by the way the victim behaves. Hence, victim resistance may end the assault in these cases.
- **Power assertive/power reassurance:** The *power assertive rapist* is confident in his actions and may view the sexual assault as an expression of manhood. The style is to befriend the victim in a non-threatening way and then to force her into sexual intercourse. The victim may have been compliant with the initial intimacy but unable to fend off the forceful sexual attack that follows. This profile is typical of 'date rapes'. By contrast, the *power reassurance rapist* is sexually insecure and thus carefully selects a vulnerable victim and the time and place of the sexual offence. Pseudo-unselfish behaviour may be shown and after the assault, the offender may ask to be forgiven and permission to contact the victim at a later date. Sometimes, power reassurance offenders take items from the victim to keep together with records of their conquests.
- **Anger-excitement/Anger-retaliatory:** the *anger excited rapist* takes pleasure from the suffering and fear of their victim and may purposely inflict pain as a part of forcing the victim into sexual intercourse. To gain confidence, the intended sexual assault is planned and rehearsed, including the use of weapons and other items to subdue the victim. However, the selection of the victim is more related to chance than careful selection. Extreme physical force and torture are common features of the anger excited offender, sometimes over a long period of time and the victim's death may be a consequence. The degradation and humiliation of the helpless victim seems to be the primary objective and this may involve abduction of the victim. By contrast, the *anger-retaliatory rapist* commits rape as an expression of inner rage or hostility towards women or other men. The sexual attack is usually unplanned and impulsive and may involve extreme physical violence over a short period of time. Sometimes the victim is a previous boy/girlfriend or spouse. In other circumstances, a victim may trigger the sexual assault because he or she looks like a previous boy/girlfriend or spouse. The rejection, breakdown and separation in previous relationships heighten feelings of insecurity and jealousy in the offender.

Overall, in comparison with other sex offenders, men who rape adult victims tend to be younger and are more likely to use aggressive force rather than coercion to overcome victim resistance. With respect to their backgrounds, rapists are more likely to have experienced a long-term relationship and less likely to have been sexually abused themselves, compared to child molesters (Hudson & Ward, 1997). The victim to perpetrator pattern seems to be particularly relevant to child molesters with 56% to 57% reporting adverse sexual experiences in childhood as compared to between 5% and 23% of rapists (Dobash, Carnie & Waterhouse, 1994; Elliott, Browne & Kilcoyne, 1995; Seghorn et al., 1987; Pithers et al., 1988).

CHILD MOLESTERS

Findings from offender surveys also give the impression that many child sexual assaults go unreported. On average men convicted of sex offences against children claim five more undetected sexual assaults, over a period of up to 6 years, for which they were never apprehended or caught (Elliott, Browne & Kilcoyne, 1995; Groth, Hobson & Gary, 1982).

CHARACTERISTICS OF OFFENDERS WHO SEXUAL ABUSE CHILDREN

The most basic categorisation of 'contact' sex offenders is to use the *age of the victim* to distinguish between those individuals who victimise adults, often referred to as '*rapists*', and those individuals who perpetrate sex offences on children (under 18 years), who are most often referred to as '*paedophiles*'. However, sex offenders who have a primary interest in children may target specific age groups. Paedophile is the term used for sex offenders who target prepubescent children, some even target very young children under three years ('nepiophilia'). The paedophile group generally find secondary sexual characteristics, such as pubic hair, unattractive and undesirable. By contrast, '*hebephiles*', are individuals who target adolescents and teenagers with developing secondary sexual characteristics. This also symbolises to them sexual innocence and inexperience (Powell, 2007). The hebephile group are also more likely to commit sexual offences against adults as well as children, especially when the adult victim appears vulnerable and/or inexperienced. Indeed, Elliott, Browne and Kilcoyne's (1995) survey of convicted sex offenders who targeted children (under 18 years) found that 7% had also offended against adults.

The *age of the offender* is also an important consideration because of the legal implications and how the case will be managed in terms of sentence and intervention. For decades, the average age of convicted child molesters has been approximately 40 years (Fitch, 1962; Elliott, Browne & Kilcoyne, 1995), although there is growing evidence for adolescent and teenage offenders committing peer and sibling abuse. Indeed, perpetrators aged 17 and younger account for one third of all allegations of sexual abuse (Glasgow, Horne, Calam & Cox, 1994; Watkins & Bentovim, 1992). Official crime statistics illustrate that approximately 23% of all sexual offences committed in England and Wales involve perpetrators aged 21 and younger but most receive community sentences (Masson & Erooga, 1999). Likewise, studies of criminal convictions in the USA report up to 20% of rapes and 30% to 50% of child sexual abuse are committed by juvenile perpetrators (Davis & Leitenberg, 1987). Nevertheless, perpetrators younger than 20 are only represented in 5% of child protection cases (US Department of Justice, 2006).

A third categorisation that is usually applied relates to the *gender of the victim*; that is females only, males only or both females and males. Victim surveys show that girls are between two and three times more likely to be sexually abused than boys (Finkelhor, 1994; Pinheiro, 2006) and this has been confirmed by reports from sex offender surveys; 58% claimed they targeted girls, 14% preferred boys and 28% targeted both boys and girls (Elliott, Browne & Kilcoyne, 1995). A history of sexual abuse in childhood appears to influence age and gender preferences of paedophiles and appears to increase the chances of sex offences against boys (Browne, 1994; Pithers et al., 1988). Retrospective studies have also revealed that 60% to 80% of sex offenders with a history of childhood victimisation began molesting children as adolescents and teenagers (Groth et al., 1982) and it has been estimated that these individuals perpetrate 50% of the sex crimes against boys and up to 20% of offences against girls (Rogers & Terry, 1984).

A fourth important category is the *relationship context between perpetrator and victim* (Faller, 1990): Firstly, 'incest' or intrafamilial abuse, where a child is in some way used sexually by a family member. Incest offenders are usually fathers, stepfathers, grandfathers, uncles and siblings and are referred to as '*intrafamilial abusers*'. Secondly, 'acquaintance' cases where the offender is known to the victim but not an immediate family member such as a baby-sitter, teacher or other persons in a professional caring capacity, friend of the family and mother's boyfriends. These are referred to as '*extrafamilial abusers*'. Thirdly, a group of child sex offenders who are also classed as extrafamilial but comprise of those individuals who are '*strangers to the victim*'.

In the child sex offender survey by Elliott, Browne and Kilcoyne (1995) it was found that approximately one third of convicted offenders were intrafamilial, one third were extrafamilial acquaintances and known to the child, and one third were strangers. However, one in three offenders in a parental role sexually abused both their own and other children. This suggests that at least one third of 'incest' perpetrators could be regarded as paedophiles with a primary 'fixated' sexual interest in children and not merely 'situational' sex offenders as suggested by Howells (1981).

Unlike other forms of child maltreatment, biological parents are also less likely to commit sexual abuse on their children than other adults. According to the American Humane Association (McDonald et al., 2005), cases of child sexual abuse represented 7% of all child maltreatment referrals in 2003. Biological parents were alleged perpetrators in only 3% of these cases. The parents' male partners were thought to be responsible for 11% of cases, other relatives 30%, foster carers 6%, child carers 23% and teachers 11%. In the other cases, the perpetrators were unknown, many of which involved a sex offender who was a stranger to the child victim.

A recent review of research on violence against children in the community by the UN Secretary General's Study on Violence Against Children estimates that between 21% and 34% of sexual assaults on children are committed by strangers (Pinheiro, 2006). The review confirms previous findings that the majority of child sexual abuse is perpetrated by some in a position of trust. For example, a recent report (John Jay College of Criminal Justice, 2004) claimed that approximately 4% of US Catholic priests had been accused of abusing 10,700 children between 1950 and 2002. The majority of their victims were boys.

The relationship between perpetrator and victim will affect the frequency and duration of the abuse, and strategies used to engage the victim in the abuse (Faller, 1990). For example, those who are family or acquainted with the victim are more likely to employ psychological strategies such as coercion and bribery, whereas strangers are more likely to rely on physical force and surprise as a means of overcoming their victims. Partly for this reason, intrafamilial and extrafamilial abusers have fewer victims than strangers to the victim. Hence, proximity in the relationship context will also influence disclosure of abuse. Close relationships are less likely to be disclosed than those that are more distant or involving a stranger.

A fifth category concerns the *type of child sex offender*, where the perpetrator is classified into one of two (or more) typologies which are related to theories of motivation for the offence. For example, Cohen, Seghorn and Calmus' (1969) described three types of child molesters in terms of their sexual motivation to abuse. Firstly, the *paedophile-fixated* offender is described as having arrested psychosocial and psychosexual development. This individual is characterised by an inability to sustain long-term relationships with adults and has an exclusive preference for children both socially and sexually. Secondly, the *paedophile-regressed* offender is described, by contrast, as *not* being preoccupied with children and able to engage in adult relationships. This person regresses into sexual activity with children in times of stress and anxiety or family breakdown. Thirdly, the *paedophile-aggressive* offender mixes sex and aggressive motives and is driven to commit sadistically violent offences to gain sexual satisfaction.

There are similarities between the various typologies and distinctions that have been put forward since Cohen et al. (1969). For example; *fixated* versus *regressed*, (Groth, 1978); *preferential* versus *situational* (Howells, 1981); or *high* versus *low fixation* (Knight & Prentky, 1990) and high deviancy versus low deviancy (Beech, 1998). However, Fisher and Beech (1994) claim that nearly a third of the men who would be identified as regressed or situational perpetrators in other classifications (and would be treated as low risk) were found in the Beech (1998) classification system to be classified as High Deviancy (and therefore high risk with associated resistance to treatment). Nevertheless, assessing risk in known perpetrators of child sexual abuse and helping them with relapse prevention cannot be accomplished without first identifying specific characteristics associated with the offence (Grubin & Wingate, 1996).

GROOMING AND THE CONTEXT OF SEX OFFENCES AGAINST CHILDREN

'*Grooming*' was a term originally used by Christiansen and Blake (1990) to describe the processes by which fathers perpetrated incestuous relationships with their daughters. However, the term has been generalised since to describe the processes and strategies that all sexual offenders use to initiate and perpetuate the sexual abuse of children. The strategies are employed by the offender to: target particular children and/or parents; create opportunities to engage and interact with child victims in a sexual way, encourage secrecy about the contact; maintain the victims in their victim role and the abusive situation; and further, to prevent disclosure both during the abuse and once the sexual relationship has ceased.

To inform prevention programmes for children a number of child sex offender surveys have been carried out (Budin & Johnson, 1989; Conte & Smith, 1989; Lang & Frenzel, 1988) These studies provided valuable information about the context in which sex offences of children occur and are maintained. For example, Elliott, Browne and Kilcoyne (1995) interviewed 91 convicted child molesters and found the following information:

In *selecting a victim*, the child being pretty was important to 42% of the offenders, and the way the child dressed was cited by 27% of the men. Being young or small were also significant factors for 18% of offenders. Hence, the physical characteristics of the child were important, but not as important as the way the child behaved, one in eight (13%) focused on innocent or trusting children and nearly half (49%) of the offenders reported they were attracted to children who seemed to lack confidence or had low self esteem. Overall, according to the offender's perceptions, the child who was most vulnerable had family problems, was alone, was non confident, curious, pretty, 'provocatively' dressed, trusting and young or small.

Recruiting a victim was related to the previous relationship the perpetrator had had with a child.

Offenders who found child victims outside their immediate families had various strategies: 35% of the men frequented places where children were likely to go to such as schools, shopping centres, arcades, amusement/theme parks, playgrounds, parks, beaches, swimming baths, fairs, etc; 33% worked on becoming welcome in the child's home; 14% 'took the chance' when a child approached them, perhaps to ask a question and 18% of the men tried to get more children by having their victims recruit other children. They did this by offering incentives to or by threatening the victim and by giving bribes and gifts to the children recruited. Just under half the offenders (46%) felt that a 'special relationship' with the child was vital (54% did not).

The *location to abuse children* varied and most offenders used more than one location. The majority said that sexual abuse took place in the offender's home (61%) or in the child's home (49%). However, 44% of the offenders also stated they abused in public places, such as toilets or in tents when children were on outdoor activities, or in secluded parks or woodlands. Less common were offences in the home of friends (13%), in the vicinity of the offender's home (6%) and in a car (4%).

The *strategies used to approach the children* or their families by offenders were also varied. Most often they offered to play games with the children, or teach them a sport or how to play a musical instrument (53%). Many also gave bribes, took them for an outing or gave them a lift home (46%). Some used affection, understanding and love (30%) and some told stories involving lies, magic or treasure hunts (14%). A few offenders simply just asked a child for help (9%). One in five offenders claimed they had gained the trust of the victim's whole family in order to be able to abuse a child. It is highly significant that 48% of the offenders isolated their victims through babysitting. On these occasions, the offenders started by talking about sex (27%) offering to bath or dress the child (20%), and/or using coercion by misrepresenting the abuse as having a different purpose (21%), such as 'it would be good for you to do this for your education' or 'this is what people do who love each other'. Eighty-four per cent of the men said that once they had developed a series of successful strategies, they approached children with that same method every time; 16% were inconsistent in their approaches and changed their strategies over time.

The *first abusive action* with the child often involved one or two immediate sexual acts. Forty per cent of the abusers said that one of the first things they had done with the child was to engage in sexual activity such as sexual touching or genital kissing, 28% slowly desensitised the child into sexual activities and 32% asked the child to do something that would help the offender, such as undressing or lying down.

The *methods used to overcome the victim's reluctance* was mixed; 19% used physical force with the child, 44% of the men used coercion and persuasion, 49% talked about sexual matters, 47% used accidental touch as a ploy and 46% used bribery and gifts in exchange for sexual touches. If the child resisted or was fearful 39% of the offenders were prepared to use threats or violence to control the child as a way of overcoming the child's anxieties. The other offenders (61%) used passive methods of control such as stopping the abuse and then coercing and persuading once again. Therefore, the majority of offenders coerced children by carefully testing the child's reaction to sex, by bringing up sexual matters or having sexual materials around and by subtlety, increasing sexual touching.

One third of the offenders (strangers to the victim) abused a child on only one occasion and then moved on to another victim; two thirds of the offenders encouraged the child's compliance and *maintain the abusive relationship* by using a variety and combination of methods. Thirty-three per cent specifically told the child not to tell; 42% portrayed the abuse as education or as a game, 24% used threats of dire consequences, 24% used anger and the threat of physical force, 20% threatened loss of love or said that the child was to blame.

With reference to the *offender's preparation for the abuse;* immediately prior to offending, 22% of the men used drugs or alcohol, 21% used pornography and 49% used fantasies about previous victims to disinhibit themselves. The other 8% contacted and talked to other offenders. One in five offenders knew where to obtain child prostitutes and illegal child pornography (videos and magazines). One in twelve kept in regular contact with other child sex offenders.

UNDERSTANDING SEX OFFENDERS

Wolf (1984) and Finkelhor (1986) have been influential in understanding the process of sexual offences against children and the importance of grooming. Wolf (1984) proposed 'cycle of offending' whereby a motivation for sexual interest in children is triggered by sexual fantasies. Once internal inhibitions are overcome, a victim is targeted and the sexual fantasy rehearsed while grooming the victim. The abuse then occurs which reinforces the fantasy or creates a fear of detection. When the fantasy is reinforced, this enhances the possibility of another sexual offence on a child (continuous cycle), which may skip some stages (short circuit cycle). If there is a fear of detection or feeling of guilt about the abuse of a child, then the offender becomes blocked and inhibited (inhibited cycle) and may stop perpetrating child sexual abuse for a period of time (Eldridge, 1998).

Similar to Wolf's ideas, Finkelhor (1984; 1986) proposed a four-stage model explaining how a perpetrator sexually offends against a child. The first two stages require the potential perpetrator to be motivated to have sexual activities with the child and to overcome any internal inhibitions to commit such acts. The third requirement is to overcome external inhibitors or obstacles, such as appropriate parenting, guardianship and protection. Lastly, the perpetrator must overcome the child's resistance and evasive behaviour (see Table 1.1). Work with a child victim and their family addresses the third and fourth aspects of this model but leaves the motivation and disinhibition of the offender intact. This demonstrates the criminogenic need to rehabilitate offenders based on a theoretical understanding of sexual offending. Table 1.1 presents other multifactorial theories that have been put forward (Marshall & Barbaree, 1990; Hall & Hirshman, 1992; Ward & Siegert, 2002; Malamuth, 1996; Thorhill & Palmer, 2000) since Wolf's and Finkelhor's models had been proposed. Single factor explanations emphasising cognitive

Table 1.1 Summary of multifactorial theories of sex offending
(adapted from Ward, Polaschek & Beech, 2006)

Theories/models	Summary
Multifactorial theories	

Finkelhor's Precondition Model (1984)	• The first multifactorial theory of child sexual abuse has been widely applied to research and practice.
	• The theory concludes that there are four underlying factors/steps (preconditions) which must be satisfied before child sexual abuse occurs:
	  1. *Motivation to sexually abuse*:
	    a) Emotional congruence: the way the offender's emotional needs are met by a child
	    b) Sexual arousal: inappropriate sexual preference and responses to children
	    c) Blockage: inability to meet sexual and emotional needs in adaptive ways
	  2. *Overcoming internal inhibitors*: disengaging in self-regulatory mechanisms which enable someone to resist the desire and urge to sexually abuse a child
	  3. *Overcoming external inhibitors*: overcoming external barriers that protects a child from sexual abuse
	  4. *Overcoming resistance of the child*: employing strategies to gain and maintain access to a child for sexual contact.

Hall and Hirschman's Quadripartite Model (1992)	• Accounts for child sexual abuse and rape but the primary focus is to capture the heterogeneity of child molesters.
	• The theory hypothesises that the following factors lead to sexually abusive behaviour against children:
	  1. *Physiological sexual arousal (state)*: deviant sexual preferences and arousal to children
	  2. *Distorted cognition (state):* thinking of children as competent sexual agents who are able to make informed decisions about sexual activities
	  3. *Affective Dyscontrol (state):* having problems with the identification and management of emotions. Ward, Hudson and Keenan (1998) called it 'emotional regulation'.
	  4. *Problematic personality (trait):* traits and vulnerabilities stemmed from adverse early experiences.

Malamuth's Confluence Model of Sexual Aggression (1996)	• A statistical model of proximate causes of sexual aggression, embedded in a combination of evolutionary, feminist and social learning precepts.

(continued)

Table 1.1 *(Continued)*

Theories/models	Summary
Marshall and Barbaree's Integrated Theory (1990)	• Developed as a *general* theory of sexual offending. • The theory attempts to explain the *aetiology* of sexual offending by looking at attachment and early experience. It is argued that adverse early experience would lead to low self-worth, poor emotional coping and problem solving and social inadequacy, which made individuals vulnerable to victimisation as well as susceptibility to inappropriate sexual behaviour and antisocial behaviour.
Thornhill and Palmer's Evolutionary Theory and Sexual Offending (2000)	• Sees rape as a consequence of mating strategies and dismisses the possible influence of culture and psychological needs (e.g. power and control). To increase the chance of their genes being passed on and their offspring surviving, males have evolved to possess intense sexual desires which increased their motivation for sexual activities and seek multiple partners. They assert that rape is likely to be a conditional strategy only employed when circumstances are judged to be favourable by the perpetrator. Factors hypothesised to increase the chances of men using rape under conducive conditions are: • *A lack of physical and psychological resources* • *Social alienation* • *Limited sexual access to females* • *Unsatisfying romantic relationships* • The theory also considers rape as a by-product of adaptations that evolved to establish sexual access to a consenting partner under Symons' (1979) suggestion that the primary adaptations causing rape are men's greater sexual drive and their predilection to engage in impersonal sex.
Ward and Siegert's Pathways Model (2002)	• Incorporates Finkelhor's, Hall and Hirschman's, and Marhall and Barbaree's theories into a more comprehensive aetiological theory for child sexual abuse. • The theory denotes that early experiences, biological factors and cultural influence result in vulnerability, which may then lead one to develop *deviant sexual preferences, intimacy deficits, inappropriate emotions and/or cognitive distortions*. These four problems can be broken down into various components and then organised into different aetiological pathways that culminate in the sexual abuse of a child. The core

(continued)

Table 1.1 *(Continued)*

Theories/models	Summary
	dysfunctional mechanisms combined with circumstantial factors would result in an offence. Currently, the model consists of five major pathways but they are kept as illustrative to allow other possible trajectories: 1. *Multiple dysfunctional mechanisms* 2. *Deviant sexual scripts* 3. *Intimacy deficits* 4. *Emotional dysregulation* 5. *Antisocial cognitions*

distortions, deficient victim empathy, deviant sexual preferences, intimacy deficits and patriarchy have also been put forward to understand the development of sexual offending. Reasons for re-offending have also been highlighted, which include a lack of relapse prevention and self-regulation strategies and poor response to treatment and intervention. For a full description of these theories and explanations, see Ward, Polaschek and Beech (2006) who attempted a unified theory of sexual offending, incorporating aspects of the above ideas (see Figure 1.1).

Although this unified theory of sexual offending has been proposed, it is obvious that sex offenders are a heterogeneous group and that exhibitionists, internet offenders, rapists, incestuous offenders and child molesters have different criminogenic needs in terms of risk assessment, management and intervention. Indeed, Fisher and Mair (1998) suggested that a satisfactory classification system for all sex offenders has limited application.

A *mental health need* has been demonstrated by the observation that 58 to 94% of sex offenders in forensic settings have a history of substance misuse, mood and personality disorders but few (less than 2%) show a history of psychosis (Langstrom et al., 2004; Leue, Borchard & Hoyer, 2004; McElroy et al., 1999; Raymond et al., 1999).

An *early intervention need* has been demonstrated by the recognition that at least a third of sex offenders began committing sexual assault during their teenage years (Elliott, Browne & Kilcoyne, 1995; Masson & Erooga, 1999) and between 50% and 80% of sex offenders acknowledges a sexual interest in children during adolescence (Abel, Osborn & Twigg, 1993). This is partly related to the fact that many have been sexually abused themselves as children (Browne, 1994).

TREATMENT PROGRAMMES

All categories of offenders require assessment and treatment (see Chapter 7 for a detailed discussion on treatment programmes). Allam, Middleton and Browne

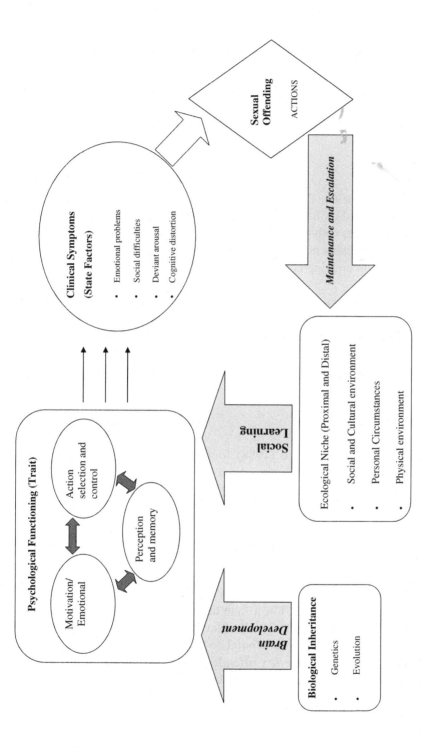

Figure 1.1 Unified theory of sexual offending (Permission from Ward, T., Polaschek, D. & Beech, A. (2006) *Theories of Sexual Offending. Chichester: Wiley*)

(1997) provide an example of the six core themes used to treat sex offenders in treatment which are:

- Cycles and cognitive distortion
- Self-esteem, social skills and assertiveness training
- Sexuality
- Role of fantasy in offending
- Victim empathy
- Relapse prevention

In a recent evaluation of the Prison Sex Offender Treatment Programme (Beech, Fisher, Beckett & Scott-Fordham, 1998), it was found that 67% of men attending showed a treatment effect with significant changes in some or all of the main themes targeted. Long term treatment (160 hours) was more effective than short term treatment (80 hours) in creating change, especially for those offenders who showed high deviancy.

Similarly, a recent audit of a community treatment programme (Browne, Foreman & Middleton, 1998) showed that 81% of sex offenders showed some improvement with all those completing a programme (63%) showing significant changes in one or more of the modules. A review of seven other community treatment programmes (Beech, Fisher, Beckett & Fordham, 1996) demonstrates that the above findings are typical.

TREATMENT EFFECTIVENESS

In Canada, Marshall and Barbaree (1988) found that treated offenders had less reconvictions than non-treated offenders both at two years follow-up (5.5% and 12.5% respectively) and four years follow-up (25% and 64% respectively). Other North American studies (Hanson & Bussière, 1998), show a reconviction rate for sexual offences of 13%, with incest offenders lower (4%) than boy victim paedophiles (21%). General recidivist rates in the same meta-analysis of 61 data sets involving 28, 972 child sex offenders found 12.2% for non-sexual violent offences and 36.3% for any offence.

Similarly, in the UK only 10% to 15% of sex offenders were reconvicted within two to four years which is, in fact, lower than most other criminal offences (Lloyd, Mair & Hough, 1994; Marshall, 1997). Nevertheless, reconviction rates for untreated sexual offenders have been found to double (from 11% to 22%) after five years (Fisher, 1994) and some sex offenders have not been re-convicted until twenty years after release from prison (Barker & Morgan, 1993). A review of juvenile offender programmes (Gerhold, Browne & Beckett, 2007) has demonstrated similar levels of effectiveness with an average of 14% sexual offence recidivism (and 44% non-sexual offence recidivism) among young offenders with a mean follow up period of five and a half years. However, measures of recidivism using reconviction data have been criticised (Friendship, Beech & Browne, 2002). Information directly from the police on alleged offences and high risk behaviours may give a better picture and more than double the actual conviction rates in terms of recidivism (Marshall, Jones, Ward, Johnston & Barbaree, 1991).

It was pointed out that a recent systematic review (Kenworthy, Adams, Bilby, Brokks-Gordon & Fenton, 2003) that only nine randomised controlled trials could be found investigating 'psychological interventions for those who have sexually offended or are at risk of offending'. Out of the nine reviewed studies, one study suggested that cognitive approach resulted in decline of offending after one year. Hence, that there is a lack of strong evidence to support the effectiveness of sex offender treatment programmes.

CONCLUSIONS

Treatment drop-out and poor response to treatment are considered the most important indicators for recidivism (Abel, Mittelman, Becker, Rathner & Rouleau, 1988; Browne, Foreman & Middleton, 1998). Indeed, those men who do not complete treatment still pose a significant risk to women and children in the community. There is little doubt that sex offences cannot be completely eradicated but assessment and treatment initiatives should significantly reduce the risk of sexual assault to women and children. Interventions with sex offenders using both assessment and treatment strategies are most effectively implemented within a multi-disciplinary framework, as the protection of women and children from sex offenders is best achieved through professional collaboration. This involves evidence-based practice which makes a clear distinction between risk management, supervision and treatment (see Allam & Browne, 1997). It is these key areas that we consider in this volume.

2

Developmental Frameworks and Functional Analysis

INTRODUCTION

The aim of a psychological assessment is to provide an understanding of why an individual has committed a sexual offence in order to aid the risk assessment process. Identifying factors, conditions and events within the individual's personal history also potentially enables practitioners to develop appropriate treatment programmes (Mash & Hunsley, 1990) in order to reduce the possibility of future offending. The use of *Antecedent-Behaviour-Consequence* (ABC) analysis serves to organise the case material into a chronological order of events illustrating the development of the offending behaviour (Gresswell & Hollin, 1992). This approach to understanding behaviour is, of course much wider than just looking at the origins of sexual offending and covers all aspects of the development of behaviour, whether it is social or anti-social. However, for the purposes of this chapter we are going to: (1) focus on the development of offending behaviours generally; (2) illustrate how a behavioural framework used to assess offending behaviour can be viewed and applied.

But before we look at these areas in more detail we will first examine some of the principles that underpin behavioural analysis in general.

BEHAVIOURAL ANALYSIS

Behavioural analysis has a number of assumptions: (1) the ontogenesis of behaviours is governed by a set of rules; (2) the importance of dynamic psychological processes; (3) the importance of learning principles; (4) the multi-factorial nature of behaviour; (5) behaviours can be changed and managed through treatment. We will now look at each of these areas in some detail.

1. Ontogenesis (Continuity of development from ovum to maturity) of behaviour is rule-based

It is argued that innate capacities (genetic, biological) and environmental events (life experiences) combine to produce a repertoire of behavioural rules for what group of behaviours best fit different and varied situations (Emde & Harmon, 1984). The combination of biology and the environment produce 'career' pathways from early childhood, through adolescence, into adulthood (Robins & Rutter, 1990). The existence of 'critical periods' (that is, a biologically determined stage of develop-ment at which a person, or animal, is optimally ready to acquire some pattern of behaviour, for example 'imprinting', Coleman, 2001) have been identified by a number of researchers (for example, Lorenz, 1966; Bowlby, 1951, 1969). These factors may change the 'continuity' of life pathways (change of rate, direction and strength, and so on), as do other life events, such as trauma (Holmes & Rache, 1967; van der Kolk, McFarlane & Weisaeth, 1996).

The central question to the prediction of life-course patterns in developmental research concerns the link between early behavioural experiences and circum-stances, and later adult behaviours. In investigating the developmental pathways from childhood to adulthood, a number of different methodological approaches are proposed. Most developmental research focuses on regularities on the individual's stability of personality characteristics over time. However, the problem with this approach is the plausibility of correlating regularities of specific traits with theories of personality (Caspi, Elder & Herbener, 1993). A second approach involves the prediction of an individual's adult behaviours based on earlier attributes (that is, early life experiences) (West & Farrington, 1977). This approach samples a broad range of childhood variables with the objective of establishing a small group of variables that are highly predictive indicators of specific outcomes in later life (for example, school drop-out, delinquency and criminality and adult psychopathology (Caspi, Elder & Herbener, 1993). Caspi et al. suggest it is also important to focus on the coherence of internal styles across social transformations in the age-graded life-course, that is to say how the individual meets developmental challenges, adapt to new settings, and the long-term consequences of these adaptational strategies' (p.14). This approach primarily combines the longitudinal assessment of individuals with the assessment of situations in order to show how early personality shapes achievements and relationships in diverse circumstances at different ages.

In this approach three distinct pathways can be identified:

(a) *Causal factors*

   Chess and Thomas (1993) suggest insight into one's own temperament characteristics is often helpful in understanding an individual and the development of insight into one's own behaviour may be useful in developing strategies to minimise undesirable expressions of temperamental trait or pattern;

(b) *Developmental factors shaped by experience*

Studies investigating into the developmental factors shaped by experience have primarily been 'adoption' studies used in estimating both genetic and environmental factors. Cadoret, Troughton, Merchant and Whitters (1990), for example, investigated the role of social events on psychopathology, arguing that environmental factors can lay the groundwork of affective symptoms for later life. Therefore, it was argued that the relevant factor that appears to affect later life affective symptomatology in males was social disruption (Bowlby, 1988), where children lack this emotional attachment, they tend to have poorer long-term outcomes in terms of emotional and intellectual development (Rutter, 1973). Continuity of anti-social behaviours over the lifespan has also been shown to be related to poor parental attachment (Fergusson & Lynskey, 1998). Farrington (1993) found that the best predictors of delinquent behaviour were troublesome behaviours at school, dishonesty and high levels of aggressiveness (compared to non-delinquent children).

(c) *Maintenance of offending behaviour*

In examining the development and maintenance of offending behaviour, Blanc (1993) argues the process that constitutes the development of persistent offending is the result of the relationship between descriptive (frequency, variety, seriousness, nature) and developmental (onset, duration and transfer from adolescent to adult) parameters. Blanc argues that this procedure demonstrates the existence of two basic processes that support the development of persistent offending; *activation* and *escalation*. The activation process refers to the way the 'development of persistent offending is stimulated as soon as it has begun and to the way its persistence is assured' (p.82). Delinquent activities within the activation process are characterised by a high level of frequency, duration and variety each based on three separate but closely interrelated mechanisms: *acceleration* between onset and frequency; *diversification* the degree of variety of offending from onset, and *stabilisation* between onset and duration.

2. Dynamic psychological processes

Individuals operate to a gratification system that attempts to satisfy basic needs, drives and appetites, and a higher affective level, the emotions of love/hate, for example. Positive and negative aspects of gratification systems often determine the choice of behaviour, which vary from one person to the next. These are 'unconscious' preferences and process that effect behaviour.

3. The importance of learning principles in understanding behaviour

Although learning principles have been applied to treatment and management programmes of offending behaviour, it is not until recently a comprehensive learning theory of criminal behaviour been developed (Lee-Evans, 1994). There are several learning paradigm systems designed to explain how we learn from experience and from acquired new knowledge of the world around us. Learning accounts of behaviour have tended to emphasise the following:

Classical conditioning (Pavlov, 1927; Watson & Rayner, 1920), which consists of the process of learning by which an initial neutral stimulus such as the ringing of a bell becomes a conditioned stimulus eliciting a particular response, such as salivation as a response by the repeated pairing with an unconditioned stimulus (for example, food), which would usually elicit the response of salivation in dogs.

Operant conditioning (Dicara, 1970; Jenkins & Moore, 1973; Skinner, 1938, 1953; Thorndike, 1898) where the relative frequency of a response increases as a result of *reinforcement* (that is, reward),[1] or decreases by the administration of an aversive stimulus (punishment).

Social Learning theories (Bandura, 1977), which has investigated how social influences can alter people's thoughts, feelings and behaviours. This approach was originally described by Bandura (1977) and others (for example, Eron, 1967; Patterson, Littman & Bricker, 1967). Bandura suggests that imitation and modelling of behaviour can sometimes occur without reinforcement, through three forms of observational learning: (i) *participant modelling*, where the individual observes and then copies the behaviour that they have seen; (ii) *vicarious learning* – with non-participant observation, that is, in written form or visual media; and (iii) *symbolic modelling* – in which behaviour and its consequences are developed and elaborated in thought or mental images.

In taking a learning principles approach to offending behaviour, four distinct schools of thought have been evoked:

(i) *Applied behavioural analysis:* This approach is based on a radical behaviourist philosophy (Morris & Braukmann, 1987; Skinner, 1938). Here the application of conditioning principles is applied to human behaviour. Criminal behaviour in this analysis is viewed as being maintained by the changes it produces in the environment which is positively reinforced through the acquisition of goods (property, sex power, and so on) acquired in the offence;

(ii) *Neo-behaviourism:* This approach is based on Pavlovian conditioning derived from the work of Wolpe (1982) and Eysenck (1982). It suggests that there are mediating cognitive states between inputs and outputs. The emphasis in this approach, with its application to criminal behaviour, is on mental events, and

---

[1]*Negative reinforcement* is said to occur when an individual escapes punishment.

that behaviour should be analysed in terms of behavioural, physiological and cognitive responses (Lang, 1970);

(iii) *Social Learning Theory: (SLT)* This approach is based on Bandura's (1977) seminal work, and provides a comprehensive theory of human behaviour drawing upon classical conditioning, operant conditioning and imitation learning. SLT emphasises internalisation in terms of affective responses to cognitive representations and evaluations of one's own behaviour, under the control of internal and external cues. Reinforcement contingencies are relevant to the *performance* of behaviour, and the *acquisition* of behaviour is primarily dependant on *imitation* through the observation of a model's behaviour;

(iv) *Cognitive-behavioural modification:* This approach includes the assumption that cognition mediates emotional and behavioural dysfunction (Lee-Evans, 1994). Therefore, cognitive-behavioural modification refers to a wide range of procedures attached to significant mental events and processes and places greater emphasis on attempts to later direct cognition as a means of changing overt behaviour.

4. The 'multi-factorial' nature of behaviour

Multi-factorial behaviour is a range of influences that determine the behaviour, either through conscious choice, unconscious choice, or in some cases, by chance. A model for the explanation and understanding of these processes is *Functional Analysis* which we will outline in detail below. As many of these contributing factors as possible need to be identified in order for functional analysis to be as accurate as possible.

5. Changing Behaviours (treatment/management)

Innate capacities/abilities (including motivations and insights) are resistant to change by present known methods. Cognitive processes can be changed by enhancing/ educating/adjusting social and interpersonal attitudes/values/beliefs of the individual. Lifestyle changes often reduce trigger situations (Lazarus & Folkman, 1984). These factors are sensitive to the offender's motivations and insight without which change is unlikely. This is an area which we will come back to in Chapter 7.

In the next section we outline the behavioural framework approach.

BEHAVIOURAL FRAMEWORKS

A number of different frameworks for the assessment of the relevant sources of information in the understanding of offending behaviour have been proposed (Mash & Hunsley, 1990). Common in other frameworks is the idea that the target behaviour is mostly best understood in terms of its relationship with past events and experiences, and how it has been shaped and modelled into the current behaviour. The most

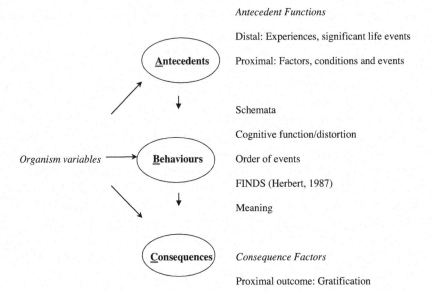

Antecedent Functions

Distal: Experiences, significant life events

Proximal: Factors, conditions and events

Schemata

Cognitive function/distortion

Order of events

FINDS (Herbert, 1987)

Meaning

Consequence Factors

Proximal outcome: Gratification

Distal Outcome: Social/Societal sanctions

Figure 2.1 Antecedents, behaviour and consequences model

accepted method of analysis is that of the Antecedent-Behaviour-Consequence (ABC) unit of analysis (Ellis, 1977; Herbert, 1987) (see Figure 2.1).

The ABC model describes a relationship between the stimulus, behaviour and its consequences. The emphasis on behavioural assessment is placed upon sampling a broad range of the client's behavioural repertoire in the different situations in which the behaviours occur. From this one can develop an understanding of the relationship between the environmental events that may provoke or maintain the index behaviour. We will now look at each of the factors outlined in Figure 2.1 in more detail.

ORGANISM VARIABLES

Without behaviour, the individual is made up organism variables. These are various physiological factors that influence the individual's development and behaviour. These can include demographic details of the individual, congenital factors, brain functioning, inherited dispositions, capacities and abilities, autonomic reactivity and the physiological consequences of acquired habits or preferences (for example, eating disorders, smoking or drug/alcohol abuse). The process of a functional analysis (see below) takes into account consideration of any physical factors that impact on the individuals' past learning history and subsequently behaviour. These include personality traits of the individual, repertoires of knowledge, cognition and behavioural skills, attitudes, values and beliefs, all of which would have had an influence upon the present day behaviour which are outlined in more detail in Figure 2.2.

Integration of formulation on:

- Formative experiences

- Innate capacities/abilities

- Situational events

- Behavioural sequences

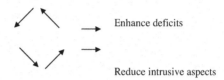

Enhance deficits

Reduce intrusive aspects

Explanation of behaviour

- Areas of intervention

- Risk of repeating behaviour

Figure 2.2 Functional analysis

ANTECEDENTS

The antecedent or stimuli to an event precede the behaviour, which then alters the probability of the behaviours, and which predicts the likelihood of punishing or reinforcing consequences (Sturmey, 1996). In examining the antecedent to an event it is relevant to consider both *distal* (that is, historical factors; Lee-Evans, 1994) and *proximal* (that is, recent events or situational) antecedent events (Herbert, 1987). Examples of distal antecedents may include organism variables such as brain functioning, sexual or physical abuse, innate capacity or abilities. The proximal antecedents describe the immediate situation which leads the individual to react or behave in the way that they have. Proximal antecedents may include such details as who was present, what was said, what time, and where, all immediately prior to the incident. Dependent upon whether the consequence is in the form of either punishment or reinforcement, the consequence can be seen as being directly related to the antecedents (that is, that which immediately precedes the behaviour). It would follow that by identifying the antecedents and controlling the consequence of the behaviour, it is possible to change the behaviour. Through classical conditioning, antecedent events can elicit conditioned responses, and through operant conditioning, antecedent events can determine response based upon discriminative stimuli.

BEHAVIOUR

The person situation interaction is the behaviour exhibited as a result of the stimulus (that is, the antecedent situation). The behaviour is seen as a sample from the entire behavioural repertoire of the individual observed in a specific situation (Sturmey, 1996). Therefore, the functional analysis serves to examine a specific target response determined by precise situational factors and conditions. Through examining in detail both the internal and external factors of the behaviour in relation to the antecedent to the behaviour it is possible to gain a clearer picture as to the processes behind the behaviour. The internal factors deal with the way in which the individual interprets new information when it is introduced to the already pre-existing information on how to behave within a certain situation (e.g., schemata, cognitive functioning, motor component and physiology). This will then determine how to react and interact within the situation. Thus, as Lee-Evans (1994) points out, there may be discordance between a phobic patient's overt-avoidance behaviour, self-report of anxiety and physiological measures of arousal. The implication for this, Lee-Evans argues, is that a comprehensive functional analysis should include an assessment of the target behaviour across all response modalities. A number of other frameworks such as *functional response, response chain* and *skill hierarchies* (Masten & Braswell, 1991; Sturmey, 1996), have also been proposed, designed to conceptualise and organise the manner in which an individual responds to situationally determined stimuli. Common among the different models is the notion that the behaviour is dynamic and that it can be viewed as part of a behavioural development (for a more detailed discussion see Evans, 1985).

The frequency, intensity, number, duration and sense/meaning (FINDS; Herbert, 1987) of the behaviour builds a behavioural framework of the incident, and in the case of there being more than one incident, it can be useful in producing a developmental framework describing how the behaviour has changed over time. As Herbert (1987) argues, this will help to establish whether there is a tendency for the problem to occur episodically, or whether there is any evidence of a clustering of behavioural events.

CONSEQUENCES

The consequences are viewed as maintaining the inappropriate behaviour through either positive (that is, gaining reward) or negative (that is, avoidance or escape) reinforcement. Like the antecedent to the behaviour, the consequences of the behaviour can be described in terms of being either immediate (proximal), or delayed (distal) to the behaviour. The proximal consequences to the behaviour are those factors that are immediate and reinforcing to the behaviour. For example, the proximal consequences of a sexual assault (depending on the motivation behind the assault) can be a feeling of pleasure, control, or power over the victim. This can be both gratifying and reinforcing, in that the desired emotion is achieved by carrying out the assault (Skinner, 1938; Thorndike, 1898). Depending on the outcome of the assault, in terms of being caught, or feelings of guilt, the distal consequences will be the social and societal sanctions imposed both by the judicial system and the social community. Typically, the target behaviour is likely to experience both short term reinforcing consequences with long term punishing consequences. The behaviour then escalates due to the immediacy of the reinforcement being more powerful than the delayed consequence. To this end, the offender's behaviour becomes impulsive, and unable to defer gratification (Lee-Evans, 1994). Therefore, the offending behaviour is more likely to be maintained through proximal reinforcement, particularly when the non-desirable consequences are delayed in terms of time and place (Wilson & Herrnstein, 1985).

The antecedent to the behaviour can be seen as a by-product of the organism variables. That is to say, the psychological development of the individual will affect how they perceive the world and therefore ultimately how they will behave. In the same way, the consequences of the behaviour will, by and large, determine how the problem behaviour develops by influencing the interpretation of the antecedent. The cycle is then repeated depending on the distal outcome of the consequences. The problem behaviour can then be seen as being part of a causal chain whereby the organism variables, the antecedence, and the consequences all contribute to the development of the problem behaviour (Sturmey, 1996).

FUNCTIONAL ANALYSIS

Any assessment of a sex offender should include a detailed functional analysis to determine the underlying motives and functions for the offending behaviour. A functional analysis is the process of bringing together all the contributing factors as a way of identifying the psychological problems behind the problem behaviour, see Figure 2.2.

Functional analysis which emphasises the behaviour serves a particular *function* for the person (Goldiamond, 1974). This de-emphasises the form the behaviour takes and shifts attention to the purposes the behaviour might serve for the individual. The function of the behaviour is therefore seen as having secondary gains by achieving a response that may not ordinarily be associated with the behaviour. Therefore, by understanding the function the behaviour serves, allows the practitioner to replace it with a more adaptive behaviour that fulfils the same functional value. This should include the actual behaviours carried out along with the accompanying thoughts and emotions. Unfortunately this is not always a straightforward task with sex offenders due to them frequently being at some level of denial about aspects of the offence and therefore not willing to be completely truthful about the areas that the assessor needs to obtain information about. Indeed, even in those offenders who are open about the level of their offending behaviours there is often a reluctance to disclose their thoughts and feelings around their offending. In order to assist in gaining the information for the functional analysis it can be helpful to provide the offender with a framework to understand the process of offending.

Currently the most useful framework is probably what is called a 'Decision Chain' (Ward, Louden, Hudson & Marshall, 1995). This model has tended to supersede earlier frameworks such as Finkelhor's (1994) preconditions or Wolf's (1984) offence cycle. A Decision Chain is a sequence of choices leading to an offence. Each choice is characterised in terms of the situation it took place in, the thoughts that made sense of and responded to the situation, and the emotions and actions that arose from these thoughts. Beech, Fisher and Thornton (2003) argue, in any analysis of offence behaviours it is important to take account of the diversity in offending, and to accommodate individuals whose firmly entrenched beliefs about the legitimacy of sexual contact with children or forced sex with adults lead them to experience positive emotions during the offence process. Decision Chains have the advantage that they can represent with equal facility sexual offences that spring from negative emotional states, and poor coping strategies (as in the Wolf cycle) and those where these negative factors are not involved (Eldridge, 1998; Laws, 1999; Ward & Hudson, 1996).

Approaches to understanding the offence process should be drawn from the work of Ward and Hudson (1998) who suggest it is possible to classify offenders according to one of four different routes to offending. These groups are defined by the individual offender's goal towards deviant sex (i.e., approach or avoidant), and the selection of strategies designed to achieve their goal (i.e., active or passive). For the *approach goal* offender, positive affective states, explicit planning and the presence of distorted attitudes about victims and offending behaviour typify the process leading to offending. While for the *avoidant goal* offender the overall goal towards offending is one of avoidance. However, self-regulation deficiencies, for example, inadequate coping skills (under-regulation) or inappropriate strategies (misregulation), ultimately result in goal failure. Consequently, negative affective states and covert planning characterise the avoidant pathway. This type of pathway can be seen as being similar to the Wolf description of the offence process.

Ward and Hudson (1998) further divide the approach and avoidant pathways into those with *active* compared to those with no *(passive)* strategies, therefore four types are defined by Ward and Hudson: approach explicit, approach automatic, avoidant active and avoidant passive. The *approach explicit* offender is one who is active and is seeking opportunities to offend and actively setting up the situation in which to offend. In contrast, the *approach automatic* (passive offender), while motivated to offend, only does so when the opportunity presents itself. The *avoidant active* offender is one who makes an effort to avoid offending but uses the wrong strategies to do this, while the *avoidant passive* offender would prefer not to offend but does nothing to prevent himself from offending.

Built into the approach of functional analysis is the process of considering not only the various determinants that help maintain the behaviour, but also those determinants that might prevent an alternative, more appropriate behaviour from developing (Lee-Evans, 1994). When brought together, the methods of assessment are used to predict the likelihood that the individual will re-offend. This is established through identifying the risk factors associated with the behaviour, the facilitators and the factors thought to prevent or inhibit the behaviour, the inhibitors. Integration of the 'factors, consequences and experiences' identifies the causes of the problem behaviour through an examination of the organism variables and the behavioural chain.

This approach involves a reconstruction and interpretation of the individual's life experiences based upon the reliable evidence available. It is a theory about how and why the person behaved the way they did in that particular situation. Having identified the conditions controlling the problem behaviour such as the facilitators and the inhibitors, the next task is to explain their origin. From this point, a behavioural treatment and management programme can be developed based on cognitive-behavioural techniques (see Chapter 7).

Clearly, the process of functional analysis calls for a detailed knowledge of the precise circumstances under which the target behaviour occurs. Given that behaviour varies across time and place, a critical issue in behaviour assessment models is that the more dissimilar the assessment situation is from the target behaviour situation, the less confident one can be that the information obtained is relevant and valid (Lee-Evans, 1994). This can be seen as a criticism of functional analysis in that it presents practical difficulties in reliable assessments of past behaviour. Depending on the level of risk, the treatment and management programme may require modifying in order to accommodate any restrictions placed on the person, this is a notion that we will examine below. The concept of assessing and categorising the level of risk a person presents of re-offending is a complex and controversial one at best. Often practitioners are sceptical about assessing a person's risk for a number of reasons due to the fact that there is always a chance that the person will re-offend. One reason for this maybe due to the concept of risk being not exclusive to forensic and criminal justice agencies, but is also found in a broad range of disciplines including business and commerce, engineering and everyday life where the definitions of *risk* and *risk assessment* are used interchangeably.

APPROACHES TO RISK ASSESSMENT

The identification of the risks posed by offenders and the factors associated with recidivism are crucial to the identification of appropriate and effective interventions designed to reduce the risk of recidivism. While this applies to all types of offending behaviour, this is particularly true for sexual offenders due to the impact of their offending on victims (Hanson, 1990; Koss, 1993). Recent advances in research have generated a lively debate concerning best practices regarding sex offender risk assessment (Janus & Meehl, 1997). Decisions pertaining to a sexual offender's dangerousness can be conceptualised in a number of different ways, but the central concern is usually risk of re-offending. It is important to note, conceptually, risk of re-offending is not the same as dangerousness, which instead refers to the severity of behaviour. Rather, risk of being reconvicted refers to the *likelihood* of being reconvicted for a new sexual offence. However, rarely is the assessment of risk as straightforward or dichotomous as is implied. More often, the assessment of risk also includes requests for information on: (1) immediacy of offending; (2) likelihood of offending; (3) frequency of offending; (4) consequences of offending.

Any assessment of the likelihood of sexual offending should be broad and involve more than a simple documentation of the level of risk. It should also contribute information that can guide risk management. The types of risk factors identified in the general risk assessment literature fall into four broad categories:

1. *Dispositional factors*, such as psychopathic or anti-social personality characteristics;
2. *Historical factors*, such as adverse developmental events, prior history of crime and violence, prior hospitalisation, and poor treatment compliance;
3. *Contextual antecedents* to violence such as criminogenic needs (risk factors for criminal behaviour), deviant social networks and lack of positive social supports;
4. *Clinical factors* such as psychiatric diagnosis, poor level of functioning and substance abuse (Andrews & Bonta, 1998; McGuire, 2000).

We will revisit these ideas in the following chapters.

CONCLUSIONS

The aim of this chapter has been to sketch out some of the theoretical ideas around the development of offending behaviours generally and to illustrate how a behavioural framework used to assess offending behaviour can be viewed and applied in sex offender risk assessment, particularly with the idea of how *functional analysis* can be used as a clinical tool used to investigate the antecedents, behaviours and consequences of the offence. This allows an assessment to be made of the process of the offence and the offence pathway that characterises the offending for that individual. Hence this type of analysis is an important first step to ascertain the type of goals and strategies a sexual offender has towards offending. In the following chapters we will illustrate how *actuarial* risk assessments can provide guidance as to the general band of risk that an offender falls into (for example, low, medium, high), *dynamic* risk assessment where research meets clinical perceptions and may include assessment of stable dynamic factors, that is, those factors that may be amenable to change in treatment such as deviant sexual interest, pro-offending attitudes, socio-affective problems, and self-management issues and acute factors, that is, those factors that may be related to imminent sexual offending.

3

Methodological Considerations in Measuring Predictive Accuracy

INTRODUCTION

Accurate assessments of levels of risk posed by sexual offenders are in high demand as decisions concerning whether an offender should be released into the community can have severe consequences both for the offender and the public. In order to increase the validity in the decision-making process, forensic practitioners are encouraged to use empirically derived actuarial risk instruments. The debate regarding accuracy of clinical judgement versus the actuarial approach is not a new one. The accuracy of clinicians making unaided clinical judgements, in relation to an offender's level of risk, has generally been found to be of low reliability, when compared with actuarial measures (Hanson & Bussière, 1996; Hood, Shute, Feilzer & Wilcox, 2002; McNeil, Sandberg & Binder, 1998; Mulvey & Lidz, 1998), and can be enhanced by using systematic/ structured risk assessment approaches (Bonta, Laws & Hanson, 1996; Dolan & Doyle, 2000; Janus & Meehl, 1997; Monahan, 1996). One of the major criticisms of clinical judgement is the apparent tendency and bias toward over-prediction (Hagen, 1997; Hood et al., 2002; Steadman, 1987), falsely predicting recidivism. In response to the clinical/actuarial debate, the literature has witnessed a surge in empirically derived actuarial risk instruments designed to assess risk of violent and/or sexual offence recidivism. It is not the purpose of this chapter to examine the predictive accuracy of actuarial risk instruments (see Chapter 5) but instead to summarise the theoretical background on the development of actuarial risk instruments.

METHODOLOGICAL CONSIDERATIONS WHEN ASSESSING RISK

Prediction in general and sexual aggression in particular, is an extremely difficult task due to the complex and multi-factorial nature of this type of crime (Borum, 1996). Any risk classification compares prediction with actual outcome, and one method to do this is by comparing recidivists with non-recidivists using a 2 x 2 contingency table (Figure 3.1). If the probability of dangerousness is over-estimated (false positive), low risk offenders are placed in treatment that is expensive and prolonged. Conversely under-estimations of risk (false negative) may lead to dangerous offenders being released without treatment where there is a high probability that a new sexual offence will be committed (Epperson, Kaul & Hesselton, 1998). However, as Hart, Webster and Menzies (1993) point out, 2 x 2 contingency tables over simplify what is a multifactorial event, and all outcomes cannot be dichotomised (for example, actual rape, attempted rape, threatened rape, and so on). Furthermore, as with actuarial risk instruments, 2 x 2 tables encourage 'absolute' judgements failing to consider qualifying statements.

At the heart of the 2 x 2 tables is the base rate for recidivism. All actuarial risk instruments are ultimately derived from 'base rates', which are usually recorded as reoffence or reconviction. So a base rate of 10% usually means that 10% of a group of sexual offenders can be expected to be reconvicted within a given time period. However, base rates are inherently ambiguous, unreliable and unstable (Koehler, 1996). It is well documented that base rates differ between ages and subgroups of offenders, increase with time (Grubin, 1998; Hanson, 1997; Hood et al., 2002; Prentky, Lee, Knight & Cerce, 1997) and vary between sexual recidivism studies from 10% to 40% (Barbaree, 1997). For example, the base rate of convictions for rapists (17.1%) is higher than that of intrafamilial offenders (8.4%) but less than that of extrafamilial offenders (19.5%). Although the recidivist rate for intrafamilial offenders was generally low, those aged between 18 to 24 years are at greater risk of recidivism (30.7%) (Hanson, 2002).

As for definitions, the base rate (BR) is the proportion of the sample that actually reoffend as noted above. The selection ratio (SR) is the proportion of the sample

OUTCOME

		Re-offenders	Non re-offenders
PREDICTION	High Risk	True Positive A	False Positive B
	Low Risk	False Negative C	True Negative D

Figure 3.1 Contingency table for predictive studies using a cohort design

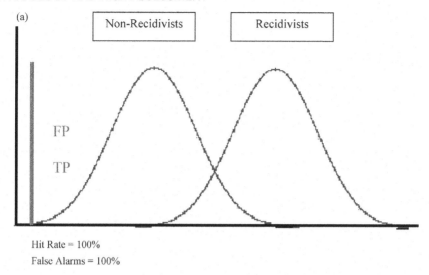

Figure 3.2a The effect of variations in the base rate: Low selection ratio Proportion of men predicted to be violent (above the line) is termed the selection ratio (hits + false alarms)

that was predicted to reoffend. The BR can be calculated as (true positive (TP) + false negative (FN))/T, T being the total sample. The SR can be calculated as (TP + false positive (FP))/T. When the SR is larger than the BR, the number of FPs will be greater than the number of FNs. On the other hand, when the BR is larger than the SR, the number of FNs will be greater than the number of FPs. The base effect of variations in the BR and SR is illustrated using the normal distribution curve. Assuming the base rates between recidivists and non-recidivists are equal, the point at which individuals are predicted to reoffend (SR) directly impacts on the accuracy of the prediction. If the SR is low, the hit rate (recidivists correctly identified) will be 100% accurate. However, this is at the cost of over predicting risk raising the FPs (Figure 3.2a). Conversely, if the SR is too high the FP rate will be reduced at the cost of a low hit rate (Figure 3.2b). To maximise the hit rate, the ST should be positioned at the point where the BR between the recidivists and non-recidivist groups overlap, maximising the TPs while minimising when the SR (Figure 3.2c).

However, Figure 3.2d illustrates the effect of the base rate on measuring predictive accuracy. The base rate in Figures 3.2a to 3.2c are assumed to be equal, where 50% of the sample reoffended and 50% did not. However, the UK base rate for sexual reconviction is estimated at 5.8% up to a two-year follow up, 6.9% up to four-years of follow up, and 17.4% at six years or more of follow up (Craig, Browne, Stringer & Hogue, in press). The effect of a low reconviction rate on the predictive accuracy of a scale can increase the FN and reduce the TP rates.

In addition to reporting TP, FP, TN and FN, the overall chance-corrected predictive accuracy is the accuracy of both positive and negative predictors taking

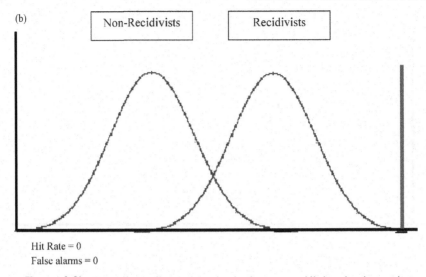

Figure 3.2b The effect of variations in the base rate: High selection ratio

prior probabilities into account (Prentky & Burgess, 2000). One method of calculating change-corrected predictive accuracy is to calculate positive predictive accuracy (PPA) and negative predictive accuracy (NPA) (Hart, Webester & Menzies, 1993). PPA and NPA are different ways of conceptualising predictive accuracy where PPA refers to the accuracy of predicting individuals that are

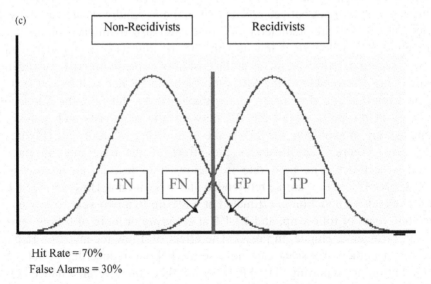

Figure 3.2c The effect of variations in the base rate: Mid-point selection ratio

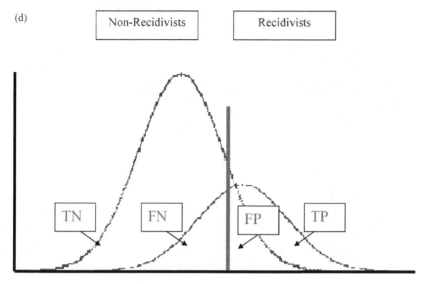

Figure 3.2d The effect of variations in the base rate: Adjusted selection ratio

dangerous while NPA refers to the accuracy of predicting individuals that are not dangerous (see Figure 3.3).

In reflecting the proportion of individuals predicted to re-offend, PPA takes into consideration the percentage of those incorrectly predicted (that is, false positives). A major difficulty in assessing risk in sex offenders is the low base rate. Szmukler (2001) illustrates how low base rates increase the probability of making a false positive error prediction. With a base rate of 6% an actuarial risk instrument with good predictive accuracy (for example, $r = 0.70$, see Janus & Meehl, 1997) would be wrong 9 times out of 10. Craig, Browne, Stringer and Beech (2004) used Szmukler's positive predictive value model to estimate the positive predictive power of a risk assessment scale. Assuming the base rate for sexual offence recidivism in the UK is at around 3% (Falshaw, 2002), and a predictive accuracy of 0.70 for a risk assessment measure (see Janus & Meehl, 1997), the same actuarial risk instrument would be wrong 94 times out of 100 (Figure 3.4).

Conversely, raising the base rate increases the probability of making a false negative error prediction, thus predicting a large number of people will not fail when in fact they will. In reality, the difficulty of predicting events increases as the base rate differs from 0.50 (Meehl & Rosen, 1955). Therefore, the accuracy of our predictions is greatest when the base rate is roughly 50%. As the base rate drops below 50% or rises above 50%, we begin to make more errors, and importantly, we begin to shift the region of error (Prentky & Burgess, 2000, p.109). Low frequency events are difficult to predict but high frequency events are easy to predict and decision-making methods are hardest and need to be highly accurate when predicting the opposite to the

Identified as	Subsequent Re-offending		
High Risk	Yes	No	Total
Yes	a	b	a + b
No	c	d	c + d
Totals	a + c	b + d	N

- **Incidence** of re-offending = (a + c)/N

- **High-risk** group = (a + b)/N

- **Positive Predictive Accuracy** (PPA) = a/(a + b): the percentage of the high-risk group who are subsequently re-offending.

- **Negative Predictive Accuracy** (NPA) = d/(c+ d): the percentage of the non-high-risk group who did not subsequently re-offend.

- **Risk Ratio** (RR) = a/(a + b)/c/(c + d): the relative likelihood of re-offending occurring in the high-risk group compared to the non-high-risk group.

- **Sensitivity** = a/(a + c): the percentage of those re-offended who were correctly identified as being high-risk.

- **Specificity** = d/(b + c): the percentage of the non-offending group who were correctly identified as not being high-risk.

- **Operating Characteristics**: refers to the performance of a test (or set of predictors) that include information on positive predictive accuracy, negative predictive accuracy, sensitivity, and specificity.

Figure 3.3 Contingency table for predictive studies using a cohort design (adapted from Leventhall, 1988)

predominant pattern. With very infrequent events the probability of making false positive errors will be high. Therefore in attempting to predict failure (that is, sexual recidivism) when the base rate is small (for example, 3%, see Falshaw, 2002), we end up predicting that a large number of individuals will re-offend when in fact they will not. This is consistent with Janus and Meehl (1997). The probability that a positive result is true varies with the base rate of the group to which to the test is being applied. With rare conditions, even the most accurate test will produce lots of 'false positives' and the large number outside the condition serves to magnify even small errors in the test (Janus & Meehl, 1997, p. 48).

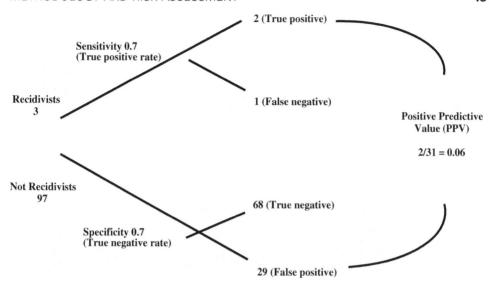

Figure 3.4 The positive predictive value: Base rate of 3% for UK sexual offence recidivism

FACTORS AFFECTING THE SEXUAL RECONVICTION RATE

The potential consequences of over estimating risk and being labelled a high risk offender may include prolonged incarceration, unnecessary supervision and participation on extended sex offender treatment programmes. There are a number of factors that may affect the sexual reconviction rate.

1. One factor affecting the sexual reconviction rate is that of 'downgrading', where sexual offences are bargained down to violent offences in order to secure a conviction. For example, Lees (1996) found that in 10 out of 19 rape cases reported in the UK, the sexual element of the crime was removed and downgraded to a violent offence. Bagley and Pritchard (2000) studied the conviction rate of child molestation and reported that intra-familial child molesters were unlikely to be convicted due to plea-bargaining. Corbett et al. (2003) examined the violent reconvictions for 104 sexual offenders (54% rapists, 11% child molesters and 35% other sexual offenders). They found that 12% of violent reconvictions were sexually motivated but that the sexual element of the offence was not recorded, and that 3% of those charged with a sexual offence were later convicted of a violent offence. Further, 60% of sexually motivated child abduction cases were recorded as violent offences and the sexual element was not recorded (Erickson & Friendship, 2002). In addition, Myhill and Allen (2002) estimate that 80% of rape offences are not reported to the police. Given the rate of detection and reconviction, Jones (2003) argues that past convictions are not the best predictor but it may be more accurate to consider past arrest or even past allegations as indicators of re-offending.

2. A further factor affecting the sexual reconviction rate is that of age of the offender (see Chapter 4). Hanson (2002) examined the relationship of age to sexual recidivism using data from 10 follow-up studies of adult male sexual offenders (combined sample of 4,673) for rapists, extra familial child molesters and incest offenders. When age of release was less then 25 years, incest offenders showed the highest recidivism rate. However, when age of release was greater then 24 years, extra familial child molesters showed the highest rate. Rapists and incest offenders showed relatively steady decline in recidivism related to age, while in contrast, extra familial child molesters showed relatively little reduction in recidivism risk until after the age of 50. Overall, sex offenders released at an older age are less likely to reoffend. Hence, sexual recidivism is found to decrease with age. These age-related decreases have been confirmed while controlling for other risk factors (Barbaree, Blanchard & Langton, 2003).

3. The definition of offending used in sexual offender reconviction follow-up studies (that is, charges, arrests, convictions, behaviours, and so on) may also affect the rate of sexual reconviction reported between studies. Falshaw, Bates, Patel, Corbett and Friendship (2003) followed 173 sexual offenders for up to six-years and compared differences in offending base rates between official (using the Home Office Offenders Index (OI); and Police National Computer (PNC)) and unofficial sources (a community-based sexual offender treatment program). The unofficial sexual recidivism rate was 5.3 times greater than the reconviction rate calculated from the OI, and 1.8 times greater than that calculated from the PNC. Using unofficial data the base rates were 6% for sexual 'reconviction', for 7% sexual 're-offending', and for 16% sexual 'recidivism' (high risk sexual offence behaviours). Similarly, Marshall and Barbaree (1988) estimated that unofficial sources show 2.4 times more re-offences than official records. The accepted underreporting of sexual offences would indicate that re-arrest rates are lower than actual re-offence rates (see Janus & Meehl, 1997). Clearly, the mechanism of how sexual recidivistic behaviour is being measured has important implications for risk assessment. Indeed, the extent to which official reconviction sources can be used as an indicator of the true official sexual reconviction rate has been questioned.

Differences in risk characteristics between sexual offender subgroups raise the question, 'to what extent can actuarial measures generalise across sexual offender subgroups?' In considering this question we explore the relationship between base rates and actuarial risk scales.

BASE RATES AND ACTUARIAL RISK SCALES

The application of actuarial risk scales to individuals with characteristics outside those of the original study group will likely limit the predictive accuracy of the scale and lead to erroneous assessments of risk from one individual to another. Such variations may, in part, be due to a systemic flaw which is more commonly known as the 'statistical fallacy' effect (Dingwall, 1989). This effect describes the process of comparing a single individual to the group data who share similar characteristics. The actuarial method compares similarities of an individual's profile to the aggregated knowledge of past events of convicted sexual offenders. By using an actuarial scale on an individual who does not share the same risk characteristics of the original study sample can have the effect of reducing the predictive accuracy of the scale. For example, most risk classification instruments include the number of previous criminal convictions, prior sexual convictions and prior non-sexual violence.

Like Rogers (2000), Doren (2002) argues that due to differences in base rates of sexual recidivism and differences in offender cohort characteristics on which actuarial measures are based, risk assessments should not be based solely on the use of actuarial measures. Indeed, it is generally accepted that sexual offender subgroups recidivate at different rates. For example, rapists (offenders with adult victims) are more likely to recidivate at a greater rate compared with child molesters (offenders with child victims) (Quinsey, Rice & Harris, 1995).

AREA UNDER THE CURVE (AUC) AND THE RECEIVER OPERATING CHARACTERISTIC (ROC) ANALYSIS

When considering the predictive accuracy of an actuarial risk scale, statistics derived from the Receiver Operating Characteristic (ROC) analysis is preferred indices of predictive accuracy and effect size (Harris, 2003; Swets, Dawes & Monahan, 2000). A comparison of *sensitivity* (true positive divided by the sum of true positive and false negatives: the percentage of re-offenders correctly identified as high-risk on assessment), with *specificity* (true negative divided by the sum of false positive and false negative: the percentage of non re-offenders correctly identified as low-risk). There is a *trade-off* between the true positives (sensitivity or hit rate) and true negatives (specificity) as follows:

- If the threshold for labelling individuals high risk, from a psychometric assessment or set of predictors, is lowered then the number of false positives or alarms increases (the percentage of non-re-offenders who are incorrectly labelled high risk).
- If the threshold for labelling individuals high risk, from a psychometric assessment or set of predictors, is heightened then the number of false negatives or misses increases (the percentage of re-offenders who are incorrectly labelled low risk).

Thus, the false alarm rate (false positives) is reciprocal to sensitivity (true positives), whereas the miss rate (false negatives) is reciprocal to specificity (true negatives). From this information the positive predictive accuracy is calculated. This identifies

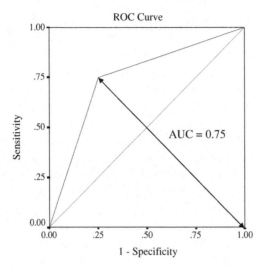

Figure 3.5 Relative operating characteristic: area under the curve = 0.75

the overall number of cases that are correctly classified as a percentage of the total number in the high-risk group (Prentky & Burgess, 2000). A perfectly accurate test would yield a ROC of 1.0 or 100% hit rate (this means there is no overlap between recidivists and non-recidivists). A ROC of 0.50 or 50% hit rate would indicate a predictive efficacy no better than chance.

The 'curve' for a perfect test would travel up the vertical axis then along the top of the box until it reaches the top right-hand corner producing a curve on the graph (Figure 3.5). A perfectly accurate test would yield an 'Area under the Curve' (AUC) hit rate of 1.0 (no overlap between recidivists and non-recidivists). In contrast, a diagonal line representing an area under the curve of 0.50 indicates a useless test with a predictive accuracy no better than flipping a coin. The AUC statistic of 0.50 indicates the prediction is at chance level (50:50) and anything above 0.50 is an increase in predictive accuracy. A typical AUC for sexual reconviction is often in the range of about 0.75 (see Craig, Browne & Stringer, 2003). In examining the effects sizes of many variables, Cohen (1988) considered $d = .20$ a small effect, 0.50 a moderate effect, and 0.80 a large effect. These would correspond to AUC indices of approximately 0.56, 0.65, and 0.72 respectively (R. K. Hanson, personal communication, 5 February 2004). Leventhal (1988) suggests that for a test or set of predictive factors to be of practical use in the prediction of child maltreatment, the receiver operating characteristics (ROC) should at least reach the following levels:

- Positive predictive accuracy: 25%
- Sensitivity: 60%
- Specificity: 90%

However, there are a number of limitations in the use of the ROC analysis that may account for variations in cross validation studies. The ROC statistic can only be applied to binary outcomes (recidivist versus non-recidivist) and cannot interpret continuous scales reflecting the severity or frequency with which recidivism occurs. Harris and Rice (2003) argue that the ROC analysis cannot account for the reliability of the data set (differences in definitions of recidivism), follow-up periods, or variations in offender characteristics.

Making ROC calculations assumes that the rates of sensitivity and specificity are equal to each other and therefore equal to the overall accuracy. That is, the accuracy in identifying recidivists (sensitivity) is the same as that in identifying non-recidivists (specificity). However, as Janus and Meehl (1997) note, prediction schemes can be calibrated to produce different rates of sensitivity and specificity. Here Janus and Meehl (1997) provide an extensive and detailed analysis of the accuracy of the actual standard or thresholds used by the judiciary in deciding which sex offenders are considered dangerous and meet the criteria for a civil commitment within the purviews of 'sexual predator' laws in the United States.

The criteria for commitment considers three aspects: that the individual has engaged in harmful sexual conduct in the past, that the individual currently suffers from a mental disorder, and that the individual will likely engage in future acts of harmful sexual misconduct (Janus & Meehl, 1997). They consider the process by which sex offender commitment courts set thresholds based on 'likelihood' or 'probability' of behaviour by an individual. They make the distinction between two groups of offenders; 'commitment class' – those offenders committed under the 'sexual predator' laws; and 'prison-release class' – incarcerated sexual offenders potentially eligible for commitment.

They examine the process by which evidence is presented to the court by the mental health professionals. If all experts agree that the individual will not reoffend sexually, the petition for commitment is dropped. However, if at least one expert judges that the individual will reoffend, the petition for commitment will proceed to trial. They note that the experts' assessments are not dichotomous (recidivist, non-recidivists) but instead make statements of probability, and if at least one expert judges the individual to be likely or highly likely to re-offend, the petition for commitment will be granted (having established the commitment criteria). They argue that probability statements are statements of groups of people to which the subject is being categorised, and to this extent, will have varying degrees of rates of recidivism depending on which category the individual belongs to. They suggest that the judicial process does not necessarily always take this into account.

After considering the literature on actuarial measures they conclude that actuarial prediction methods need to demonstrate accuracy rates of 0.70 (good) or 0.75 (benchmark) in order for the court to make valid and reliable judgements on commitment. Further calculations from the literature reveal sexual and violent recidivist rates of 20%–45% for the 'commitment class' and 20% for the 'prison-release class' of which a special group of 5% assumes a recidivism rate of 75%. Having considered the base rate and accuracy of actuarial measures at 0.70, Janus and Meehl (1997) translates the probability of recidivism in the 'commitment class' between 37% and 66%, and 23% to 50% for the commitment class by base rate of the 'prison release class' and special group. This, they argue, is below the benchmark of 75% accuracy. They conclude that the judiciary typically commits people using a far lower threshold for potential dangerousness than the courts claim to be their standard.

In exploring the sensitivity and specificity of risk measures, Janus and Meehl (1997) cite Hanson, Steffy and Gauthier's (1993) use of a 'risk checklist' assigning scores from 0 to 5 for each child molester in the study. Of those who scored 5, 77% were reconvicted of a sexual or violent offence, and by definition a cut-score of 5 using the same risk checklist would yield a court commitment of 77% of sexual offenders. Sensitivity would be 15%, meaning that the commitment process would allow 85% of all recidivists to go free. They argue that, 'specificity would be a near perfect 97% – almost all non-recidivists would be correctly identified (1997, p. 58). However, they argue that Hanson et al.'s results cannot be applied to the court commitment process due to having lower recidivism base rates (41% – sexual and violent recidivism) and limitations in the ability to generalise the results from Hanson et al.'s sample.

However, Doren and Epperson (2001) offer a critique of Janus and Meehl's analysis specifically addressing assumptions in the calculations in base rates and the single cut-scores. Doren and Epperson suggest that Janus and Meehl (1997) miscalculated the base rate scores due to not taking into account the predominant type of sexual offender referred for commitment. They argue that the people referred for potential commitment, and especially those actually committed, show a larger proportion of child molesters than does the overall set of incarcerated sex offenders. Rates from 63% to 88% translate to an average base rate of 47.2% to 50.4% for people in the commitment class, and from 45.6% to 48.9% for the 'prison-release class'. Rightly, they argue that the bulk of Janus and Meehl's analysis is based on the 'commitment class' and assume that the rate is the same for the 'prison-release class'. Doren and Epperson argue that having considered the revised base rate of at least 50%, the standard of 70% is achieved and 75% is approached. Using the revised base rates, Doren and Epperson concluded that the judiciary does employ standards in keeping with the court's stated claims and the apparent intentions of the sex offender commitment laws (2001, p. 51).

Turning to the cut-scores, Doren and Epperson (2001) argue that Janus and Meehl were misguided in assuming a dichotomy of risk based on a singly cut-score. They cite several psychometric and actuarial measures that offer a range of scores relating to extent and severity of the problem. Indeed, the majority of actuarial risk measures offer guidelines of recidivism associated with confidence levels of risk based on relative costs of false positive and false negatives. As Doren and Epperson report, increasing the cut-scores decreases the false positive rate at the expense of increasing the false negative rate. However, cut-scores can be increased to minimise the probability of a false positive prediction when the costs of false positive predictions outweigh the costs associated with false negative prediction (Doren & Epperson, p. 50). Therefore, the selection ratio (those in the sample scoring above the cut-score) will vary and fixing specificity equal to sensitivity would not be a requirement of the applied use of actuarial risk instruments.

APPLYING GROUP DATA TO INDIVIDUALS

The actuarial method compares similarities of an individual's profile to the aggregated knowledge of past events of convicted sexual offenders. However, the extent to which cohort data can be applied to individual characteristics and sex offender subgroups has been questioned (Craig, Browne & Stringer, 2004). Where the sample is large, the margin of error for this group estimate is very small. However, as the sample numbers decrease, the margin of error gets larger. Like Rogers (2000), Litwack (2001) and Silver and Miller (2002) urge caution when using actuarial risk assessment tools for predicting interpersonal violence. Firstly, they argue actuarial tools are designed primarily to facilitate the efficient management of institutional resources rather than to target individuals or social conditions in need of reform. Secondly, the group-based nature of actuarial prediction methods may contribute to the continued marginalization of populations already at the fringes of the economic and political mainstream.

Hart, Michie, and Cooke (2007) recently considered the 'margins of error' in group versus individual prediction of violence. Assuming that for a given actuarial risk category group estimates of violence risk are binomial proportions, Hart et al. calculated the 95% confidence intervals (CI) for the Static-99 (Hanson & Thornton, 2000) and the Violence Risk Appraisal Guide (VRAG, Quinsey, Harris, Rice & Cormier, 1998). For group estimates, in respect of Static-99, the 95% CI's for score categories ranged from 8 to 19 percentage points in width, with a mean of about 13 percentage points. With regard to the risk categories (zero to 6) in the Static-99, categories 0, 1, 2 and 3 had overlapping 95% CI's; categories 4, 5 and 6+ had 95% CIs that overlapped with each other but not with those of categories 0–3. Thus, the Static-99 yielded only two distinct group estimates of risk: low and high. Looking at the VRAG, the 95% CIs for score categories ranged from 13 to 30 percentage points in width, with a mean of about 20 percentage points. With regard to risk categories (zero to 9) in the VRAG categories 1–4 had overlapping 95% CIs, categories 5–7 overlapped with each other, but not with those of categories 1–4, category 8 did not overlap with those of categories 1–6, but did overlap with that of category 7, and category 9 did not overlap with those of categories 1–7, but did overlap with that of category 8. These findings suggest that the VRAG risk categories yield three reasonably distinct group estimates of risk: low, moderate, and high. However, when calculated for individual estimates, the 95% CIs were much greater. For the Static-99, the 95% CIs for score categories ranged from 82 to 89 percentage points in width, with a mean of about 86 percentage points. For the VRAG, the 95% CIs for score categories ranged from 79 to 89 percentage points in width, with a mean of about 85 percentage points. Put simply, the 95% CIs for score categories within each test overlapped almost completely, indicating that their risk estimates did not differ significantly. Hart et al. argue that at the individual level, the margins of error were so high as to render the test results virtually meaningless, having little, if any, practical value when estimating risk.

However, Doren (2007) offers a critique of the Hart et al. (2007) study based on four methodological principles. The first principle considers that the utility of any statistical procedure is compromised when invalid assumptions are made. Doren argues that the formulas for upper and lower limits in computing confidence intervals, as listed by Hart et al., were derived with the presumption of group data application (that is, at a very minimum, n > 1). This can be seen in the formulas themselves where a figure (θ) is necessary for the 'proportion of recidivists in the category'. Hart et al. report, 'When considering groups, the probability is defined in frequentist terms as the proportion of people who will commit violence. . .and the margin of error is uncertainty regarding the proportion of people who will commit violence. However, these definitions do not make sense for individuals, who either will or will not commit violence' (p. 61). Doren argues that the analysis in using the formula presumes that a 'proportion' of a 'group' where n = 1 can be expressed in something other than 0% and 100%. Doren points out that Hart et al. report 'in between' figures (based on group data) to do their computations. An n = 1 application of the statistical formulas used violates assumptions inherent in those formulas. Hence, results derived are not directly interpretable. The second principle considered by Doren is the principle of using multiple sources of data and using more data, both of which are better than using a single data source. The computations of 95% CI for group data were based solely on the developmental studies for each instrument (that is, the VRAG and Static-99). Doren argues that Hart et al. drew conclusions based solely on those data, ignoring the fact that other data were available (for example, from Doren, 2004, for the Static-99). Using smaller versus larger samples serves to result in confidence intervals that are larger than would be determined if more existing data were used. Doren suggests by ignoring existing data served to increase the size of computed confidence intervals unnecessarily. The third principle considers the repeated supportive cross-validations of the empirical findings represent reality better than one statistically derived finding. Hart et al. conclude that there is no differentiation across any of the studied actuarial levels when 'individual confidence intervals' are computed. Doren suggests that if this were true, then we should expect to see some degree of variability across studies in the relative rank ordering of the risk levels, due to this degree of individual variability. He argues this is not found either for the VRAG or the Static-99, where the rank orders for recidivism rates have regularly been found to be linear and the AUCs (a measure of the relative rank ordering of the risk levels) quite consistently are significantly different from chance. Indeed, he argues that regular empirical results contradict what Hart et al. suggest being true. The fourth principle considers that prediction involves 'either-or' statements, while individual risk assessments are described in proportions. Doren argues that Hart et al. use these concepts interchangeably. For instance, they state 'the difficulties of predicting the outcomes for groups versus individuals – whether in the context of games of chance or of violence risk assessments – are intuitively obvious' (p. 63). However, Doren points out that the authors' earlier quoted statement (from p. 61) rejected this overlap in concepts when it came to individuals. Hart et al. indicate the belief that proportional concepts do not apply to individuals. The inherent contradiction from this view and the findings from the authors' analysis can be seen in the fact that the 'individual confidence intervals' are regularly in proportional terms (Doren, 2007). Doren suggests that once you conclude that proportional concepts do apply to individuals (that is, risk assessments are appropriately described in proportional terms that are different from predictions), Hart et al.'s conclusions become questionable. For example, the conclusion that 'individual prediction errors are extremely large' (p. 63) does not speak to the accuracy of risk assessments that are in more proportional terms. Doren argues that the analysis within Hart et al.'s study says nothing about the accuracy of actuarial risk assessment instruments within the risk assessment context.

Like Doren (2007), Mossman and Sellke (2007), and Harris, Rice and Quinsey (2007) also express concern over Hart et al.'s study. Mossman and Sellke (2007) argue that Hart et al. were incorrect to view 'individual risk' as something different from 'group risk'. Harris et al. (2007) argue that Hart et al.'s study is statistically flawed by conflating test reliability and validity. The first error related to using confidence intervals to assess the 'precision' or 'margin of error' for an individual test result. However, confidence intervals were not designed for this purpose but rather the standard error of measurement which is the margin of error associated with a single person's true score would be more appropriate. Harris et al. argue that much research is based on aggregated data of many single observations of behaviour, and yet to use a single case as evidence conveys only a little scientific information. Indeed, the notion that it is wrong to base individual decisions on 'group data' has been refuted (Grove & Meehl, 1996; Quinsey et al., 2006). Harris et al. note that Hart et al. use the terms 'precision' and 'accuracy' interchangeably. However, test accuracy (i.e., validity) is assessed in terms of sensitivity, specificity, and the trade off between these two. As Harris et al. note there are more than 40 independent tests of the accuracy of the VRAG and approximately 40 replications, involving more than 13,000 cases, of the Static-99. Contrary to the assertions of Hart and colleagues, VRAG scores have been shown to predict the speed and severity of violent recidivism. Harris et al. argue that the statistical argument by Hart and colleagues does not refute these empirical results supporting the accuracy of actuarial risk assessments. By conventional standards, average predictive effects (in terms of the sensitivity-specificity trade off) are large and are distributed as expected by psychometric principles and the laws of probability. Harris et al. argue that classification accuracy is the standard in assessing the kind of 'precision' attempted by Hart and colleagues. In most tests of the VRAG, there have been no statistically significant differences between the observed rates and those expected on the basis of the proportions provided as norms (Harris & Rice, in press), especially given known variation predicted by Bayes' Rule. Harris et al. conclude that, the undeniable superiority in accuracy of actuarial systems over known alternatives means they must be used where available and the abandonment of decision making on risk will only worsen the practice of clinicians who must make decisions about the risk of violent recidivism.

As we have attempted to do in this chapter, Harris et al. rightly note that it is important to understand that the reliability and validity of actuarial instruments are independent of their use in particular schemes for sentencing and managing offenders.

CONCLUSIONS

The research has demonstrated the predictive validity of actuarial risk assessment scales over that of clinical judgement and this has led to a proliferation of actuarial assessments. Although actuarial risk assessment scales have shown to be good predictors of long-term risk they have a number of limitations. Practitioners using actuarial scales in adversarial settings (for example, courts, parole hearings) must do so with caution and have a thorough understanding of methodological limitations of the technology and possible errors and inaccuracies of reporting actuarial risk estimates in individual cases. Data relating to actuarial estimates should be presented alongside dynamic changes in a person's risk which is likely to reflect a more idiosyncratic assessment of risk rather than relying on mechanistic predictions. Although the research supports the use of some actuarial measures, they only describe part of the picture and may not necessarily be sufficient for all types of offenders. Indeed, the use of actuarial scales should be restricted to those individuals who share characteristics consistent with the original study sample. Any deviation from the cohort data is likely to lead to anomalous outcomes in levels of predicted risk.

PART II

Static risk factors

4

Static Factors Associated with Sexual Recidivism

INTRODUCTION

Risk factors can be divided into two types, *static* and *dynamic* factors, with dynamic factors being subdivided into *stable* and *acute* risk factors.

- *Static* risk factors are useful for evaluating long-term risk, but because it is historical in nature it cannot be used to assess changes in levels of risk over time. Examples of static risk factors include age at first conviction, victim characteristics (that is, unrelated, stranger, or male child), developmental and offence history and history of diagnoses.
- *Dynamic* risk factors are enduring factors linked to the likelihood of offending that can nevertheless be changed following intervention. Dynamic factors can be subdivided into *stable* and *acute* factors.
- *Stable Dynamic* factors are those factors which are relatively persistent characteristics of the offender which are subject to change over long periods of time such as levels of responsibility, cognitive distortions and sexual arousal.
- *Acute Dynamic* factors are rapidly changing factors that change day-by-day or hour-by-hour such as substance misuse, isolation, victim acquisition behaviours and negative emotional states, the presence of which increase risk.

Most actuarial risk assessment scales primarily use static risk factors and several static factors have repeatedly been demonstrated to predict sexual recidivism. In a review of the literature Craig, Browne, Stringer and Beech (2005) examined 26 studies on sexual offence recidivism ($n = 33,001$) and identified 17 static factors that were associated with sexual offence (Table 4.1). These included prior

Table 4.1 Static risk factors associated with sexual offence recidivism

Static Risk Factors

Developmental Factors	Victim Factors	Sexual Interest Factors	Forensic Factors	Clinical Factors
Juvenile sexual offences	Extra familial victim	Non-contact sexual offences	Past criminal history	Lower IQ
Poor family background	Male victim	Deviant sexual interest[1]	Past sexual convictions	Marital/relationship history
Victim of sexual abuse	Stranger victim	Sexual arousal to children[3]	Past violent convictions	Discontinuation in community Treatment programmes
Age-at-first-offence	Multiple victims	Paraphilias (Atypical Sexual Outlets)	Time spent in custody	Diagnosis of Personality Disorder Psychopathy[2]
Age-at-release (inversely related)	Unrelated victim		Number of previous sentencing occasions	
				Emotional congruence

NOTE:
[1]Deviant sexual arousal has been measured using the definition of Sexual Deviance recorded in the Sexual Violence Risk -20 (Boer et al., 1997) manual and criteria in the Diagnostic and Statistical Manual for Mental Disorders – Fourth Edition-TR (DSM-IV-TR, 2000).
[2]The diagnosis of Psychopathy assessed using the Psychopathic Checklist-Revised (that is, a score of 30 or more; Hare, 1991) was considered a static risk factor.
3The measure of sexual arousal toward children using the penile plethysmography was considered a static factor as it is enduring and resistant to change.

criminality (Broadhurst & Maller, 1992; Browne, Foreman & Middleton, 1998; Långström & Grann, 2000; Proulx et al., 1997; Rice, Harris & Quinsey, 1990; Thornton & Travers, 1991; Worling & Curwne, 2000), prior sexual offences (Hanson & Bussière, 1998; Hanson, Scot & Steffy, 1995; Hanson, Steefy & Gauthier, 1993; Quinsey, Rice & Harris, 1995), Psychopathy (Hanson & Harris, 1998; Långström & Grann, 2000; McGuire, 2000; Rice, Harris & Quinsey, 1990; Serin, Mailoux & Malcolm, 2001; Seto & Barbaree, 1999; Worling, 2001), age and time spent in custody (Broadhurst & Maller, 1992; Browne et al., 1998), and paraphilias and deviant sexual interests (Hanson & Bussière, 1998; Hanson & Harris, 1998; Proulx et al., 1997; Quinsey, Rice & Harris, 1995; Worling & Curwen, 2000).

Hanson, Scott and Steffy (1995) found static factors that predicted sexual recidivism among child sex offenders were prior offence type and victim type, different from the predictors of non-sexual recidivism (low education, youth, violence). Extra familial male victim factors were closely related to recidivism in several studies (Frisbie & Dondis, 1965; Proulx et al., 1997; Hanson et al., 1993) though Prentky et al. (1997a) found that sex of the victim was not predictive of recidivism. Criminal lifestyle variables were strong predictive measures (Hanson & Harris, 1998; 2000c) but it seems logical that those already known to authorities are more likely to be detected in future. Broadhurst and Maller (1992) concluded that sex offenders are not specialist [unique] offenders but the factors significantly related to recidivism were true of the general prison population. It must be noted, however, that their study was based on static risk factors, relating to previous criminal history, so these findings may be expected. Moreover, predictors of violent recidivism (for example, juvenile delinquency, age, prior offences and personality disorder) were the same as those who predict recidivism in the general population of non-sexual criminals. This may go some way to explain why some actuarial risk measures for sexual offenders were found to be better predictors of general offending behaviour rather than specific offending patterns such as sexual or violent offences (see Craig, Browne & Stringer, 2003a). In a recent actuarial risk assessment evaluation study (Craig, Beech & Browne, 2006a), only one out of six measures (Rapid Risk Assessment for Sexual Offence Recidivism: RRASOR, Hanson, 1997) obtained greater accuracy in predicting sexual reconviction than for violent or general reconviction. However, in a retrospective study, Långström and Grann (2000) reviewed all forensic psychiatric evaluations. Consistent with previous studies, factors that predicted general recidivism were not the same as those associated with sexual recidivism. Previous sex offences, poor social skills, male victims, and two or more victims in index offence were all risk factors associated with sexual recidivism. Early conduct disorder, previous convictions, psychopathy, and the use of death threats or weapons at the index sex offence were predictors for general criminality.

PERSONALITY DISORDER, PSYCHOPATHY AND SEXUAL DEVIANCE

In an attempt to define personality-based subgroups of sexual offenders, Worling (2001) assessed 112 adolescent sex offenders over a six-year follow-up using the California Psychological Profile (CPI, Gough, 1987), a protocol designed to assess 20 variables related to both interpersonal and intrapersonal functioning. Four-group typologies of adolescent male sex offenders were reported; Antisocial/ Impulsive; Unusual/Isolated; Overcontrolled/Reserved; and Confident/Aggressive. A small difference was observed between groups regarding familial relationships to the victim, attributable to having younger siblings in the family. Offenders prone to selecting intra familial victims were also more likely to have younger siblings in their families. Antisocial/Impulsive offenders were the most likely to have received criminal charges for their index sexual assaults, and to have been recipients of abusive physical discipline. Although there were no significant differences between groups with respect to sexual assault recidivism, the two more pathological groups, Antisocial/Impulsive and Unusual/Isolated offenders, were most likely to have been charged with a subsequent violent (sexual or non-sexual) or non-violent offence.

Factors such as a diagnosis of Psychopathy,[1] deviant sexual interests and offence history are consistently associated with sex offender recidivism (Hanson & Hariss, 1998; Quinsey, Rice & Hariss, 1995; Rice, Hariss & Quinsey, 1990; Serin, Mailloux & Malcolm 2001). Gretton et al. (2001) administered the youth version of the PCL-R (PCL:YV, Forth, Kosson & Hare, 2003) to 220 adolescent males in an outpatient sex offender treatment programme. It was reported that offenders with high PCL:YV scores and penile plethysmography evidence of deviant sexual arousal prior to treatment were at very high risk for general reoffending.

In examining the interaction between psychopathy and treatment behaviour and recidivism, Seto and Barbaree (1999) found that there was no difference between rapists, incest offenders and extra familial child molesters in their scores in treatment behaviour. Rapists were more than twice as likely to commit any kind of offence as child molesters but did not differ in their likelihood to commit a new

---

[1]Psychopathy measured using The Hare Psychopathy Checklist-Revised (PCL-R: Hare, 1991). The PCL-R is a standardised rating scale for the assessment of psychopathy in forensic populations. It examines behaviours and inferred personality traits related to a widely understood clinical concept of psychopathy. Psychopathy is a severe personality disorder characterised by a set of affective, interpersonal and behavioural features, which include the selfish, callous and remorseless use of others, deficient affective experience, and an impulsive irresponsible lifestyle, which may include antisocial behaviour. The PCL-R score is made up of two factor scores: Factor 1 (interpersonal/affective) and Factor 2 (socially deviant lifestyle). Each of these factors breaks down into two sub-factors or facets. Factor 1 can be divided into two facets of Interpersonal (e.g. glibness/superficial charm; grandiose sense of self-worth) and Affective (e.g. lack or remorse or guilt; shallow affect; lack of empathy). Factor 2 can be divided into two facets of Lifestyle (e.g. lack of realistic long term goals; parasitic; irresponsibility) and Antisocial (poor behavioural controls; criminal versatility) (Hare, 2003).

serious offence. Neither PCL-R nor treatment behaviour predicted general recidivism but was significantly related to serious recidivism (a new violent or sexual offence). However, men who scored higher in psychopathy and displayed good treatment behaviour were almost three times as likely to commit any kind of new offence, and five times more likely to commit a serious re-offence than men in the other group combinations. This is consistent with previous research where high PCL-R scorers who displayed good treatment behaviour re-offended at a higher rate (Hare, 2002; Rice, Harris & Cormier, 1992; Quinsey, Harris, Rice & Cormier, 1998). However, in a replication study Barbaree, Seto and Langton (2001a) found no relationship between high PCL-R scores and displays of good treatment behaviour and subsequent recidivism. Indeed, in contrast to Seto and Barbaree's earlier findings, Richards, Casey and Lucente (2003) examined the treatment behaviour of 404 incarcerated females in a substance abuse treatment efficacy study using the PCL-R. Psychopathy scores were significantly associated with poor treatment behaviour and Factor 1 scores better predicted new charges once released into the community. Kiehl, Hare, McDonald and Brink (1999) also reported that those offenders with higher Factor 1 scores (affective and interpersonal traits) were at higher risk of recidivism following treatment. Hare (2002) suggests that high Factor 1 PCL-R scorers may actually learn manipulative behaviour of other skills in treatment that increase their risk for serious recidivism (Quinsey, Khanna & Malcolm, 1998).

Like Seto and Barbaree (1999), Serin, Mailloux and Malcolm (2001) assessed the relationship between psychopathy (Factors 1 and 2), deviant sexual arousal and recidivism in a sample 68 incarcerated sexual offenders followed up post release for seven years. Unlike Kiehl et al. (2000), recidivists had significantly higher Factor 2 scores than non-recidivists although it is not clear whether Factor scores are related to type and nature of reoffending. Although recidivists did not differ from non-recidivist in terms of sexual deviance, child molesters had slightly higher mean arousal scores than rapists. Rapists had significantly worse survival times[2] than child molesters. Those offenders considered high risk (scored above 15.5 on the PCL-R) were less successful than those in the low risk group and those offenders who had higher indices of deviant sexual arousal coupled with higher PCL-R scores, recidivated sooner and more often than those of similar levels of deviance with lower PCL-R scores. This is consistent with previous findings regarding patterns of sexual offender recidivism (Rice & Harris, 1997; Rice et al., 1990; Quinsey et al., 1995). However, it is worth noting that a PCL-R cut score of 15.5 is not considered sufficient for a diagnosis of Psychopathy. In using the PCL-R, the cut score used in North America and Canada is 30, while in the UK male prison population it is 25

---

[2]Survival analysis is a statistical technique used to determine the average time spent in the community prior to recidivating, given certain predictor variables and controlling for unequal time to fail.

(Hare, 1991). It follows then by using cut scores lower than that of the diagnostic minimum can lead to misleading interpretations of the overall findings.

Porter et al. (2000) investigated whether psychopathy would contribute to the understanding of the heterogeneity of sexual violence. The PCL-R was administered to 329 incarcerated sex offenders and nonsexual offenders categorised according to the nature of their crimes. Mixed rapist/child molesters and rapists were more psychopathic than pure child molesters, although all sex offender groups showed elevated Factor 1 scores. A high proportion (64%) of offenders who had victimszed both children and adults were psychopathic, indicative of a criminal whose thrill seeking is directed at diverse sexual victims (appropriately called a sexual psychopath). This is broadly consistent with Woodworth and Porter (2002) who investigated the relationship between psychopathy and the characteristics of criminal homicides committed by a sample of 125 Canadian offenders. It was found that homicides committed by psychopathic offenders were significantly more instrumental (that is, associated with premeditation, motivated by an external goal, and not proceeded by a potent affective reaction) or 'cold-blooded' in nature, whereas homicides committed by non-psychopaths often would be 'crimes of passion' associated with a high level of impulsivity/reactivity and emotionality.

There is an argument that psychopathy should be considered as a stable dynamic risk factor as it changes with age and in some circumstances, intervention. Porter, Birt and Boer (2001) administered the PCL-R to 317 Canadian federal offenders (224 low scorers and 93 scoring within the psychopathic range) and using the diagnostic cut score of 30 investigated the complete criminal career and community release profiles. Adult crimes were coded according to age at commission as well as violent, non-violent, or non-sexually violent. Changes in performance following release into the community also were examined. Offenders scoring within the psychopathic range consistently committed more violent and non-violent crimes than their counterparts for about three decades, spanning their late adolescence to their late 40s. However, the numbers of non-violent criminal offences committed by high PCL-R scorers declined considerably after age 30 relative to violent offences, which declined and then rebounded in the late 30s before a major reduction was evidenced. Adulthood high PCL-R scorers failed during community release significantly faster than did low scorers. The release performance of low PCL-R scorers improved with age, whereas the opposite was seen for high scorers. Further, offenders scoring high on the PCL-R did not show a lower charge to conviction ratio with age, suggesting that they may not have been getting better at manipulating the legal system.

It is a widely held belief that psychopathic individuals are extremely difficult to treat, if not immune to treatment. However, Salekin (2002) reviewed 42 treatment studies on psychopathy and found little scientific basis for the belief that psychopathy is an untreatable disorder. Three significant problems with regard to the research on the psychopathy treatment relation cast doubt on the treatability of this disorder. Salekin found there is considerable disagreement as to the defining characteristics of psychopathy, that the aetiology of psychopathy is not well understood, and that there are relatively few empirical investigations of the psychopathy treatment relationship and even fewer efforts that follow up psychopathic individuals after treatment. Skeem, Monahan and Mulvey (2002) also question the position that individuals with psychopathy typically are viewed as incurable. Based on a sample of 871 civil psychiatric patients (including 195 'potentially psychopathic' and 72 'psychopathic' patients), they explored the relationship with psychopathy, receipt of outpatient mental health services in real-world settings, and subsequent violence in the community. The results suggest that psychopathic traits do not moderate the effect of treatment involvement on violence, even after controlling statistically for the treatment assignment process. Psychopathic patients appear as likely as non-psychopathic patients to benefit from adequate doses of treatment, in terms of violence reduction. However, it is not clear to what extent Porter et al.'s (2001) or Skeem et al.'s (2002) results extend to sexual offenders.

Hildebrand, de Ruier and de Vogel (2004) examined the role of psychopathy and sexual deviance in predicting recidivism in a Dutch forensic psychiatric sample of 94 rapists. The sample was followed-up for up to 23.5 years. The base rate for sexual recidivism was the lowest at 34%, compared with violent nonsexual recidivism at 47%, for violent including sexual recidivism at 55% and for general recidivism at 73%. They found for all types of offending, those scoring high on the PCL-R (≥ 26) were significantly more often reconvicted than other offenders. They found the psychopathic and nonpsychopathic offenders differed significantly with respect to sexual recidivism. In their study the determination of sexual deviance was based on the operational definition of sexual deviance used in the Sexual Violent Risk-20 (SVR-20, Boer et al., 1997) (see Chapter 5). This was based on the persons' documented history of offending and/or the acknowledgement of sexual deviance during treatment. Sexual deviance was found to be a significant predictor of sexual reconviction and survival analysis revealed that psychopathic sex offenders with sexual deviant preferences are at substantially greater risk of committing new sexual offences than psychopathic offenders without deviant preferences, or nonpsychopathic offenders with or without sexual deviance. They also found, consistent with the Hanson and Bussière (1998) meta-analysis, the total number of prior convictions (sexual, violent nonsexual, general) was found to be a significant predictor of recidivism (sexual, violent non-sexual and general). Although marital status was found to be a predictor of sexual recidivism, substance abuse was only a significant predictor for violent non-sexual reoffending. Age-at-first offence and marital status did not add incremental variance over psychopathy for the prediction of violent non-sexual, violent or general reconviction. Consistent with previous research, Hildebrand et al. found that the presence of deviant sexual preferences was significantly related to an increased risk of reconviction for a sexual offence.

Summary findings this research indicate sexually deviant psychopathic rapists recidivate more often and faster with a sexual offence that other groups of rapists. Hildebrand et al.'s research highlights the importance of combining assessments of psychopathy and deviant sexual interest when assessing risk on sexual offenders.

AGE AND SEXUAL RECIDIVISM

Although a number of research studies indicate a negative correlation with age and sexual offence recidivism, the effect of age on sexual and violent reconviction remains unclear with some studies producing contradictory results. Hanson (2002) examined the relationship of age to sexual recidivism using data from 10 follow-up studies of adult male sexual offenders (combined sample of 4,673) for rapists, extra familial child molesters, and incest offenders. When age of release was less than 25 years, incest offenders showed the highest recidivism rate. However, when age of release was greater than 24 years, extra familial child molesters showed the highest rate. Rapists and incest offenders showed relatively steady decline in recidivism related to age; while in contrast, extra familial child molesters showed relatively little reduction in recidivism risk until after the age of 50. Overall, sex offenders released at an older age are less likely to reoffend. Hence, sexual recidivism is found to decrease with age. The recidivism rate of intra familial child molesters was generally low (less than 10%), except for the intra familial offenders in the 18 to 24 year old age group, whose recidivism risk was comparable to that of rapists and extra familial child molesters. Barbaree, Blanchard and Langton (2003) re-examined Hanson's (2002) results and found age-related decreases in recidivism while controlling for other risk factors. They followed 468 sex offenders released into the community were followed for an average period of over five years. The effects of age-at-release were examined using survival curves. Offenders released at an older age were less likely to recommit sexual offences and that sexual recidivism decreased as a linear function of age-at-release. Recidivism rates were highest at younger ages for child molesters and lowest for incest offenders. They found by the age of 60 or 70 years there was a uniformly low sexual recidivism rate for rapists, child molesters and incest offenders. When Barbaree et al. examined the five-year recidivism rate in respect of 'age bands' of offenders they found a drop in sexual recidivism rates from 16.7% for the youngest band to 3.82% for the over 50 age band. They also examined the effects of age on sexual arousal and sexual recidivism in sex offenders. Erectile responses were measured in a sample of 1,431 sex offenders using volumetric phallometry during presentations of visual and auditory depictions of prepubescent, pubescent and adult males and females. The maximum degree of arousal was plotted over the age of the offender at the time of the test. Age was a powerful determinant of sexual arousal and a line-of-best-fit indicated that arousal decreased as a reciprocal of the age-at-test.

However, Doren (2002) draws attention to an important caveat when interpreting this data. The findings by Hanson do not say anything about what happens by aging specifically for high risk offenders. Different untested assumptions lead to different conclusions about the effect of age on risk, meaning no empirically supported conclusion can be drawn in this regard from the Hanson study. Thornton and Doren (2002) studied 724 UK adult males who served prison sentences for sexual offences and divided their age into five-year intervals measured at time of release from prison. Over a 10-year follow-up risk was measured based on the number of times the person was sentenced for a sexual offence (1 time, 2 times, or 3+ times). They found the 3+ sentence occasion offenders showed an average 10-year sexual reconviction rate of 46%. This is consistent with the RRASOR where a score of 4 corresponds to a probabilistic estimate of 48.6% reconviction in ten-years, and a score of 6+ in Static-99 corresponds to a probabilistic estimate of 45% reconviction in ten-years. Age at release still mattered in lowering recidivism rates for lower (1 sentencing occasion) and moderate (2 sentencing occasion) risk levels, but the highest risk level (3+ sentencing occasions) showed no lowering of recidivism rates from ages 25–59 at time of release. They note in the highest age category (60+ years), there was virtually no recidivism for any of the three risk level groups. However, sample numbers were small and generalisation may still be an issue.

Age and risk of sexual recidivism have also been considered in a number of actuarial risk measures (for a review of actuarial risk measures see Chapter 5). As Thornton (2006) points out, Static-99 (Hanson & Thornton, 2000) and RRASOR (Hanson, 1997) dichotomise age on release contrasting the 18 and 24 band (higher risk) with older ages (lower risk). The Minnesota Sex Offender Screening Tool-Revised (MnSOST-R, Epperson et al., 1999) dichotomises age at release contrasting age 30 and below (higher risk) to age 31 and above (lower risk). The Risk Matrix 2000 (RM2000, Thornton et al., 2003) risk scale differentiates the age bands of 18–24 at the highest risk, ages 25–34 as intermediate risk, and ages either under 18 or older than 34 as the lowest level risk. From the literature there appears to be consensus that the 18–24 age band represents the higher risk group whereas the 60+ age band are the lower risk group. Although the assumption appears to be that there is a uniform decline in risk associated, a closer look at the research challenges this assumption. Thornton (2006) argues that one of the difficulties in interpreting analyses of effect of age for the middle years of life group (that is, 25–59) is that studies that calculate correlations between age and recidivism use data from outside the middle years to strongly constrain the line that is fitted for offenders in the middle years.

Hanson (2006) used a combined sample of 3,425 subjects derived from eight studies which were organised into age bands 18–30s, the 40s, the 50s and 60+ for subjects age at release. Using a survival analysis sexual recidivism was determined for a period of five years. In keeping with earlier studies a statistically significant linear inverse relationship between age-at-release and sexual recidivism was found.

However, using a Chi-square analysis between age bands and sexual recidivism revealed significant results between 18–30s and 60+, but not between the 40s and 50s. He found the two middle years groups (40–49 and 50–59) had essentially the same recidivism rates. He used Static-99 to assess the subject's actuarial risk at the time of release into the community. The degree of historically assessed risk related to general antisociality did not alter the effects of age at release.

Thornton (2006) argues it is particularly important to control for other factors as well as actuarial factors since existing studies on the relationship between age and recidivism are really comparing groups that also differed on their age on sentence. He argues that older offenders on release are not simply the younger offenders grown up. He argues that younger offenders who have already been sentenced for sexual offences on several occasions are not only demonstrating youth and a certain number of sexual priors, they are also demonstrating a fast rate of sexual offending while an offender in his 50s with a similar number of sexual priors will not only be older, but have demonstrated a much slower rate of offending. A further confusion in this area is the differing follow up periods between studies. In an attempt to address some of these methodological issues Thornton (2006) followed a sample of 752 sexual offenders over a 10-year period. As an indicator of sexual deviance he used the number of prior sexual sentencing occasions and as an indicator of general criminality he used prior convictions for non-sexual violence. An integration of the data led to a number of what appeared to be contradictory results. He found age on release was positively correlated with prior sexual sentencing occasions and negatively correlated with prior non-sexual violence. Sexual offenders released at a younger age tended to be general criminals while those released at a later age were more likely to be sexual specialists. Only when age on release and prior criminal history was controlled for did a significant linear relationship between age and sexual recidivism emerge. The form of the relation between age on release and sexual recidivism varied depending on the number of prior sexual sentencing occasions in the offender's history. For those with only one prior sexual sentencing occasion the effect of age was characterised with a gradual decline in sexual recidivism. For those with no prior sexual sentencing occasions age on release and sexual recidivism was unrelated. In contrast, for those with two or more prior sexual sentencing occasions, there was a significant cubic trend. For highly repetitive sexual offenders the effect of age was described as involving an initial very high sexual recidivism rate for those released between 18 and 25, a substantial reduction in this rate (from about 80% to just under 50%) for those released after that age, with no subsequent decline until age 60 when the rate falls again (Thornton, 2006).

Barbaree, Langton and Peacock (2005) further expanded on their earlier research in 2003 and tested for the effect of age-at-release on recidivism for high risk offenders using the two dimensions of sexual recidivism described by Doren (2004); sexual deviance and general antisociality. When controlling for high risk the effect of age-at-release was the same for high versus low risk offenders as measured by the general antisociality factor. However, when high risk measured using the sexual deviance factor it showed an increased effect of age-at-release compared to the effect on lower risk sexual offenders. In one of the biggest studies to date, Langan et al. (2003) conducted a study of nearly 9,700 prison released sexual offenders categorised into brackets 18–24, 25–29, 30–34, 35–39, 40–44 and 45+. A three-year rearrest rate for any type of sexual offending was recorded and it was found there was no difference in recidivism rates between any of the age categories except when comparing the oldest (45+) to any other age group. The only downward trend in sexual offending was sometime after age 44. As Doren (2006) points out these results are in keeping with Hanson (2006) and Thornton (2006) where there appears to be some type of plateau in the rates of sexual offending in the older offender category.

Fazel et al. (2006) followed 1,303 sexual offenders for an average of 8.9 years and reported rates of repeated offending (sexual and violent) for four age bands (<25, 25–39, 40–54, and 55+ years). They found those aged 55 years and over sexually reoffended at a rate of 6.1%, compared with a rate of 10.7% for those aged under 25 years. Although there appeared to be a drop in sexual reconviction rates between from 9.4% for the age band 25–39 to 5.6% for the age band 40–54, the reconviction rate increased to 6.1% for the older age band 55+.

Craig (2007) followed 131 offenders (85 sex offenders and 46 violent offenders) over a two and five year period. The sample was grouped into four age bands (i.e.,<24, 25–34, 35–44, and 45+ years) and rates of sexual, violent, sex and violent (combined), and any offence reconviction was compared. There was an almost liner relationship between age and rate of reconviction with the youngest age band (<24 years) presenting the greatest risk of reconviction and the older age bands (45 + years) presenting the lowest reconviction rate. At five years follow-up the youngest age band were significantly more likely to be reconvicted of new sex and violent offences (combined) than any other age band. In relation to sexual reconviction, there was a plateau effect in the middle age bands with the oldest age band obtaining the highest sexual reconviction rate compared with all other age bands at five years follow-up. Although these findings support the view that lower aged sex and violent offenders pose greater risk than their older aged counterparts, this was not true for sexual reconviction at five years follow-up. Even when controlling for the actuarial risk item age 18–24.99 years, the youngest age band were significantly more likely to be actuarially assessed (that is, Static-99) as high risk and were more likely to target victim strangers, be single, and display non-sexual violence during the index offence. Static-99 correctly identified moderate-high and high risk young offenders in 40% of cases compared with identifying low risk older offenders in 64% of cases.

The results from Craig (2007) are consistent with Barbaree et al. (2003) and Fazel et al. (2006) who reported a drop in sexual recidivism rates for the youngest age group compared to the oldest. However, in Craig's study, although there is a linear relationship between age and violent, sex and violent (combined), and any reconviction, this was not true in terms of sexual reconviction at five years follow-up. While the sexual reconviction rate at five years follow-up is effectively the same between the three age bands 25 to 44 years (6.7%, 8.8% and 6.7% respectively), the oldest age group were reconvicted at a greater rate (14.3%). Although this trend is broadly consistent with Fazel et al. (2006), these results are in contrast to earlier studies and may be explained by differences in sample characteristics in Craig's study. However, similar to Hanson (2006) and Thornton (2006), Craig found a plateau effect within the middle age band (35–44 years), particularly at five years follow-up with regard to sexual, violent and any reconviction when compared with the older age band. Hanson (2006) found the two middle years groups (40–49 and 50–59) had essentially the same recidivism rates and found the moderate-high offenders in their 40s had lower recidivism rates than the moderate-high offenders ins their 50s. Thornton (2006) argues that one of the difficulties in interpreting analyses of effect of age for the middle years of life group (that is, 25–59) is that studies that calculate correlations between age and recidivism use data from outside the middle years to strongly constrain the line that is fitted for offenders in the middle years.

Much of the research relating to the effect of offender age on sexual recidivism has involved the offender's age-at-release. However, Harris and Rice (2007) investigated the relationship between recidivism and three different measures of offender age; age-at-release, age-at-index-offence and age-at-first-offence. While all three age measures were found to correlate significantly with violent recidivism (including sexual and non-sexual), a regression equation showed that age-at-first-offence was the most important factor among the different age measures. It appeared that age-at-first-offence may be more important than age-at-release relative to violent recidivism. In extending this area of research they then replaced age-at-first-offence with that of age-at-release on the RRASOR and Static-99 risk scales. It was found when the age-at-first-offence was used showed an equal or improved correlational result. Harris and Rice argue this age measure may better reflect the offenders 'life course persistent antisociality' reflecting a long pattern of interpersonal violence. Someone with a young age-at-first-offence will either still be young at the time of the risk measure, or now be older and reflect a lifelong pattern of offending (Doren, 2006). It would appear therefore that offender age-at-release may be an inferior measure compared to age-at-first offence relative to sexual recidivism. In trying to further explain the relationship between age and sexual recidivism, Doren (2006) offers a comprehensive review of the more recent studies (Barbaree, Langton & Peacock, 2003, 2005; Hanson, 2002, 2006, Harris & Rice, 2007; Langan et al., 2003; Thornton, 2006). He concludes when offenders' risk is not considered, age-at-release generally shows some type of reduction in recidivism in the older age categories. However, when the offenders' risk is considered, it mattered how the risk was being measured.

Measures of general antisociality did not show differential effects of age on sexual recidivism rates, whereas risk related to sexual deviance did. Doren draws attention to the opposing results from Thornton (2006) and Barbaree et al. (2006) in respect to the interaction between high sexual deviance risk and age-at-release and suggests methodological and sampling differences may account for these results. In summarising these results Doren discusses the practical use of this area of research. He argues that age-at-release should be considered as a protective factor beyond current actuarial risk assessments for offenders driven by general antisociality. However, there is little change in recidivism across age-at-release 40–59 years and the effect of age-at-release on high risk offenders at age-at-release 60+ is unknown. Nevertheless, it is also true that an offender with a young age-at-first-offence still can represent high recidivism even at a much older age-at-release. Harris and Rice's results would suggest offender's risk should be assessed based on age-at-first-offence rather than age-at-release and Barbaree et al. and Langan results suggest practitioners should consider whether or not the offender participated in treatment or offended against a child to know how to incorporate age-at-release into a risk assessment. Due to the wide disparity of findings it is difficult to know how to best incorporate offenders' age and its relationship to sexual recidivism. If we were to consider a cut-off age, historical research would seem to indicate risk can be presumed to decrease with age. Although Barbaree et al.'s results indicate an age-40 threshold for the absence of high risk, this is in contrast to Hanson (2006) and Thornton (2006). From these studies sexual recidivism risk diminishes in the oldest age-at-release category studied, age 60+. However as Doren points out, Thornton only had eight subjects aged 60+ and Hanson had 11 in the same age category whereas Barbaree et al.'s sample included 16 subjects aged 51+ in the high risk bracket. It is clear due to the disparity between studies that it is difficult to draw any firm conclusions on how age should be understood in terms of risk of sexual recidivism.

CONCLUSIONS

A review of the studies on sexual recidivism reveals a consistent pattern of static risk factors including prior criminal history, deviant sexual interests, prior sexual offending, non-contact sexual offences, personality disorders, Psychopathy, age-at-release, age-at-first-offence, victim stranger and unrelated victim, and extra familial male victims as being positively associated with sexual recidivism. Many actuarial risk scales tend to be heavily reliant on static factors and may be of limited use in the case of first time offenders whose current offence may be unusual or have sadistic elements. Recent research on the factor structure of actuarial risk items reveals identifiable factors of which deviant sexual interests, antisocial orientation and detachment appear to be the most prominent in predicting sexual recidivism. It has been consistently demonstrated that young offenders pose the greatest risk of being reconvicted of sex and violent offences and are more likely to be identified actuarially as high risk offenders. Consistent with previous research, there is some suggestion of a plateau effect in reconviction rates for the middle age group offenders. The accurate assessment of the impact of an offenders' age on sexual recidivism risk is likely to be highly valuable to evaluators and forensic practitioners involved in the long term assessment of sex and violent offenders. While the growing body of research suggests the younger age bands pose the greatest risk of sexual and violent reconviction, how age is assessed, is yet to be determined. There appears to be some support for the adjustment of actuarial scores based on the passage of time, although any adjustment would need to be empirically determined rather than relying on clinical judgment. Continued research into the effect of age on recidivism risk and actuarial scales may produce actuarial adjustment scales by which actuarial scores can be adjusted using empirically derived tables given certain variables (for example, age and passage of time since last offence).

5

Actuarial and Clinically Guided Measures

INTRODUCTION

Professionals working with sex offenders are often called on to assess the risk they present. These assessments are normally concerned either with the risk of further sexual offences or with the risk of future violence of any kind. To carry out this task the professional can use an actuarial risk predictor or clinical judgement. Actuarial instruments are empirically derived but are essentially atheoretical in character, in that they provide no guidance on which psychological risk factors underlie risk and hence no indication of how risk can be reduced or when such a reduction in risk has taken place (say through successful treatment). Clinical judgement may allow a decision to be made at an ideographic level, but has until recently been both idiosyncratic and unfounded in research. In the last few years very real attempts have been made to draw these approaches together, both in general risk assessment (that is, Andrews & Bonta, 1995) and its application to sexual offenders (Beech, Erikson, Friendship & Hanson, 2002; Thornton, 2002).

The aim of this chapter is to describe what would be needed to carry out a thorough assessment of the likelihood that an individual will offend sexually. Clinicians may also be concerned that an individual may offend violently. This assessment is beyond the remit of this chapter, except to note that there are a number of violence risk assessments currently available such as the Violence Risk Appraisal Guide (VRAG, Quinsey, Harris, Rice & Cormier, 1998) and the HCR-20 (Webster, Douglas, Eaves & Hart, 1997). It should also be noted that the systems currently discussed below generally do not systematically take into account victim characteristics, but look at the likelihood of any further sexual offending rather than a specific reoccurrence of the original sexual offence.

We would argue that any assessment of the likelihood of sexual offending should be broad and involve more than a simple documentation of the level of risk. It should also contribute information that can guide risk management. The types of risk factors identified in the general risk assessment literature fall into four broad categories: (1) *dispositional factors*, such as psychopathic or anti-social personality characteristics; (2) *historical factors*, such as adverse developmental events, prior history of crime and violence, prior hospitalisation, and poor treatment compliance; (3) *contextual antecedents to violence* such as criminogenic needs (risk factors for criminal behaviour), deviant social networks and lack of positive social supports; (4) *clinical factors*, such as psychiatric diagnosis, poor level of functioning and substance abuse (Andrews & Bonta, 1998; McGuire, 2000)., which will be discussed in later chapters, therefore, it should be borne in mind that in any comprehensive risk assessment for any type of future sexual/non-sexual violence the clinician should seek to determine the presence or absence of each category of these risk factors (McGuire, 2000). We will not examine actuarial and clinically guided approaches to risk assessment, more dynamic approaches will be examined in Chapter 6.

ACTUARIAL RISK ASSESSMENT MEASURES

Objective risk scales using combinations of predictor variables, through the use of statistical techniques (such as stepwise regression and discriminant function analysis) have become increasingly important in this area (for example, Hanson, Steffy & Gauthier, 1993; Hanson, Morton & Harris, 2003; Harris & Rice, 2003). The procedure involves discerning the variables predictive of recidivism and assigning them relative weights to determine low, medium and high-risk cases by score. However, the replicability of such factors must be questioned, as it is difficult to determine whether the identified variables can generalise to other populations than those on whom it is tested it was also developed (Craig, Browne & Stringer, 2004). The next section reviews some of the more common scales used for assessing risk of reconviction in sexual offenders. A comparison of the predictive accuracy of the scales reviewed here, relative to the other scales, is presented in Table 5.1. Estimates of predictive accuracy of the risk scales are presented in terms of Area's Under the Curve (AUC) of the Receiver Operating Characteristic (ROC) (see Chapter 3). The AUC indices are the preferred measure of predictive accuracy (Harris, 2003). In order to facilitate comparisons across follow-up studies that have used different measures of effect size, Rice and Harris (2005) provide a table of effect size equivalencies for the three most common measures: ROC area (AUC), Cohen's d, and r. Rice and Harris (2005) argue, that d values pertain only to variables scored on an interval scale. When the non-dichotomous variable is ordinally scaled, r or AUC should be used.

Table 5.1 AUC results for the SORAG, SACJ, RRASOR, Static-99, Risk Matrix-2000-Sexual/Violent, MnSOST-R, MASORR and SVR-20 risk assessment scales

| Risk Scale | Author | | Recidivism (Area Under the Curve: AUC) | | |
		n	Sexual	Violent*	Any**
SORAG	Barbaree et al. (2001)	215	0.70	0.73	0.76
	Bartosh et al. (2003)	167	0.71	0.64	0.74
	Bélanger & Earls (1996)	57	0.82		
	Firestone et al. (1999)	558	0.65		
	Hanson & Morton-Bourgon (2004)	5,103	0.48d	0.75d	0.79d
	Harris et al. (2003)	396	0.66	0.73	
	Harris & Rice (2003)	51	0.90		
	Hartwell (2001)	164	0.67		0.70
	Langton et al. (2007)	269		0.67	
	Looman (2006)	258	0.69	0.69	
	Nunes et al. (2002)	258	0.65	0.69	
	Rice & Harris (2002)	82	0.81	0.76	
	Quinsey et al. (1998)	618	0.62		
SACJ	Thornton (1997)	533	$r = 0.33$		
SACJ-Min	Craig et al. (2006a)	85(so)	0.52	0.58	0.57
		131(sv)	0.54	0.59	0.59
	Hanson & Thornton (2000)	1208	0.67	0.64	
RRASOR	Barbaree et al. (2001)	215	0.76	0.65	0.60
	Bartosh et al. (2003)	186	0.63	0.73	
	Craig et al. (2006b)	85	0.48	0.71	0.55
	Hanson (1997)	2592	0.71		
	Hanson & Morton-Bourgon (2004)	5,103	0.59d	0.34d	0.26d
	Hanson & Thornton (2000)	1208	0.68	0.64	
	Harris et al. (2003)	396	0.59	0.56	
	Harris & Rice (2003)	55	0.79		
	Sjöstedt & Långström (2000)	1400	0.72		
	Sjöstedt & Långström (2002)	51	0.73	0.62	
	Sjöstedt & Grann (2002)	1288	0.73		
	Thornton et al. (2003)	429	0.70		
Static-99	Barbaree et al. (2001)	215	0.70	0.70	0.71
	Bartosh et al. (2003)	186	0.63	0.72	0.69
	Beech et al. (2000)	53	0.73		
	Craig et al. (2004)	121	0.59	0.59	0.55
	Craig et al. (2006a)	85	0.52	0.69	0.57
	Craig et al. (2006c)	119	0.67		
	Craig et al. (2007)	119	0.66		
	Friendship et al. (2004)	2557	0.70	0.70	
	Hanson & Morton-Bourgon (2004)	5,103	0.63d	0.57d	0.52d
	Hanson & Thornton (2000)	1208	0.71	0.69	
	Harris et al. (2003)	396	0.62	0.63	
	Harris & Rice (2003)	37	0.84		

(*continued*)

Table 5.1 *(Continued)*

Risk Scale	Author	Recidivism (Area Under the Curve: AUC)			
		n	Sexual	Violent*	Any**
	Langstrom (2004)	1,303	0.75	0.72(NSV)	
	Looman (2006)	258	0.63	0.56	
	Nunes et al. (2001)	588	0.70	0.74	
	Nunes et al. (2002)	258	0.70	0.69	
	Sjöstedt & Långström (2000)	1400	0.76	0.74	
	Sjöstedt & Grann (2002)	1273	0.75		
	Thornton (2001)	117	0.92		
	Thornton & Beech (2002)	121	0.91		
	Thornton et al. (2003)	429	0.73		
RM2000/S	Craig et al. (2006a)	85 (so)	0.59	0.64	0.61
		131(sv)	0.55	0.58	0.66
	Craig et al. (2004)	121	0.56	0.55	0.60
	Thornton et al. (2003)	647(t)	0.77		
		429(u/t)	0.75		
RM2000/V	Craig et al. (2006a)	85 (so)	0.65	0.86	0.75
		131(sv)	0.53	0.84	0.76
	Craig et al. (2004)	121	0.55	0.68	0.70
	Thornton et al. (2003)	429		0.80	
		311		0.78	
MnSOST-R	Epperson et al. (1998)	274	0.77		
	Epperson et al. (2000)	220	0.73		
	Barbaree et al. (2001)	215	0.65	0.58	0.65
	Hanson & Morton-Bourgon (2004)	5,103	0.66*d*		
MASORR	Barbaree et al. (2001)	215	0.61	0.58	0.62
SVR-20	Craig et al. (2006a)	85 (so)	0.54	0.53	0.56
		131(sv)	0.49	0.56	0.62
	Craig et al. (2006d)	153 (sv)	0.48	0.56	0.60
	Hanson & Morton-Bourgon (2004)	819	0.77*d*		0.52*d*
	Sjöstedt & Långström (2002)	51	0.49	0.64	

NOTE:
(s/v)   Sex and violent offenders
(s/o)   Sex offenders
(t)   Treated sample
(u/t)   Untreated sample
*   Including sexual offences
**   Including sexual, sexual violent, non-sexual violent, non-sexual non-violent
d: Effect size values: According to Cohen (1988) *d* values of 0.20 (AUC = 0.56) are considered small, those of 0.50 (AUC = 0.62) medium, and those of 0.80 (AUC = 0.72) large.

1. Sex Offender Risk Appraisal Guide (SORAG: Quinsey, et al., 1998)

In predicting recidivism among sexual offenders, Quinsey et al. (1998) acknowledge the methodological flaws, which often dog this area of research. Sexual offenders are often charged with attempted murder, homicide, common assault, or even burglary following plea-bargaining and the two outcome variables, violent and sexual offending, are much less distinct. Quinsey et al. used two primary definitions of recidivism: (1) *Sexual Recidivism* defined as any charge or conviction for an offence against another person that clearly involved sexual contact; (2) *Violent Recidivism* defined as any offence that involved violence, and as such, violent recidivism included all sexual recidivism (p. 156). Quinsey et al. argue that there are commonalties and differences in the variables that predict violent and sexual recidivism (such as psychopathy, criminal history and marital status). However, they argue that it is the variables such as prior sexual offences, and victim injury that have been positively related to violent and sexual recidivism, but not among offenders in general. From this, they attempted to construct a special sex offender instrument – the Sex Offender Risk Appraisal Guide (SORAG) with the aim to predict at least one reconviction for a sexual offence. The best predictive accuracy for SORAG is an AUC of 0.90 (Harris & Rice, 2003) (see Table 5.1). For a discussion on the Area Under Curve statistic see Chapter 3.

2. Structured Anchored Clinical Judgement Scale (SACJ: Thornton, 1997, reported by Grubin, 1998)

The SACJ is a brief scale for assessing the risk of sexual and violent recidivism. The SACJ was designed so the assessment of risk can change over time as more information about an offender becomes available. Instead of weighting the items it uses a stepwise approach broken down into three steps, in order of ease of access of information. The first step categorises offenders into one of three levels of risk (high, medium and low) based on the following convictions; previous or current sexual offences; previous or current non-sexual violent offences; and more than three past convictions of any sort. The second step considers eight items: stranger victims, any male victims, never married, convictions for non-contact sex offences, substance abuse, placement in residential care as a child, deviant sexual arousal and psychopathy. The SACJ was designed to be used even when there is missing data. The minimum information required is the Step 1 variables and the first four variables from Step 2 as amended for use with the police service (SACJ-Min). In a validation sample, the SACJ-Min correlated 0.34 with sex offence recidivism and 0.30 with any sexual or violent recidivism (Hanson & Thornton, 2000). These results are consistent with that of the Rapid Risk Assessment of Sexual Offence Recidivism (RRASOR: Hanson, 1997) scale. The final part of the SACJ (Step 3) considers information that is unlikely to be obtained except from sex offenders who enter treatment programmes (for example, treatment drop-out, improvement on dynamic risk factors, see Chapter 6). In a

16-year follow-up of 533 sex offenders released from Her Majesty's Prison Service, the SACJ correlated well with sexual recidivism ($r = 0.33$). Moreover, 9% (N = 15) of low risk offenders (N = 162), 23% (N = 53) of those categorised as medium risk (N = 231) and 46% (N = 64) of high risk (N = 140) were convicted of a new sexual offence, suggesting the usefulness of the SACJ as a risk measure. There have been few validation studies using this scale and most of them have used the shortened version, SACJ-Min. In the Static-99 validation study Hanson and Thornton (2000) reported AUC indices of 0.67 for sexual reconviction and 0.64 for violent reconviction for this scale. However, in a later study by us (Craig et al., 2006b) we found AUC indices of 0.52 for sexual reconviction, 0.57 for violent reconviction and 0.58 for general reconviction, suggesting that the measure works better in predicting non-sexual offences. We would also note that this instrument is brief and easy to use.

3. *Rapid Risk Assessment for Sex Offence Recidivism (RRASOR: Hanson, 1997)*
   The briefest scale reported here is the *RRASOR*. The advantage this scale has over the other scales, is that it used data from seven different follow-up studies that were then cross-validated on a different sample, thus not only was the sample size large but the studies originated from various countries (Canada, the United States and the United Kingdom). Based on a wide range of risk predictors drawn from the Hanson and Bussière (1996) meta-analysis of 61 sexual recidivism studies ($n = 28,972$), a stepwise regression selected the best predictors of sex offence recidivism. The four main factors selected were those variables that accounted for unique variance: prior sexual offences, age, victim gender and relationship to victim. Based on a system of assigning points to the presence of such variables, the scale ranges from 0 (first time incest offenders, over the age of 15) to six (paedophilic offender with four or more previous convictions and released prior to the age of 25 who has offended against extra familial male victims). The RRASOR showed a moderate level of predictive accuracy across all samples with the average correlation significantly better than the best single predictor (prior sexual offences, $r = 0.20$. The estimated five-year sexual offence recidivism rate was 13.2% (N = 2,592), which was very close to the 13.4% estimate (N = 2,592) provided in Hanson and Bussière's (1996) meta-analysis. In a validation sample RRASOR correlated 0.28 (AUC = 0.68) with sexual offence recidivism and 0.22 (AUC = 0.64) with any violent recidivism (Hanson & Thornton, 2000). More recently, Barbaree et al. (2001) reported AUC = 0.76 ($r = 0.26$) for sexual recidivism and AUC = 0.65 ($r = 0.20$) for violent recidivism. The best predictive accuracy for RRASOR is an AUC of. 79 (Harris & Rice, 2003). Although the scale is simple and easy to use it provides limited information to justify its use in isolation and sole reliance on actuarial risk scales can only be justified when the scale considers a sufficient number of relevant predictor variables. The RRASOR was not intended to provide a comprehensive assessment of all the

factors relevant to the prediction of sexual offender recidivism, but instead is designed to screen offenders into levels of risk.

4. *Static-99 (Hanson & Thornton, 2000)*
Further analysis of RRASOR and SACJ revealed that the two scales were assessing related but not identical constructs. It was argued that a combination of both scales would predict better than either original scale creating *Static-99* as a new scale (Hanson & Thornton, 2000). It consists of ten items: prior sex offences, prior sentencing occasions, convictions for non-contact sex offences, index non-sexual violence, prior non-sexual violence, unrelated victims, stranger victims, male victims, lack of a long-term intimate relationship and whether the offender is aged under 25 on release (or now, if the offender is in the community). In the development study Static-99 was correlated ($r = 0.30$) with sexual recidivism. Although by empirical standards a correlation of 0.30 is not particularly high, Hanson and Thornton (2000) discount the argument that it is sufficient to reject Static-99, arguing that '…*most decision makers are not particularly concerned about the "percent of variance accounted fo"'. Instead, applied risk decisions typically hinge on whether offenders surpass a specific probability of recidivism*' (pp. 129–30). Hanson and Thornton argue that such a specific probability of recidivism was identified by Static-99 in that a sub-sample (approximately 12%) of offenders whose long-term risk for sexual recidivism was greater than 50%. However, Hanson and Thornton note Static-99 is intended to be a measure of long-term risk potential, and given the absence of dynamic risk factors, would not be suitable to select treatment targets, measures of change or predict when sexual offenders are likely to recidivate. The Static-99 risk scale is perhaps one of the most widely used and researched actuarial risk assessment scale and is currently used in Canada, the United Kingdom, United States of America and Australia. The best predictive accuracy for Static-99 is an AUC of 0.92 (Thornton, 2001) and 0.91 (Thornton & Beech, 2002).

5. *Risk Matrix 2000 – Sexual/Violence (Thornton, Mann, Webster, Blud, Travers, Friendship & Erickson, 2003)*
In a recent development in actuarial measures, Thornton et al. (2003) re-examined the Structured Anchored Clinical Judgment Scale (SACJ; see Grubin, 1998, Hanson & Thornton, 2000) and created a two-dimensional risk assessment system for sex offenders referred to collectively as Risk Matrix 2000. The revised system has two scales, one for measuring risk of sexual recidivism – Risk Matrix 2000/Sexual (RM2000/S), and one for measuring risk of non-sexual violent recidivism – Risk Matrix 2000/Violent (RM2000/V) in sexual offenders, both of which are widely used in the British Prison and Probation Services. The RM2000/S and RM2000/V scales were constructed to yield four summary risk categories: Low, Medium, High and Very high. The scores of both RM2000/S and RM20000/V

can be combined to give a composite risk of reconviction for sexual or non-sexual assaults – Risk Matrix 2000/Combined (RM2000/C). In developing the Risk Matrix-2000 scales, the authors referred to the Hanson and Bussière (1998) meta-analysis as it was felt this study offered a more complete guide to the literature, containing more precise and representative estimates of the predictive accuracy of individual factors than would be obtained from any individual study. The RM2000/S uses a two-step system to risk assessment. Step 1 contains three risk items (number of previous sexual appearances, number of criminal appearances and age) the sum of which is translated into a risk category. Step two considers four aggravating risk factors (any conviction for sexual offence against a male, any conviction for a sexual offence against a stranger, any conviction for a non-contact sex offence, and single – never been married), the presence of two or four aggravating factors raises the risk category by one or two levels respectively. Thornton et al. (2003) validated the predictive accuracy of the RM20000/S on two UK samples, treated ($n = 0.647$) and untreated ($n = 429$) sex offenders and obtained AUC of 0.77 and 0.75 in predicting sexual reconviction respectively. In contrast to the RM2000/S, the RM2000/V contained risk items that were selected on *a priori* grounds for inclusion and include; age on release, amount of prior violence and a history of burglary. Validated on two samples followed-up over 10 years ($n = 311$) and between 16–19 years ($n = 429$), RM2000/V obtained AUC of 0.78 and 0.80 in predicting non-sexual violent reconviction respectively. There has been relatively little independent research using the Risk Matrix-2000 scales although Craig and colleagues cross validated the scale in a series of research studies. They found that the RM2000/S scale predicted sexual reconvictions as well as Static-99 and RRASOR. However, they also found that the RM2000/V was a better predictor of sexual reconviction than the RM2000/S and also a very good predictor of violent reconviction with AUCs of 0.86 (Craig, Beech & Browne, 2006). However, in their study they found that the RM2000/V did not correlate with other sexual reconviction risk scales adding support to the notion that RM2000/V appears to measure facets of behaviour different to that of sexual offending, in terms of deviant sexual interest and appetite, but consistent with other aspects of sexual recidivism such as non-sexual violence. The concept of a 'dual dimension' to sexual offending will be returned to later in this chapter.

6. *Minnesota Sex Offender Screening Tool-Revised (MnSOST-R: Epperson, Kau, & Hesselton, 1998)*
Developed by the Minnesota Department of Corrections, this is a 16-item scale. This covers: number of sexual convictions, length of sex offending history, whether the offender was under any supervision when a sex offence was committed, any sex offence committed in a public place, use or threat of force, multiple acts on a single victim, different age groups of victim, offended against a

13–15 year old and being at least 5 years older than the victim, stranger victims, anti-social behaviour as an adolescent, substance abuse, employment history, discipline history while incarcerated, chemical dependency while incarcerated, sex offender treatment while incarcerated, age at release. Epperson, Kaul, and Hesselton (1998) argue that as the pattern of offending is different for intra familial sex offenders than for other sexual offenders, they developed a revised version of the scale the MnSOST-R for use with extra familial sex offenders and rapists using a sample of 274 sex offenders. In a six-year follow-up study, arrests rather than convictions were used as the defining feature since these were seen as more proximal to actual offence data. The revision process took consideration of more recent research to identify additional variables to those already discerned and a new item scoring and selection system eliminated all clinical predictions by replacing them with actuarial methods. A revised tool of 17 items correlated with sexual recidivism ($r = 0.27$) and had an area under the ROC curve of 0.77 (D. Epperson, personal communication in Hanson, 2001b). However, a validation study of MnSOST-R using a Canadian offender population reported that MnSOST-R was unsuccessful in predicting sexual recidivism with an AUC of 0.65, much lower than for the Minnesota population (Barbaree et al., 2001). It can be seen that this scale has been developed for use with prisoners and covers a broader range of items than many of the other scales. It is, however, notably harder to score than scales like RRASOR, Static-99 and RM2000 and makes assumptions about the availability and nature of sexual offender treatment and chemical dependency treatment that may not apply outside Minnesota. The scale performed well (AUC $= 0.76$) when tested in Minnesota by its authors (Epperson, 2000) but rather less well when cross-validated by independent researchers in a Canadian sample. In the latter sample, however, its predictive accuracy was still significant, AUC $= 0.70$ (Langton, Barbaree, Harkins, Seto & Peacock, 2002). Bartosh, Garby, Lewis and Gray (2003) investigated the validity of Static-99, RRASOR MnSOST-R and SORAG in predicting recidivism and found that the effectiveness of each instrument varied depending on offender type. Static-99 and SORAG were both significantly predictive of sexual and/or violent reoffending when examining extra familial child abusers. In terms of extra familial molesters, the RRASOR did not establish significance for sexual recidivism. However, when incest offenders were considered, the RRASOR neared significance in terms of sexual recidivism (ROC $= 0.727$, $p = 0.07$) and sexual and/or violent recidivism (ROC $= 0.843$, $p = 0.05$) but was not significant in terms of violent or any reoffence. For intra familial (incest) offenders, all four instruments were at least moderately predictive of sexual recidivism, but only the Static-99 and the SORAG were highly predictive of violent recidivism. None of the four instruments established consistent predictive validity with regard to rapists or non-contact sexual offenders. Only the MnSOST-R failed to illustrate significant ROC values with regard to either sexual or violent reoffending. When the

MnSOST-R was confined to extra familial offenders, the scale was significant only in predicting any recidivism (ROC = 0.688, $p < 0.01$). Similarly, for rape offenders and non-contact offenders, the MnSOST-R neared predictive validity only in terms of any recidivism (ROC = 0.671, $p = 0.05$; and 0.705, $p = 0.08$) and did not establish significance in terms of any other categories of recidivism. Despite the fact that ROC analysis is relatively unaffected by base.

7. *Juvenile Sex Offender Assessment Protocol (J-SOAP: Prentky, Harris, Frizzel, & Righthand, 2000)*

The Juvenile Sex Offender Assessment Protocol (J-SOAP, Prentky, Harris, Frizzell & Righthand, 2000) is a subscale of which was based on the Childhood and Adolescent Psychopathy Taxon scale (Harris, Rice & Quinsey, 1994) and developed to assess risk of re-offending in juvenile sexual offenders. The 23-item protocol consists of four rational scales, Scale I Sexual Drive/Sexual Preoccupation; Scale II Impulsive, Antisocial Behaviour; Scale III Clinical/Treatment and Scale IV Community Adjustment. The risk assessment protocol was completed on 96 juvenile sex offenders at intake and again at time of discharge 24-months later. Due to the small sample size, which included eight known recidivists, only three of who were sexual recidivist, Prentky et al. were unable to demonstrate predictive validity due to the low base rate for sexual recidivism (4%). Although the four component scales yielded good reliability (0.75–0.86), the Sexual Drive/ Sexual Preoccupation scale was weak in differentiating those who did not re-offend from other high-risk categories than compared to the Impulsive, Antisocial Behaviour scale. It is argued that this may be due to the paucity of information contained in archival documents, as there is often limited recorded information on sexual drive and preoccupation (Prentky et al., 2000). However, those juveniles who were placed because of 'Poor Community Adjustment' had a higher Impulsive, Antisocial Behaviour score than those considered high risk and those deemed high risk were identified due to their sexualised behaviour reflected in Scale I. J-SOAP is clearly in the early stages of development and validation and Prentky et al. are currently testing and revising this protocol.

CRITICISMS OF ACTUARIAL SCALES

Although research has demonstrated the usefulness of using actuarial scales to assess risk of sexual reconviction in sexual offenders, there are a number of criticisms of the actuarial approach (Hart, Laws & Kropp, 2003). There is great variability between risk scales as a result of applying aggregate group data to an individual whose characteristics may differ from those in the original study sample. It is therefore not clear to what extent actuarial measures can be used to generalise across sex offender sub-groups, such as sexual offenders with learning disabilities.

For example, most actuarial risk measures include factors such as, number of previous criminal convictions, prior sexual convictions and prior non-sexual violence. However, as Green, Gray and Willner (2002) found, sexual offenders with learning difficulties were more likely to be convicted of a sexual offence if they had targeted children and males as victims. Sex offenders with differing victim characteristics were less likely to have been convicted and thus would not have a history of prior convictions. In these circumstances, actuarial measures may underestimate the risk of those offenders diverted from the criminal justice system to mental health services. Actuarial risk scales can only be applied to individuals who share characteristics consistent with the cohort data and any deviation from the original study population will impact on the predictive accuracy of the scale. Grubin and Wingate (1996) argue that empirical evidence from one population does not necessarily translate to another, and that most prediction scores cluster at around 40%. Similarly, for behaviours with low base rates, prediction in ignorance of the relevant base rate can lead to error. When applied to behaviours amongst the population as a whole, predictions based upon data about infrequent events limited to small groups will lead to error. This error is exacerbated when meta-analytical methods are used to identify risk predictors. As Grubin and Wingate (1996) suggest, meta-analysis is not particularly good at demonstrating multi-variant effects which require methodologies of a more complex type. The rigid use of actuarial measures does not represent the general view of forensic research and several authors have developed a comprehensive view of risk assessment employing the benefits of actuarial methods while recognising the importance of considering behaviour contextually. Heilbrun (1997) suggests that risk appraisal can be divided into two approaches. The 'prediction model' focuses on the probability of a specified event occurring within a given time period, and the 'control model' considers those factors that reduce the risk of an event occurring. Heilbrun argues that risk assessment can be enhanced in the prediction model by utilising static (that is, historical, non-changeable risk factors: useful for evaluating long-term risk), or dynamic factors (that is, enduring factors linked to the likelihood of offending that can nevertheless be changed following intervention). The control model would seek to identify dynamic factors in order to manage risk and reduce sexual or violent recidivism.

Beech et al. (2003) note the following about actuarial risk assessment. First, actuarial scales yield a probability, not a certainty, of future recidivism. Second, since existing instruments have been developed around official recidivism events, the probabilities associated with each risk category inevitably underestimate true re-offence rates. Thus, an individual with a low actuarial risk classification may nevertheless sometimes be likely to offend (for example, an incest offender with continuing access to a past victim). Third, if the clinician relies totally on actuarial instruments this may lead them to ignore unusual factors that are relevant to the individual case. Fourth, actuarial estimates of risk may be misleading for unusual individuals with characteristics that were not well represented in the samples used to construct or test the actuarial instruments. Fifth, existing actuarial instruments seek to estimate long-term risk and take no account of acute risk factors that might indicate imminent re-offending. Sixth, existing actuarial instruments do not indicate which factors need to be addressed in treatment for risk to be reduced. Despite these limitations, static actuarial instruments presently represent the most cost-effective way of dividing convicted offenders into groups that differ in overall long-term risk, and hence in their need for custodial, supervision, or treatment resources to manage that risk. We will now examine structured clinical approaches to risk assessment.

STRUCTURED CLINICAL JUDGEMENT SCALES

In contrast to actuarial risk measures, structured clinical approaches to risk assessment are primarily based on the clinicians own judgment of the offender's risk (see Chapter 2). This approach does not use actuarial scales to estimate an offender's risk but clinical experience and knowledge of offending behaviour.

1. Sexual Violence Risk-20 (SVR-20: Boer, Hart, Krop, & Webster, 1997)
   Boer, Hart, Kropp and Webster (1997) assessed the risk of sexual violence by selecting 20 factors, from an extensive list, that could be comprehensively divided into three main sections to formulate *Sexual Violence Risk-20* (SVR-20). Factors include: a) *Psychological Adjustment* – sexual deviation, victim of child abuse, cognitive impairment, suicidal/homicidal ideation, relationship/employment problems, previous offence history (non-sexual violent, non-violent), psychopathy, substance use problems, and past supervision failure; b) *Sexual Offending* – such as high-density offences, multiple offences, physical harm to victims, use of weapon, escalation and cognitive distortions, c) *Future Plans* – whether the offender lacks realistic plans and has negative attitudes towards instruction. Boer, Hart, Kropp and Webster (1997) developed the SVR-20 more as a set of guidelines to improve assessments of risk for sexual violence. It is unknown whether judgements based on the SVR-20 have any predictive validity and further research is needed to demonstrate its effectiveness. They note that the SVR-20 risk factors are not intended to be used as an actuarial scale. Instead, they suggest that evaluators should consider the SVR-20 and any other case-specific factors deemed important, and should integrate them in an unstructured or clinical manner (p. 336). More controversially, the authors claim, 'it is both possible and reasonable for an evaluator to conclude from the presence of a single risk factor that an individual is at high risk of sexual violence' (Boer, Wilson, Gauthier & Hart, 1997). Grubin and Wingate (1996), however, have criticised the use of single variables as having no inherent meaning, in that they only indicate association rather than imply causation. Although the scale was

never designed as an actuarial predictor, its accuracy at predicting sexual recidivism has been tested in a number of studies. The AUC indices for the SVR-20 in predicting sexual reconviction range from 0.48 to 0.54 although Craig et al., (2006a; 2006d) and Sjöstedt and Långström (2002) both found that the SVR-20 was a better predictor of violent reconviction than of sexual reconviction.

2. *Statistics Information on Recidivism Scale (SIR: Bonta, Harman, Hann & Cormier, 1996b)*
Bonta, Harman, Hann and Cormier (1996b) have demonstrated the use of the *Statistics Information on Recidivism Scale* (SIR) for prevalence decisions by the Correctional Services of Canada. This 15-item scale related to criminality, first conviction, age at conviction, mental status and social functioning was constructed using a sample summation technique, where weighting an item was based on the difference between the recidivism rate for offenders with that particular characteristic and the overall recidivism rate. The scale has proved useful as a measurement of risk for general recidivism among sexual offenders but is less effective at predicting sexual offending. This indicates that different sets of factors are involved in predicting sexual recidivism than those that predict general and non-sexual violent recidivism (Hanson & Bussière, 1998). Moreover, the SIR is composed of static risk factors so is limited in its provisions regarding potential for treatment intervention, while risk level changes may go undetected. Other risk procedures have been recommended for SIR to include changeable (dynamic) factors, for example, The Level of Service Inventory-Revised (Andrews & Bonta, 1995). However, such procedures may prove a time consuming endeavour.

3. *The Risk for Sexual Violence Protocol (RSVP, Hart, Kropp, Laws, Klaver, Logan & Watt, 2003).*
Devised by, Stephen Hart, Randall Kropp, Richard Laws and colleagues in Canada and the UK the *Risk for Sexual Violence Protocol (RSVP)* represents the most evolved form of structured professional judgement in the risk assessment and management field. Like the HCR-20, and SVR-20, the RSVP does not employ actuarial or statistical methods to support decision making about risk. Rather it offers a set of guidelines for collecting relevant information and making structured risk formulations. The RSVP protocol is an evolved form of the Sexual Violence Risk-20 (SVR-20, Boer et al., 1997) and is based on a rejection of actuarial approaches to the assessment of risk of sexual violence. Laws (2006) offers a critique of the SVR-20 as having inadequate coverage of the problem, poor focus on risk management and missing information. Similar to the SVR-20, the RSVP identifies the potential risk factors (presence) and makes a determination of their importance to future offending (relevance). However, in addition to the SVR-20, the RSVP provides explicit guidelines for risk formulation, such as

risk scenarios and management strategies. The inclusion of risk formulation adds to the likely completion time for the RSVP and, as such, and may take much longer to complete than other guided risk measures. The RSVP assumes that risk must be defined in the contact in which it occurs and regards the primary risk decision as preventative, considering steps which are required to minimise any risks posed by the individual. Laws (2006) emphasises the RSVP is not a predictor but a system of managing risk right now including both static and dynamic risk factors. The target population for the RSVP is male 18 years or more with known or suspected history of sexual violence, older male adolescents (16–17 years), and women with known or suspected history. The protocol is not suitable for children or young adolescents. The RSVP is a 22-item protocol divided into five domains including sexual violence history, psychological adjustment, mental disorder, social adjustment and manageability. The RSVP should not be used to determine whether someone committed acts of sexual violence in the past, nor to provide an estimate of specific likelihood or probability that someone will commit acts of sexual violence in the future. The RSVP highlights information relating to clinical problems discouraging any overall risk scores. Information is structured in numbers of steps: case information, presence of risk factors, relevance of risk factors, risk scenarios (possible futures), risk management strategies and summary judgements. The RSVP has good inter-rater agreement and concurrent validity but should be used as a long-term measure to inform case management. However, it has yet to be empirically validated. The RSVP extends current clinically-guided risk assessment measures and is likely to be a valuable tool when assessing and managing risk in sexual offenders.

4. *Assessment of Risk Manageability for Individuals with Developmental and Intellectual Limitations Who Offend (ARMIDILO; Boer, 2004; 2006)*
Although literature has witnessed great advances in the assessment and treatment of sexual offenders, much of this research has been primarily based on main-stream non-learning disabled offenders and there are relatively few descriptions of treatment studies or risk assessment systems designed and standardised on sexual offenders with learning disabilities. To bridge this gap in research, Boer and colleagues (2004; 2006) recently developed a clinically guided dynamic risk assessment system for sex offenders with learning disabilities. The ARMIDILO, used with an actuarial test and an appropriate structured clinical guideline is part of an assessment procedure which combines the assessment of risk and risk manageability in one assessment. The items in the ARMIDILO are distributed amongst staff/environment and client dynamic factors, both of which are further differentiated into stable and acute dynamic groups. Empirically-derived variables are related to an outcome measure (such as recidivism). The scale provides a structure for the data gathering process and data reporting enhancing as much as possible objectivity. The scale provides likelihoods for re-offending within

certain time-frames and allows easy comparison of any one offender to other offenders when using the same test. It also allows test users to derive a treatment or management plan due to inclusion of dynamic risk factors which can change. All items are as related to risk as they are to manageability in institutional or community settings. Each assessment will require the assessor to determine which variables are of most relevance to their client and determine which items are or are not indicative of elevated risk for the client. The items are mostly dynamic and have borrowed liberally from the STABLE and SONAR scales of Hanson and Harris (2001). The scale is divided into three steps: Step 1 considers the use of a static actuarial test for a baseline measure of risk. Boer (2006) argues the RRASOR has been shown to be an effective actuarial tool for use with sex offenders with learning disabilities. Step 2 looks at applying a structured guided assessment to risk using the Sexual Violence Risk-20 (SVR-20; Boer et al., 1997) or the Risk for Sexual Violence Protocol (RSVP, Hart, Kropp, Laws, Klaver, Logan & Watt, 2003), both systems being quite similar to each other (~85% content overlap, similar coding rules, risk level decision rules, and so on). Boer argues that there is more data to support the use of the SVR-20, with learning disabilities, non-learning disabled, mentally disordered and other client groups (for example, aboriginal). In the SVR-20, High, Moderate and Low risk are defined in terms of treatment and supervision needs and the degree of need for a risk management plan. In the ARMIDILO, risk manageability is defined as the overall current dynamic risk manageability estimate, which is the offender's ability to manage his dynamic factors, adjusted by the individual's structured clinical risk estimate and actuarial risk baseline (higher risk, less adjustment and vice versa). Step 3 considers the estimate of how manageable the client is with using the ARMIDILO risk items. Similar to other structured guidelines, Boer suggests items may be scored for validation purposes: '+2' (a problem), '+1' (may be a problem), and '0' (neutral) or use 'yes', 'maybe', 'neutral', or 'no problem' when using the guideline for clinical purposes. Boer argues the items can also be conceptualised as protective factors, decreasing risk. Hence, an item could be scored '−2' – a definite protective factor, '−1' – a possible protective factor, whereas '0' remains neutral, or use 'definite protective factor (DPF)', or 'possible protective factor (PPF)', or 'neutral', when not a protective or risk increasing factor. The stable and acute risk factors are as follows:

Stable Dynamic Items (staff and environment)
- Attitude toward learning disabled clients; communication among supervisory staff; client-specific knowledge by supervisors; consistency of supervision; and environmental consistency.

Acute Dynamic Items (staff and environment)
- New supervisory staff; monitoring of client by staff; victim access; and environmental changes.

Stable Dynamic Items (client)

- Attitude toward and compliance with (a) supervision and (b) treatment; knowledge of behaviour pattern, risk factors and relapse prevention plan; sexual knowledge and self-management; mental health problems; time management and goal-directedness; substance abuse; victim selection and grooming; general coping ability and self-efficacy; relationship skills (a) intimate (b) others; use of violence or threats of violence; impulsiveness; and client-specific stable factors.

Acute Dynamic Items (client) assessed <3-months

- Social support/relationship changes: to self/other harm; changes to substance abuse pattern; changes in sexual preoccupation; changes in emotional regulation; changes in victim-related behaviours; changes in attitude/behaviour towards intervention; changes in ability to use coping strategies; changes in routine; and client-specific acute dynamic factors.

The predictive accuracy of the ARMIDILO is yet to be determined, although the scale is likely to prove a useful method for structuring dynamic risk related information for sexual offenders with learning disabilities.

FACTOR STRUCTURE OF ACTUARIAL RISK SCALES

In Craig, Beech and Browne's (2006a) evaluation study of six actuarial risk scales examined the predictive accuracy of RRASOR, Static-99, SVR-20, SACJ-Min and RM2000/S and RM2000/V on 85 sex offenders and 46 violent offenders over an average follow-up period of 105 months. They found a cross-over effect in offending. Of the sex offenders 9.4% were reconvicted for a violent offence compared with 17.6% who were reconvicted for a sexual offence. Of the violent offender sample 28.5% were reconvicted for a violent offence compared with only 2.2% who were reconvicted for a sexual offence. These results are consistent with prevailing thinking that deviant sexual interests and antisocial orientation are important predictors of sexual recidivism (Hanson & Bussière, 1998, Hanson & Morton-Bourgon, 2005). These results suggest a dual dimension to sexual offending. Support for this comes from Roberts, Doren and Thornton (2002). Roberts et al. investigated the inter-relationships between several actuarial sex and violent risk measures (RRASOR, Static-99, MnSOST-R, VRAG) and the Psychopathy Checklist-Revised (PCL-R; Hare, 1991) and revealed two distinct dimensions relating to sexual reconviction; 'deviant sexual interests' and 'anti-social/violent personality characteristics'. On the basis of their findings the authors argue that there are two underlying drives toward sexual recidivism: (1) *Paedophilic Deviance/ Sexual Repetitiveness*, diagnosable and illegal sexual desires, and (2) *General Criminality/Antisocial-Violence*. They suggest that RRASOR and Static-99 may actually measure different aspects of sexual and violent offending. The RRASOR correlated with diagnosable paraphilias but not with anti-social behaviour. Whereas exclusive Static-99 items correlated with diagnosable anti-social personality disorder and high PCL-R scores but was negatively correlated with paedophilia. The RRASOR scale tended to correlate with sexual deviance dimensions, whereas other actuarial instruments tended to correlate with the general violence dimension (Doren, 2001; Quackenbush, 2000). They conducted a factor analysis on 10 actuarial items from the risk scales and three identifiable factors emerged: *General Criminality, Sexual Deviance* and *Detachment.* Items reflecting burglary, prior burglary, young age, and any prior nonsexual violent offences loaded highly on the first named factor. Items loaded onto the sexual deviance factor included any prior sexual offences, non-contact sex offences and male victim. The detachment factor was associated with stranger victim, and single (never married).

Langton, Harkins, Peacock and Barbaree (2003, August) conducted a principle component analysis of 31 non-redundant actuarial items from four actuarial risk scales (SORAG, two items; RRASOR, two items; Static-99, two items; MnSOST-R, 10 items) and one guided clinical risk instrument (VASOR, six items; McGrath, Hoke, Livingston & Cumming, 2001). Langton et al. found three distinct factors: *Sexual Deviance, Lifestyle Maladjustment/Instability* and *Detached Predatory Behaviour.* Langton et al. (2003) reported that different actuarial factors differentially predict different recidivism outcomes. Their Sexual Deviance factor significantly predicted sexual recidivism, while their factors Lifestyle Maladjustment/ Instability, and Detached Predatory Behaviour significantly predicted violent recidivism. Seto (2005) also conducted a principle component analysis on 19 actuarial items in an attempt to improve predictive accuracy by combining actuarial items. Three factors were identified, *Antisociality, Atypical Sexual Interests* and *Demographics.* More recently, Barbaree, Langton and Peacock (2006) also conducted a principle component analysis on the actuarial items from RRASOR, Static-99, VRAG, SORAG and MnSOST-R on 311 sexual offenders. Six identifiable factors were revealed; *Antisocial Behaviour, Child Sexual Abuse, Persistence, Detached Predatory Behaviour, Young and Singl,* and *Male Victim(s).* The Antisocial Behaviour factor was the largest single factor in terms of the number of items loading (10 items) and the proportion of variance accounted for (11.38%). The items loading on this factor include: criminal convictions, impulsivity, juvenile delinquency, substance abuse, and violence. Sexual deviance was reflected in four separate factors representing different aspects of sexual deviance, including atypical sexual preferences (Child Sexual Abuse, Male Victims), the number of previous sexual crimes (Persistence), and distant or non-existent personal relationships with victims (Detached Predatory Behaviour). In total, these four factors attracted loadings from 21 items and accounted for a combined proportion of variance of 28.1%. The Antisocial Behaviour factor obtained an AUC index of 0.68 at predicting violent recidivism whereas the child sexual abuse, persistence and young and single factors obtained AUC of 0.61, 0.62, and 0.62 respectively for predicting sexual recidivism. Barbaree et al. found the only factor that did not reflect either criminality or sexual deviance was to do with age, marital status and employment stability. They explain this by saying younger offenders are less likely to be married and employed in a stable job. As already discussed above, although recent empirical findings indicate that sexual recidivism declines with age it is well known that most crime is committed by younger offenders. Barbaree et al. examined the relationship between the factors and actuarial scales and found that the VRAG and SORAG were strongly associated with Antisocial Behaviour whereas the RRASOR was strongly associated with the Persistence factor. These findings are consistent with Roberts et al. (2002) and Doren (2002). Barbaree et al. argue that since RRASOR loads almost exclusively on the sexual deviance factors (Persistence, Child Sexual Abuse, Male Victims and Detached Predatory Behaviour) with a near zero loading on Antisocial Behaviour, then RRASOR can be seen as primarily an assessment of sexual deviance. They argue that VRAG can be seen primarily as an evaluation of antisocial behaviour as it was most strongly loaded on the Antisocial Behaviour and having low loadings on the sexual deviance factors. In contrast, the SORAG, Static-99 and MnSOST-R showed moderate correlations across the antisocial behaviour and sexual deviance factors.

Understanding the factor structures of various actuarial risk assessment measures are likely to assist clinicians in assessing the dual dimensions associated with sexual offending. Doren (2002) argue that due to the factor structures of the actuarial scales and the fact they appear to measure different aspects of sexual offending, then clinicians should routinely use two or more actuarial risk scales when carrying out risk assessment evaluations. It is likely this approach to risk assessment will yield information both in terms of antisocial behaviour and mental health diagnosis as well as an indicator of deviant sexual interests.

CONCLUSIONS

The 'actuarial only' proponents contend that accurate risk appraisal demands the use of statistically based models omitting clinical judgement (Quinsey et al., 1998). Risk appraisal would therefore be simplified by the use of an instrument that statistically identifies relevant factors producing a score, which translates into categories of risk, that is, 'low, medium, or high'. Here estimates of risk are based on specific, objective information as opposed to clinical opinion. However, the absence of any clinical input when assessing risk can have profound effects on the results. Sreenivasan et al. (2000) cite the case of the serial killer Jeffrey Dahmer who killed 17 people. Utilising the RRASOR instrument, Dahmer would have scored 2 (14.2% 5-year risk for sexual re-offence). The critical clinical variables such as diagnoses (sexual deviance) tend not to be well represented in actuarial instruments.

In terms of post-treatment risk, clinical judgement has been shown to be a poor predictor of recidivism over actuarial instruments such as VRAG and SORAG. Sexual offenders who score high on the PCL-R and who behaved well in treatment are more likely to commit a new offence of some kind, and much more likely to commit a new serious offence (Seto & Barbaree, 1999). As treatment behaviour is usually incorporated into clinical judgements, non-actuarial assessment may underestimate the risk posed, particularly in offenders with psychopathic traits.

By their nature, actuarial models tend to be limited to static or historical variables and are not targeted towards assessing patient treatment potential or management. Actuarial measures are designed to make absolute predictions of a specified behaviour within a specific time period and tend not to measure dynamic change based upon motivation, insight or intervention, producing estimates of probabilities of re-offence with less emphasis on confidence intervals. Although the California Actuarial Risk Assessment Tables for Rapists and Child Molesters (CARAT, cited by Sreenivasan et al., 2000) developed by Schiller and Marques (1999) have attempted to develop actuarial tables, it is limited by small cell numbers and lacks external cross-validation (Sreenivasan et al., 2000).

Nevertheless, actuarial risk assessments differ greatly in their predictive accuracy ranging from $r = 0.09$ to $r = 0.45$. One possible explanation for this may relate to certain assumptions made in the development of actuarial risk instruments in relation to sexual behaviour and risk. The population bases for actuarial models are not representative of the population or individual to whom the model is being applied, impacting on the generalisability of the model. VRAG and SORAG are based upon Canadian prisoners and psychiatric patients, while RRASOR and Static-99 risk factors were identified using a meta-analytical technique based on 61 data sets from 1943 to 1995 spanning several different countries. As with treatment studies and recidivism, there was no uniform definition of outcome, whether recidivism referred to re-offending, arrest or conviction. Indeed, legal definitions may have changed in the 52-year period when RRASOR and Static-99 instruments are based.

The literature is rich in studies identifying static predictor variables such as offence history, but it is only recently that recidivism studies have started to explore dynamic risk factors. Current actuarial prediction instruments are largely based on static or historical factors. This would appear to provide only half the picture. By considering dynamic factors such as treatment effects, motivation, insight, sexual deviance and general psychological problems, alongside *actuarial* static risk classification, may provide a more global and valid assessment of an offender's risk for sexual recidivism.

PART III

Dynamic risk factors

6

Dynamic Factors Associated with Sexual Recidivism

INTRODUCTION

Dynamic risk assessment is where research meets clinical perceptions, and may include assessment of *stable* dynamic factors, that is, those factors that may be amenable to change in treatment such as deviant sexual interest, pro-offending attitudes, socio-affective problems and self-management issues; and *acute* dynamic risk factors. In other words, those factors that may be related to imminent sexual offending. Much is known about the *static* risk factors associated with increased risk (see Chapter 5), but less is known about which characteristics need to change in order to reduce risk, or what changes in dynamic factors increase, or decrease, a person's risk (Beech, Fisher & Thornton, 2003). However, a number of researchers have begun to consider dynamic factors as part of an overall structured approach to risk assessment combined with actuarial systems in an attempt to improve predictive accuracy, for example in the Minnesota Sex Offender Screening Tool-Revised (MnSOST-R, Epperson, Kaul & Hesselton, 1998), and the structured clinical judgement instrument: The Sexual Violence Risk-20 (SVR-20; Boer, Hart, Kropp & Webster 1997). However, unlike the literature on static risk factors, there appears to be less agreement on which dynamic risk factors should be measured, which may also explain why dynamic factors are not included in many current risk assessment instruments.

How dynamic variables are measured has also been criticised. Harris and Rice (2003), for example, are of the opinion that dynamic predictors need to be able to demonstrate an incremental contribution (assessed for at pre-release and again at follow-up) to be included in actuarial measures. While they accept assessing for attitudes in sexual offenders can contribute to developing a formulation of offending behaviour, the inclusion of dynamic with historical variables actually decrease predictive accuracy in their own work. Also, although dynamic factors have been included in various meta-analytical studies (Hanson & Bussière, 1998), they have not performed as well as static risk factors. However, this picture appears to be changing (Craig, Thornton, Beech & Browne, 2007; Hanson, 2005). With that in mind, the aim of this chapter is to examine what are the dynamic risk factors, and whether there is any additive value in including dynamic factors into risk assessments.

IDENTIFYING DYNAMIC RISK FACTORS

Some of the earliest work examining dynamic/clinical risk factors has been reported by Hanson, Steffy and Gauthier (1993), who reported that sexual offenders felt more in control of their lives, more extraverted, reported less subjective distress, were less hostile, had a less depressed mood and improved self-esteem after therapy. From this pattern of results, Hanson et al. concluded that the factors associated with a life-long pattern of offending needs to be targeted in treatment to reduce risk.

More recently, Hanson and Bussière (1998) have examined what putative risk factors are strongly related to sexual recidivism. They examined what factors, static and dynamic, are strongly related to sexual recidivism in a meta-analytical review of 61 different studies (country of origin: 30 United States, 16 Canada, 14 United Kingdom, 2 Australia, 2 Denmark, 1 Norway), produced between 1943 to 1995, amounting to 28, 972 offenders. Most of the studies examined mixed groups of adult sexual offenders (55 mixed offence types, only 6 child molesters; 52 samples of adults, only 6 adolescents; 3 both adolescents and adults). Approximately one half of the samples (48%) were from sexual offender treatment programmes. The most common measures of recidivism were reconviction (84%), arrests (54%), self-reports (25%) and parole violations (16%). The average follow-up period was four to five years. On average, the sex offence recidivism rate was 13.4% (n = 23, 393; 18.9% for 1,839 rapists and 12.7% for 9,603 child molesters). The recidivism rate for nonsexual violence was 12.2% (n = 7, 155), but there was a substantial difference in the nonsexual violent recidivism rates for the child molesters (9.9%; n = 1, 774) and the rapists (22.1%; n = 782). When recidivism was defined as any reoffence, the rates were predictably higher: 36.3% overall (n = 19, 374), 36.9% for the child molesters (n = 3, 363), and 46.2% for rapists (n = 4, 017). This is consistent with UK data (Falshaw et al., 2003).

Predictive accuracy was calculated using r because it is readily understood and the statistical procedures for aggregating 'r' are well documented (Hedges & Olkin, 1985; Rosenthal, 1991), but is the average correlation coefficient, using Pearson's r. Cramer and Howitt (2004) note that this correlation efficient (as an expression of effect size) gives the proportion of variance accounted for across the two variables if this co-efficient is squared. Correlation coefficients can also easily be calculated from effects sizes from different studies by transforming using the Fisher z transformation of Pearson's correlation. Hanson and Bussière found that the strongest predictors of sexual recidivism were characteristics related to sexual deviance and, to a lesser extent, general criminological variables. Specifically, measures related to sexual deviance include phallometric assessment of sexual preference for children ($r = 0.32$), prior sexual offences ($r = 0.19$), phallometric assessment of sexual preference for boys ($r = 0.14$), young age at offence ($r = 0.13$), any prior offences ($r = 0.13$), and never having been involved in a long-term relationship ($r = 0.11$).

In the UK Craig, Browne and Stringer (2003a) examined 26 studies on sexual offence recidivism ($n = 33,001$) from which they identified 14 *stable* dynamic risk factors, as shown in Table 6.1, found to be associated with sexual offence recidivism.

It can be seen from Table 6.1 that the stable dynamic risk factors can be organised into the following groups: sexual, affective and clinical factors. The distribution of risk items is consistent with structured risk assessment frameworks described in this chapter. Prominent are the risk factors associated with sexual interest including deviant sexual urges, sexual interest in children, paraphilias (atypical sexual outlets) and sexual pre-occupation. Measures of affect and emotional regulation (socio-affective functioning, anger, emotional identification with children, and low self-esteem) and clinical factors (pro-sexual assault attitudes, poor self-management skills, lack of empathy, impulsivity and hostility) were all associated with sexual recidivism. These factors are consistent with those reported by Hanson and Bussière (1998).

Table 6.1 Stable dynamic risk factors associated with sexual offence recidivism from Craig et al. (2003)

Sexual Interest Factors	Affective Factors	Clinical Factors
Deviant sexual urges	Socio-affective functioning	Pro-sexual assault attitudes
Sexual interest in children (PPG)	Low self-esteem	Poor self-management skills
Paraphilias	Anger	Lack of empathy
Sexual preoccupation	Emotional identification with children	Impulsivity
		Hostility
		Personality disorder

NOTE: Penile Plethysmography (PPG) was considered a stable dynamic risk factor as changes in phallometrically assessed deviant sexual arousal following intervention are often short lived and return to deviant arousal profiles.

Meanwhile probably the most up-to-date analysis has been reported by Hanson and Morton-Bourgon (2004, 2005), who completed an up-dated meta-analysis from Hanson and Bussière's (1998) study. Here, Hanson and Morton-Bourgon reviewed 82 different studies (country of origin: 35 United States; 26 Canada; 12 United Kingdom; 2 Austria; 2 Sweden; 2 Australia; and 1 each from France, the Netherlands, and Denmark), produced between 1943 and 2003. Of these studies, 41 (50%) were unpublished. Thirty-five studies were the same as those included in Hanson and Bussiere's (1998) review, 10 studies contained updated information (for example, longer follow-up periods, new analyses), and 37 studies were new. Most of the studies examined mixed groups of adult sexual offenders (72 mixed offence types, 69 child abusers, 2 rapists, 1 exhibitionist; 67 predominantly adults, 15 adolescents; all male). All the offenders had committed offences that meet contemporary definitions of sexual crimes (that is, old studies containing homo-sexuals were excluded). The offenders in 31 studies came from treatment pro-grammes. On average, the observed sexual recidivism rate was 13.7% ($n = 19,267$; 73 studies), the violent non-sexual recidivism rate was 14.3% ($n = 6,928$; 24 studies), the violent recidivism rate (including sexual and nonsexual violence) was 14.3% ($n = 11,361$; 29 studies), and the general (any) recidivism rate was 36.2% ($n = 12,708$; 56 studies). In measuring the predictive accuracy of risk factors Hanson and Morton-Bourgon reported Cohen (Cohen, 1988) d values, which is an index of effect size, where the means of one group (non-recidivists) are subtracted from the recidivist group and divided by the pooled standard deviation of the two groups. According to Cohen, effect size values of 0.20 are considered 'small', values of 0.50 are considered 'medium', and values of 0.80 are considered 'large'. The value of d is approximately twice as large as the correlation coefficient calculated from the same data. The strongest predictors of sexual recidivism were sexual deviancy (d. = 0.30) and antisocial orientation (d. = 0.23). Antisocial orientation (antisocial personality, antisocial traits, history of rule violation) was the major predictor of violent non-sexual recidivism (d. = 0.51), violent (including sexual) recidivism (d. = 0.54) and any recidivism (d. = 0.52). Consistent with the findings from Hanson and Bussière's (1998) study, measures of deviant sexual interests were all significantly associated with sexual recidivism: any deviant sexual interest (d. = 0.31), sexual interest in children (d. = 0.33), and paraphilic interests (d. = 0.21). Sexual preoccupations (paraphilic or non-paraphilic) were also significantly related to sexual recidivism (d. = 0.39), as were high (feminine) scores on the Masculinity-Femininity scale of the Minnesota Multiphasic Personality Inventory (MMPI, Hathaway & McKinley, 1943) (d. = 0.42). Sexual interests in children was a significant predictor of sexual recidivism (d. = 33), as was the general category of any deviant sexual interest (d. = 0.24). However, a phallometric assessment of sexual interest in rape/violence was not significantly related to sexual recidivism. The promising dynamic risk factors included variables related to sexual deviancy (any deviant sexual interest, sexual preoccupations), antisocial personality (antisocial personality disorder, $d = 0.21$, psychopathy as measured by the hare Psychopathy Checklist-Revised (PCL-R, Hare, 1991), $d = 0.29$), and antisocial traits (general self-regulation problems $d = 0.37$, employment instability $d = 0.22$, hostility $d = 0.17$). The potentially misleading risk factors were negative family background, internalisation of psychological problems, and poor clinical presentation (for example, denial, low motivation for treatment). Overall, they found that the variables that predicted sexual recidivism were similar, but not identical, to the predictors of non-sexual recidivism. Sexual deviancy and antisocial orientation were the major predictors of sexual recidivism for both adult and adolescent sexual offenders, although sexual deviancy was unrelated to non-sexual recidivism.

A STABLE DYNAMIC FRAMEWORK

Thornton (2002) has reported a useful framework for stable dynamic risk factors, suggesting that they fall into four specific domains: sexual interests, distorted attitudes, socio-affective functioning and self-management problems. This observation, that sexual offenders have problems, to a greater or lesser extent across these four domains is probably not too surprising given that nearly everybody thinks, feels, manages their behaviour and emotions (to a greater or lesser extent). We will now examine each of these domains in more detail.

SEXUAL INTERESTS DOMAIN

McGuire, Carlisle and Young (1965) proposed that any abnormal sexual behaviour was the direct product of a deviant sexual preference. This proposal evolved to become the [deviant] 'sexual preference hypothesis' (Lalumière & Quinsey, 1994), that is, men who engage in sexually deviant behaviours do so because they prefer them to socially acceptable sexual behaviours. This domain refers to both the direction and strength of sexual interests and considers offence-related sexual preferences and sexual preoccupation both factors identified as predictive of sexual recidivism (Hanson & Bussière, 1998; Hanson & Morton-Bourgon, 2005; Pithers, Kashima, Cumming & Beal, 1988; Proulx et al., 1999). This area of risk refers to the direction and strength of sexual interests, although it should be pointed out that individuals do not necessarily act on their interests. Equally, normal sexual interests do not necessarily imply that someone has not or will not offend.

Four forms of dysfunction in this domain are distinguished in this domain, in relation to men who have offended sexually against adults and/or children, divided into the following categories in the Structured Assessment of Risk and Need

(SARN, Webster et al., 2006), employed by the English and Welsh Prison Service (see below):

- *Sexual preoccupation (obsessed with sex)*, which refers to the intensity of the offender's sexual interests, such as repeated sexualisation of non-sexual situations or focusing on the sexual aspects of a situation or thinking excessively about sex. Sexual preoccupation has been identified as a predictor of risk in a number of studies (for example, Beech, 1998; Firestone et al., 1999; Hanson & Harris, 2000a);
- *Preferring sex to include violence or force*, which refers to a preference for coercive sex over consenting sex. Thornton (personal communication) notes that here a preference for coerced sex over consenting sex would be seen as rape-preference, while a significant sexual arousal response to someone else's pain, humiliation, or terror can be seen as sexual sadism;
- *Sexual Preference for children* Some men are more sexually attracted to children than they are to adults. Their sexual thoughts and fantasies are about children as often as they are about adults, or are more often about children, or are only about children;
- *Other offence-related sexual interests*, specifically paraphilias (that is, deviant sexual interests).

The assessments probably most commonly used for the assessment of sexual interests are the Penile Plethysmograph (PPG), response-time based measures, psychometric assessment, and to a lesser extent the Polygraph. The PPG measures changes in penile circumference or volume in response to audio or visual stimuli. It has been subject to criticism due to the invasive nature of the assessment and concerns over the appropriateness of using images of children. More recently the use of computerised images or auditory material has helped alleviate this problem but there are also concerns over the significance of the results. In addition, there are problems of individuals being able to fake their responses by suppressing responses to deviant stimuli. Nevertheless, appropriately chosen PPG indices (Harris, Rice, Quinsey, Earls & Chaplin, 1992) do show large mean differences between sexual offenders and non-offenders. And PPG indices, especially those indicating a sexual preference for children are predictive of sexual recidivism (Hanson & Bussière, 1998). In North America the PPG is routinely used in many treatment programmes, including those for adolescent offenders, but its use in Britain is limited, being used in some prisons and psychiatric facilities for mentally disordered offenders.

There have also been attempts to develop alternative measures of sexual preference using response time. The Abel Assessment measures the length of time an individual looks at a particular image. It is marketed in North America and is reported in some research studies (for example, Abel, Huffman, Warberg & Holland, 1998; Abel, Lawry, Karlstrom, Osborn & Gillespie, 1994). It is less intrusive than the PPG and seems to relate to past offending as well as the PPG does but has not yet been related to sexual recidivism. Affinity as similar system has been developed in the UK by David Glasgow (Glasgow, Osbourne & Croxon, 2003).

The Polygraph, an instrument for the simultaneous recording of several involuntary physiological activities, including pulse rate and perspiration, is used widely in North America to facilitate judgements about whether someone is being truthful, and may be the next system in the UK. Combined with a sexual history questionnaire, it seems to facilitate fuller disclosure of past offending and so may indirectly indicate the direction of sexual interests (Ahlmeyer, Heil, McKee & English, 2000). However, its usefulness is dependent upon the employment of highly trained polygraphers, which limits its availability.

Clinical interview, without the polygraph, has also been found to be effective in identifying problems in this domain (Webster et al., 2006). Some psychometric tests might also be considered useful in the measurement of sexual interests such as the Multiphasic Sex Inventory (Nichols & Molinder, 1984). However, the problem with any such self-report measures is that the results are dependent upon the offender being honest about his sexual interests (Beech, 2001).

DISTORTED ATTITUDES DOMAIN

This domain refers to sets of beliefs about offences, sexuality or victims that can be used to justify sexual offending behaviour. Distorted beliefs in sexual offenders are well supported within the literature (Beech, Fisher & Beckett, 1999; Hanson & Harris, 2000a; Hanson & Scott; 1995; Pithers et al., 1988; Ward et al., 1995) as offence precursors in child abusers (Beech, Fisher, & Beckett 1999; Hanson, Gizzarrelli & Scott, 1994; Hanson & Scott, 1995). There is some, more limited, evidence of their relevance to rapists (Beech, Ward & Fisher, 2006; Bumby, 1996; Hanson & Scott, 1995; Malamuth & Brown, 1994) and sexual murderers (Beech, Fisher & Ward, 2005; Beech, Oliver, Fisher & Beckett, 2005).

Generally, Hanson and Harris (2000a) found distorted attitudes to be offence precursors, and both Bakker, Hudson, Wales and Riley (1998) and Firestone et al. (1999), in their samples, report that those who sexually reoffended sexually had higher scores on Abel and Becker Distortions scale (Abel, Becker & Cunningham-Rathner, 1984) than those who had not reoffended. Additionally, measures of pro-offending attitudes were predictive of sexual recidivism by both Beech et al. (2002), Craig et al. (2007) and Thornton (2002).

A number of different forms of distorted attitudes specifically related to sexual offending against adult women and children are identified in this domain divided into the following categories from the SARN (Webster et al., 2006), used by the National Offender Management System (NOMS) in the UK.

- *Adversarial sexual attitudes (believing men should dominate women sexually)*
  Here, there is a belief that men should dominate or control women and that

the proper role for women is to be submissive to men. Thornton (personal communication) notes that women who fail to accept male dominance are seen as being disrespectful and the man is seen as justified in acting in a way that restores the proper order of things;

- *Child abuse supportive beliefs* Some men believe that it is sometimes acceptable to behave in a sexual way with a child. This might be because they have the idea that the child did not stop them or 'seemed' interested about sex. It might be that the offender thought that sex would be a helpful thing to do, for example, to teach the child about sex, or at least this would not be harmful. They see some children as ready for sex, or think they are just showing love for the child;
- *Sexual entitlement* (believing that you have a right to sex) The idea here is that a man having a sexual 'need' entitles him to gratify it. The man expressing this belief may assert that his sex drive is unusually strong and that it is more painful for him to be sexually frustrated than it is for a woman/child to acquiesce to his wishes;
- *Rape-supportive (justifying) beliefs* Here men believe that rape can be justified or at least be made not so inappropriate if the woman has behaved badly. Therefore rape is seen by men holding these beliefs as something that can appropriately be used to teach a woman a lesson, instil respect, or simply as something that she deserved;
- *Women are deceitful beliefs (beliefs that women cannot be trusted)* Here the offender holds the view that women are deceitful, manipulative, corrupt or exploitative. Again there are two common variants (a) that women's surface behaviour does not indicate their true feelings and (b) that women have a hostile exploitative attitude towards men.

A number of psychometric measures have been developed to assess attitudes supportive of sexual assault/ pro-offending attitudes, such as the Justifications Scale of the Multiphasic Sex Inventory (MSI, Nichols & Molinder, 1984); The Abel and Becker Cognitions Scale (Abel et al., 1984); The Bumby RAPE and MOLEST scales (Bumby, 1996); The Children and Sex: Cognitive Distortions Scale (Beckett, 1987); the Burt Rape Scales (including rape myths. adversarial sexual attitudes, acceptance of interpersonal violence against women, sex role stereotyping, Burt, 1980); Hostility towards women scale (Check 1984). While, Beech (Beech et al., 2005; Beech et al., 2006) notes the usefulness of interview in assessing underlying rapists/sexual murderers dysfunctional schemas. We would also suggest that the Implicit Association Task, which is a cognitive measure of deep seated attitudes, and is a well known paradigm in social psychology, may be useful in assessing distorted attitudes in sexual offenders (Gray et al., 2005).

SOCIO-AFFECTIVE FUNCTIONING DOMAIN

This domain refers to the ways of relating to other people and to motivating emotions felt in the context of these interactions. Negative emotional states such as anxiety, depression and low self-esteem (Pithers et al., 1988; Proulx et al., 1999), and especially anger (Hanson & Harris, 2000a), have been found to be offence-precursors. Factors such as low self-esteem, loneliness and external locus of control also seem to distinguish child molesters from comparison groups (Beech, Fisher & Beckett, 1999). Thornton argues that at least four aspects of socio-affective functioning are relevant to sexual offending in the SARN (Webster et al., 2006).

- *Grievance thinking* (suspicious, angry, vengeful towards others) This cluster of problems involves a combination of frequently seeing oneself as having been wronged, suspiciously scanning the environment to see who is going to wrong one in the future, and brooding angrily over past or anticipated wrongs. It also involves a reluctance to see or accept other people's point of view, a tendency to righteously insist on imposing one's own interpretation of a situation on others. Grievance thinking can contribute to offending in at least two ways: it can provide a source of motivation for angry/revenge seeking offences; and it can motivate behaviour that leads to high risk situations;
- *Inadequacy* This cluster of problems involves a combination of low self-esteem, subjective feelings of loneliness and an external locus of control. This cluster of problems has also been described as social inadequacy (Beech et al., 2003);
- *Lack of emotional intimacy* (not having an intimate relationship) Here lack of intimacy is seen as leading to offending by creating an unsatisfied need for emotional intimacy that the offender seeks to satisfy through offending, and by removing the inhibition against offending that loyalty to an intimate relationship would create;
- *Distorted intimacy balance* (being more emotionally open/comfortable with children than with adults). Here some men feel scared of having relationships with adults. They feel more confident about getting on well with children. They feel that children accept them, like them and enjoy their company. They feel they have more in common with children and they feel happier when involved in activities with children than with adults. They may choose to work with children, or have hobbies that children are interested in. They may feel that they are themselves more like a child than an adult.

These factors have been found to be typically more marked in analyses comparing the more repetitive sexual offenders to less repetitive sexual offenders (for example, Thornton, 2002), or in analyses comparing convicted sexual offenders to non-offenders (for example, Fisher, Beech & Browne, 1999). Similar socio-affective factors have been identified as acute offence-precursors. For example, Pithers et al. (1988) found various kinds of negative affect (anger, anxiety, depression and low self-esteem) to play this role, as did Hanson and Harris (2000a). Hence some of these factors seem to be both stable and acute dynamic factors. Meta-analytical results support the recidivism relevance of emotional congruence/over-identification with children and to a lesser extent hostility (Hanson & Morton-Bourgon, 2005).

Beech et al. (2003) suggest that the following psychometric scales may be useful in the assessment of problems in this domain: the Children and Sex: Emotional Congruence Scale (Beckett, 1987); The UCLA Loneliness scale (Russell, Peplau & Cutrona 1980; Thornton Self Esteem Questionnaire (Thornton, Beech & Marshall, 2004; Webster et al., in press); the Underassertiveness/Aggressiveness scales of the Social Response Inventory (Keltner, Marshall & Marshall, 1981); The Nowicki-Strickland Locus of Control Scale (Nowicki, 1976); The Novaco Anger Scale (Novaco, 1975); the Dissipation-Rumination Scale (Caprara, 1986); the Hypermasculinity Inventory (including calloused sexual attitudes (Mosher & Sirkin, 1984). Clinical interview has also been found to be effective in identifying problems in this domain (Webster et al., 2006). However, as noted above, the problem with any such self-report measures is that the results are dependent upon the offender being honest about his sexual interests. There is currently some work using the emotional. Stroop (1935) assesses the affective valence of emotionally laden words to individuals (Smith & Waterman, 2004) that may be useful in the assessment of problems in this domain. Although this work is very much at the preliminary stage at the current time.

SELF-MANAGEMENT DOMAIN

This domain refers to problems in general self-regulation. Self-regulation involves restraining immediate impulses in the service of longer-term or wider interests of the self. The mechanism, according to Ross and Fabiano (1985), is that criminals carry out anti-social acts due to a failure to insert a stage of reflection between impulse and action. Failures in self-regulation may derive from a number of sources.

Failures to regulate are divided into the following categories in the current version of the SARN (Webster et al., 2006).

- *Lifestyle impulsiveness/impulsive unstable lifestyle.* This type of behaviour involves well-established habits or attitudes that do not support self-regulation. More specifically, it involves a persistent and generalised tendency to make impulsive, irresponsible, anti-social, rule-breaking decisions. Lifestyle impulsivity has been identified as predicting reoffence amongst rapists (Prentky & Knight, 1991). Lifestyle impulsivity is measured partly by Factor 2 of the PCL-R (Hare, 1991), which has been found to predict sexual recidivism in rapists (Rice & Harris, 1997). Impulsivity has also been seen as a general problem that affects many types of offender (McGuire, J. 2000);
- *Poor problem solving (not knowing how to solve life's problem)* This is a problem with many different types of offenders where inappropriate strategies are used to solve problems;

- *Poor emotional control (out of control emotions/urges)* This is noted as a form of impulsivity where an individual appears withdrawn and over-controlled, but where aggressive impulses periodically surface as unpredictable expressions of violence.

In terms of measuring this domain as noted above sections of the PCL-R (Hare, 1991) would appear useful. Beech et al. (2003) also suggest that there are self-report instruments that have been constructed to measure the impulsivity such as the Barratt Impulsivity Scale (BIS-II, Barratt, 1994), as well as performance tasks such as the Porteus mazes (Porteus, 1955) that may be useful in assessing this domain.

ORGANISING DYNAMIC FACTORS INTO ASSESSMENTS OF SEXUAL DEVIANCE

Two systems in the United Kingdom have been developed that look at stable-dynamic factors. The Sex Offender Treatment Evaluation Project (STEP) test battery (Beech et al., 1999) used by Probation Services to measure *deviancy* in child abusers and the SARN (Thornton, 2002; Webster et al., 2006), used to assess all offenders in the English and Welsh Prison Service, and eventually in the Probation Service, under the NOMS system. These two systems of dynamic risk assessment are briefly described below.

DEVIANCY CLASSIFICATION (BEECH, 1998)

The deviancy construct in the STEP test battery was developed by Beech (1998) who classified child abusers according to their levels of problems on a battery of psychometric measures, assessing problems in child abusers in Domain 1 (strengths of deviant sexual interests), Domain 2 (distorted attitudes/beliefs), and Domain 3 (inadequacy emotional congruence, intimacy deficits and self-esteem problems). Two main types of child abusers were identified using this system in terms of their psychometric profiles were termed *High* and *Low deviancy* in terms of the differences between the groups and non-offenders on a number of psychometric measures (Fisher, Beech & Browne, 1999).

Here deviancy equates to the degree of deviation of scores from non-offender means, rather than deviancy being used in a pejorative sense. Specifically, *High deviancy* men were found to have significantly higher levels of distorted attitudes about children and sex than *Low deviancy* men and show significantly poorer empathy for victims of sexual abuse than non-offenders. Other significant differences between *High deviancy* and non-offending men indicate that they are reporting difficulty in forming intimate adult attachments, while perceiving their emotional needs could be better met by interacting with children than adults. The *High deviancy* group were also found to be significantly more under-assertive and to have significantly lower levels of self-esteem than non-offenders. In contrast, *Low deviancy* offenders did not show globalised cognitive distortions about children nor did they show high levels of emotional identification with children seen in *High deviancy* offenders. The *Low deviancy* group also showed significantly higher levels of social adequacy problems than non-offenders, although this was not as marked as in the *High deviancy* group.

Beech (1998) reported that *deviancy* tended to be associated with specific demographic factors. *High deviancy* offenders tend to have more victims, were more likely to have a previous convictions for a sexual offence, were more likely to have abused males or both males and females, and to have offended in an extra-familial setting or in both intra-familial and extra-familial settings. While *Low deviancy* men were much more likely to have committed offences against one or two victims within the family.

STRUCTURED ASSESSMENT OF RISK AND NEED (SARN, THORNTON, 2002; WEBSTER ET AL., 2006)

The SARN uses clinical ratings assessing 16 dynamic risk factors, categorised into each of Thornton's four risk domains, as discussed in detail above. It should be noted that Webster et al. report a high levels of inter-rater reliability using this clinical rating system of the four risk domains shown in Table 6.2.

It can be seen from Table 6.2 that there is considerable overlap between the Beech and Thornton classification systems. The major problems in Thornton's Domains 2 and 3, and the sexual obsessions component of Domain 1, essentially equate to Beech's *High deviancy* group. However, the SARN system is more wide-ranging and is more complex requiring considerable historical and clinical information, but gives a broader picture of the problems offenders have than Beech's more limited classification of child sexual abusers. However, it should be noted that the term *deviancy* (Thornton & Beech, 2002) has been widened to express the extent to which the offender's functioning is dominated by the psychological factors that contribute to his offending. Here, in *High deviancy* men the dynamic risk factors underlying offending are relatively intense and pervasive, that is an individual showing problems within at least three of the four risk domains. While in *Low deviancy* men the dynamic risk factors are relatively weak in intensity and circumscribed in their effect, and hence has problems in two or fewer risk domains.

STABLE 2000 (HANSON & HARRIS, 2000B)

Hanson and Harris also developed a system with both stable and acute risk factors (see below). Originally called SONAR this system has now been renamed in two parts STABLE and ACUTE 2000 (see below) (Hanson & Harris, 2000b; Hanson & Harris, 2000c). STABLE 2000 assesses six stable dynamic dimensions: significant social influences, intimacy deficits, attitudes supportive of sexual assault,

Table 6.2 Dynamic risk factors of SARN by domain: HMPS SOTP version[1]

Domain/risk factor title	Brief description of risk factor
Sexual interests domain	
Sexual preoccupation	An obsession with sex so that sex is an unusually salient activity.
Sexual preference for children	A preference for sexual activity with pre-pubescent children over adults.
Sexualised violence	A preference for coerced sex rather than consenting sex.
Other offence-related sexual interest	Any other socially deviant sexual interest, which seemed to play a crucial role in committing the offence.
Distorted attitudes domain	
Adversarial sexual attitudes	A view of heterosexual relationships where the male is seen as dominant and the female as submissive.
Sexual entitlement	The egocentric belief that if a man desires sex, he is entitled to have it.
Child abuse supportive beliefs	Beliefs that justify sexual activity with children or minimise the seriousness of such offending.
Rape-supportive beliefs	Beliefs that justify or excuse rape of adult women.
Women are deceitful beliefs	Beliefs that women are deceptive, corruptive or exploitative.
Social and emotional functioning domain	
Inadequacy	Subjective feelings of loneliness, low self-esteem and an external locus of control.
Distorted intimacy balance	Preferring to meet emotional intimacy needs through relationships with children rather than adults.
Grievance thinking	A thinking style characterised by suspiciousness, anger, vengefulness and a failure to see others' point of view.
Lack of emotional intimacy	Failure to achieve emotionally intimate adult relationships, whether desired or not.
Self-management domain	
Lifestyle impulsiveness	A pattern of making impulsive and irresponsible decisions.
Poor problem solving	Failure to employ cognitive skills to solve life problems.
Poor emotional control	Uncontrolled outbursts of emotion.

[1]Table 6.2. provided by the Offending Behaviour Programmes Unit of the English and Welsh Prison Service.

co-operation with supervision, sexual self-regulation (for example, sex drive/ pre-occupation, sex coping and deviant sexual interests) and general self-regulation. Hence STABLE 2000 factors are broadly consistent with the deviancy framework. These items are scored, 0, 1, or 2, to produce scale where those scoring 0 to 4 are considered Low risk (n = 307), those scoring 5 to 8 as moderate risk (n = 333), and those scoring 9 to 12 as high risk (n = 86) (Hanson, 2005). The scale has been evaluated in a prospective study called – the Dynamic Supervision Project (reported by Harris & Hanson, 2003; Hanson, 2005). This study running between year 2001 and 2006 followed over 1000 under community supervision, who have sexually offended against children or adults in all Canadian provinces, all three Canadian territories and the Correctional Service of Canada, Alaska and Iowa. STABLE-2000 were assessed every six months. Currently the inter-rater reliability of STABLE 2000 has been reported by Hanson (2005) as very good (ICC = 0.90), and the predictive accuracy being reasonable (AUC = 0.76), for a sexual offence, and slightly better (AUC = 0.77) for any sexual offence or breach.

In terms of using these systems, it can be seen from this brief review that Beech's *deviancy system*, the SARN and STABLE 2000 all highlight sexual interests, pro-offending attitudes and intimacy deficits, socio-affective deficits (for example, under assertiveness, low self-esteem and emotional loneliness). The SARN and STABLE 2000 systems also address general self-regulation, although the latest version of the SARN is probably the broadest in its scope.

EVIDENCE FOR THE USEFULNESS OF ASSESSING STABLE DYNAMIC RISK FACTORS

Thornton and Beech (2002) examined the extent to which psychological *deviance* predicts sexual recidivism interacts and also compared the accuracy of a static and dynamic risk assessment. Here, they compared the accuracy of the deviancy assessment to assess stable dynamic factors and Static-99 (Hanson & Thornton, 2000) to assess static factors, on two samples of sex offenders (121 men assessed prior to participating in a brief cognitive-behavioural prison programme in England and Wales and 53 male adult sex offenders assessed prior to participating in brief community treatment programme (Beech et al., 2002). Here, Thornton and Beech found that as a predictor of sexual recidivism, the problems in the number of dysfunctional domains obtained moderate accuracy (AUC ranging from 0.83 to 0.85) compared with Static-99 (AUC ranging from 0.91 to 0.75) over a four-year follow-up period. The recidivism rates by static risk and number of dysfunctional domains (*higher/lower deviancy*) categories are shown in Table 6.3.

It can be seen from Table 6.3 that the overall reconviction rate of the sample was 11% (19 out of 174). In terms of identifying the relative contributions of statistical and psychological relationships to subsequent risk it can also be seen from Table 6.3

Table 6.3 Reconviction rates in Static-99 risk and psychological deviance categories

	Total sample	High risk Static-99	Medium-High Static-99	Medium-Low Static-99	Low risk Static-99
Higher deviance(3+ dysfunctional areas of problems)	14/41 (34%)	8/12 (67%)	5/13 (39%)	0/7 (0%)	1/9 (11%)
Lower deviance(0-2 dysfunctional areas of problems)	5/133 (3%)	1/9 (11%)	3/23 (13%)	0/45 (0%)	1/56 (2%)
Total sample	19/174 (11%)	9/21 (43%)	8/36 (22%)	0/52 (0%)	2/65 (3%)
Reported five year recidivism levels by Static-99 risk-band score (Hanson & Thornton, 2000)	**18%** **(195/1086)**	**39%** **50/129**	**28%** **(82/290)**	**10%** **(43/410)**	**5%** **(14/257)**

that the reconviction rates by statistical risk categories were: High risk: 43%; Medium-High: 22%; Medium-Low 0%; Lower risk. These data accord fairly well with five-year predicted recidivism rates from Hanson and Thornton (2000) for High risk men, but are somewhat lower than the predicted rates for Medium-High, Low-Medium, and Low risk men from Hanson and Thornton (2000), as shown in the bottom row of Table 6.3. While for the assessment of psychological *deviance*, as can be seen from the second column of Table 6.3, over ten times more *Higher deviance* (34%) were reconvicted for sexual offence than *Lower deviance men*. This difference was statistically significant. As for the combination of the two approaches, it was found that both the statistical approach and psychological factors made an independent contribution to the prediction of sexual recidivism, thus, combining the two allows better prediction than either factor on its own. This is particularly illustrated by the finding that 67% of the men deemed as higher deviance and high risk were reconvicted for sexual offence within four years from the original assessment.

Consideration of the length of the follow up in this study suggests that for the Medium-High statistical risk/high psychological deviance combination (39%) is associated with a level of reconviction that is the same as that reported for High Static Risk offenders by Hanson and Thornton (2000) for a five-year follow up period. While for the Low risk/*Higher deviance* sample these were found to, more or less, recidivate at the same level as the Static-99 Medium risk sample reported by Hanson and Thornton (2000).

More recently, Craig et al. (2007) considered the effectiveness of psychometric markers of risk in approximating the *deviancy* domains and how these measures of dynamic risk could be used to predict sexual reconviction compared with actuarial risk. Here, four scales of the Multiphasic Sex Inventory (MSI; Nichols & Molinder, 1984) and six scales of the Special Hospitals Assessment of Personality and Socialisation (SHAPS; Blackburn, 1982) were administered to 119 sexual offenders. These scales were selected clinically on the basis of theoretical relevance to the Thornton's stable risk domains as follows: MSI Sexual Obsession and Paraphilia scales were used to assess the *Sexual Interests* domain; the MSI Cognitive Distortions and Immaturity and Justifications scales were used to assess the *Distorted Attitudes* domain; the SHAPS Anxiety, Hostility, Depression and Aggression scales were used to assess the *Socio-Affective Functioning* domain; and the SHAPS Psychopathic Deviate and Impulsivity scales were used to assess the *Self-Management* domain. The SHAPS and MSI scales were then combined with a principle component factorial procedure which produced a single factor for each domain. Actuarial risk was again measured using Static-99, which was later organised into three sub-scales: *Sexual deviance* (prior sexual convictions, male victims, non-contact sexual offences, non-relative and stranger victims); *General Criminality* (index non-sexual violence, prior non-sexual violence, and four or more sentencing occasions); and *Immaturity* (young age at offending).

It was found that these actuarial domains correlated with different aspects of the psychological risk factors. Specifically the *Sexual Interests* domain correlated ($r = 0.26$, $p < 0.01$) with the *Sexual Deviance* subscale of Static-99, the *Socio-Affective* domain correlated with the *Immaturity* Static-99 subscale ($r = 0.25$, $p < 0.01$), and the *Self Management* domain correlated with both the *General Criminality* ($r = 0.29$, $p < 0.001$) and the *Immaturity* ($r = 0.28$, $p < 0.01$) subscales of Static-99. No significant relationship was found between the *Distorted Attitudes* domain and any of the Static-99 subscales.

A Psychological Deviance Index (PDI) was calculated by standardising each of these scale scores for a domain. A domain was counted as dysfunctional if its average standard score was greater than zero. This means the number of dysfunctional domains index could be calculated running from 0 to 4. In measuring the risk assessment properties of the four dynamic risk domains, the *Sexual Interests* domain obtained a large effect in predicting sexual reconviction over two-years (AUC $= 0.86$), and five-year follow-up periods (AUC $= 0.72$). The *Self Management* factor obtained moderate results (AUC $= 0.71$) in predicting sexual reconviction at two years. In comparison, Static-99 obtained moderate accuracy in predicting sexual reconviction, at two-years (AUC $= 0.66$) and five years (AUC $= 0.60$). When the rates of sexual recidivism were compared with the PDI, it was found that the increase in rates of sexual recidivism mirrored the increase in the degree of PDI. As the PDI increased from, zero, one, two, three and four, the rates of reconviction were 3%, 10%, 8%, 14%, and 26% respectively. However, when the PDI was grouped into Low (0), Moderate (1–2) and High (3+) categories, it was found the degree of PDI and rates of reconviction were linear at 3%, 18% and 40% respectively (Figure 6.1). When the PDI and Static-99 were entered into a

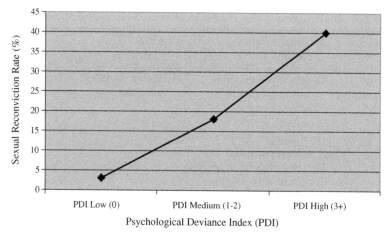

Figure 6.1 Psychological Deviance Index (PDI) and sexual reconviction

logistic regression analysis it was found that the PDI made a statistically significant contribution to prediction of sexual reconviction independent of Static-99 at five-year follow-up.

However, it should be noted that both of these studies share a common sample of 53 child abusers originally reported by Beckett, Beech, Fisher and Fordham (1994) and Beech et al. (2002), in the combined results from Thornton (2002), Thornton and Beech (2002), and Craig et al. (2007), as does Hanson (2005), support the usefulness of assessing stable dynamic psychological factors to assess the level of risk and treatment need (see Chapter 7) of sexual offenders.

IDENTIFYING ACUTE DYNAMIC RISK FACTORS

Craig, Browne and Stringer (2003a) identified 13 *acute* dynamic risk factors (see Table 6.4) that have been found to be associated with sexual offence recidivism.

It can be seen from Table 6.4 that the acute dynamic risk factors fall into the following groups: sexual interests, treatment behaviour, clinical factors and contextual factors.

Harris and Hanson (2001) explored *acute* dynamic predictors of risk in sexual offenders. Here, they collected information via interviews with community supervision officers and file reviews. They found significant differences between the recidivists and the non-recidivists on most of the acute factors examined in this study. Specifically, compared to non-recidivists, recidivists were more frequently unemployed, were more likely to abuse drugs and/or alcohol during the course of supervision where the level of substance abuse increased just before recidivating. They also found that recidivists were more likely to have ever used anti-androgens (sex-drive-reducing medications) than non-recidivists. Recidivists were more likely

Table 6.4 Acute dynamic risk factors associated with sexual offence recidivism

Sexual Interests Factor	Treatment Behaviour Factors	Clinical Factors	Contextual Factors
Frequency of sexual fantasies	Delinquent behaviour during treatment	Affective disorders Substance use	Isolation Recent unemployment
	Poor treatment co-operation		Deviant social influences
	Poor co-operation with supervision		Chaotic lifestyle
	Deterioration in awareness of high risk situations and relapse prevention strategies		Poor social support
			Relationship problems
	Short duration of treatment programme		
	Deterioration in dynamic risk during treatment		

to dropout or otherwise were considered treatment failures compared to the non-recidivists. Substance abuse problems during supervision were also more common among recidivists. Not surprisingly, the recidivists tended to view themselves as posing little risk of committing new sexual offences and took fewer precautions to avoid high-risk situations.

Conversely, supervising probation officers perceived the non-recidivists' social environment to have more positive than negative social influences whereas the pattern was reversed for recidivists. Non-recidivists were also described as being more co-operative with supervision and having less chaotic lifestyles than the recidivists.

As for the immediate build-up to offending in recidivists, Hanson and Harris (2000a) report that in the period of one month prior to the offence, there was a marked alteration in several of the acute dynamic factors. The recidivist's appearance and compliance with supervision deteriorated. There were also increased negative mood, anger and psychotic symptoms, one month prior to the reoffence. Hence it would appear that such factors signal an escalation in the offender's level of risk. Similarly, deterioration in awareness and relapse prevention strategies following a return to the community have also been described as dynamic risk factors of sexual offence recidivism (Fisher, Beech & Browne, 2000).

ASSESSING ACUTE DYNAMIC RISK FACTORS

Hanson and Harris have also developed ACUTE 2000 (Hanson & Harris, 2000c) which is the acute counterpart of STABLE 2000 (Hanson & Harris, 2000b), which covers the following acute risk factors: victim access; emotional collapse (that is, evidence of severe emotional disturbance/ emotional crisis), collapse of social supports; hostility; substance abuse; sexual preoccupations and rejection of supervision. The final factor in this system is what Hanson and Harris term a 'unique factor' in that some offenders have unique characteristics that represent a real risk factor for that offender. The type of factors that could be important for an offender could be such events as: a specific date or event (that is, an anniversary) that causes an emotional response, pain or discomfort – possibly triggering alcohol or drug abuse; homelessness, contact with a specified family member, health problems of a cyclical nature that may enter and leave the offender's situation with little warning, and being bothered by intrusive thoughts regarding their own victimisation.

Hanson and Harris have examined the performance of the ACUTE-2000 variables in their Dynamic Supervision Project (Hanson, 2005; Harris & Hanson, 2003). This study running between year 2001 and 2006 followed 1000 sex offenders. Risk factors were monitored and recorded by supervising probations trained in the use of the scale. Static factors were also assessed at initial assessment, Stable dynamic risk factors, using STABLE-2000 were assessed every six months (see above) and acute factors were assessed after every supervision of the offender. The results so far indicate good reliability between supervising officers scoring ACUTE-2000 risk factors ($ICC = 0.89$) with reasonable predictive accuracy being for ACUTE-2000 (AUC $= 0.74$) for sexual offences (Hanson, 2005).

CONCLUSIONS

The aim of this chapter was to outline the current position regarding the assessment of stable and acute dynamic risk factors and the evidence base for their usefulness, in that considering dynamic factors alongside actuarial static risk classification, may provide a more global and valid assessment of an offender's risk for sexual recidivism. Trait or psychological dispositional factors assessed at pre-release may also help identify individuals exhibiting characteristics of psychological deviance who may require greater supervision. The current trend in research suggests that taking into account dynamic psychological problems (such as low self-esteem, emotional identification with children and justifications for sexual offending) and assessments of psychological and sexual deviance alongside static risk classification contributes to offender's risk for sexual recidivism. Redefining our understanding of what dynamic factors represent may be the genesis for future research into incorporating dynamic factors into actuarial systems spawning a new generation of risk scales (Mills, 2005). Therefore, a more global assessment of risk, including a combination of risk assessment approaches (actuarial scales with research guided clinical judgement, and clinically adjusted actuarial approaches) as part of a comprehensive approach to risk appraisal (see Chapter 10), may be the future of risk assessment. As Hanson (2005) observes, the tone of the risk assessment literature has changed from the validity of carrying out risk assessments to debating the best method of risk assessment.

Also we would note that common among the dynamic risk assessments systems reviewed here is a theoretical assumption that *stable* risk factors (for example, such as pro-sexual assault attitudes and sexual interest in children) interact with *acute* states (e.g., victim acquisition behaviours and deterioration in lifestyle stability) leading to an increased risk of sexual reoffending. This is consistent with theoretical model postulated by Beech and Ward (2004), which we will examine in Chapter 8.

7

Treatment and Sexual Recidivism

INTRODUCTION

The aim of this chapter is to give an overview of what current treatment of sex offenders consists of and to point out how heavily influenced this approach is by current concepts in risk assessment and the general criminogenic principles of 'What Works' for offenders. We will also outline current treatment provisions in prisons and the community in the UK. This chapter ends with a discussion on the difficulties of ascertaining whether we can currently scientifically measure whether treatment actually works.

APPROACHES TO TREATMENT

Treatment of sexual offenders has undergone a series of changes from the early attempts using unstructured psychoanalytic techniques to modern day highly structured groups-based treatment. Wood, Grossman and Fichtner (2000) note that these approaches broadly fall into three categories: insight-oriented, psycho-analytic therapy, behavioural and cognitive-behavioural therapy. Brown (2005) notes that the above broadly reflect the approaches to treatment in the broader criminogenic literature from 'nothing works' (Martinson, 1974), to 'something works' (Gendreau & Ross, 1979), to the current 'What Works' literature (Andrews & Bonta, 2003; McGuire, 1995), which is about what works, for whom, and in what circumstances. We will now examine each of these broad approaches to treatment in a little more detail.

Early descriptions of sex offender treatment would appear, according to Brown (2005), to describe a humanistic psychoanalytic approach (early work reported in Frisbie, 1969; Frisbie & Dondis, 1965). This type of approach provided little in terms of reducing recidivism rates of sexual offenders. In fact Laws and Marshall (2003) point out that 'treated' offenders actually had higher rates of recidivism than untreated offenders. With the advent of behaviour therapy in the 1960s success was starting to be reported in treatment using behaviour modification techniques to suppress deviant arousal (McGuire, Carlisle & Young, 1965). Beech and Mann (2002) note that for a number of years treatment was limited to behaviour modification (where aversive conditioning using electric shock or aversive odours was commonplace) and social skills training. However, with the rise of cognitive treatment for depression and anxiety, attention turned to the thought processes of sexual offenders and the role of cognitions, specifically 'cognitive distortions' (Abel et al., 1989) in offending, that is, pro-offending attitudes and beliefs used by sexual offenders to justify their offending and minimise any guilt they may feel. Work on challenging these thoughts began to be incorporated into treatment, along with a focus on developing empathy for the victims of abuse. The inculcation of empathy was seen as vital in tackling any victim-blaming attitudes or denial of the harm caused by abuse (Abel, Blanchard & Becker, 1978), and the development of empathy was seen as important in reducing the likelihood that an individual would sexually recidivate. By the mid-1980s the concept of relapse prevention, first developed in the addictions field by Marlatt and Gordon (1985), was adapted for application in work with sexual offenders (Marques, 1982; Pithers et al., 1983). The relapse prevention approach signified a combination of cognitive and behaviour therapy (CBT).

To give a brief synopsis of CBT, the behavioural component addresses the overt and covert behaviour of an individual, drawing upon the principles of learning theory. Originally, as noted above, behavioural therapy was confined to the use of procedures to alter behaviour, that is, rewarding desired behaviours and punishing unwanted behaviours, but has since broadened out to include modelling (demonstrating a desired behaviour) and skills training (teaching specific skills through behavioural rehearsal). The cognitive component of CBT therefore addresses the thoughts or cognitions that an individual experiences, which are known to affect mood state and hence have an influence upon subsequent behaviour. The cognitive aspect of therapy therefore aims to encourage an individual to think differently about events, thus giving rise to different affect and behaviour. The use of self-instruction and self-monitoring, and the development of an awareness of how one thinks affects how one feels and behaves, are vital components in cognitive therapy.

By combining these two approaches, CBT provides a comprehensive approach to treating sex offenders. Group, rather than individual work has also been the usual method of delivery of CBT for sexual offenders. The group work approach is seen as being suitable for all types of sexual offender. Beech and Fordham (1997) have outlined the benefits of being in a group, and group work, as the following: groups provide an environment that can offer both support and challenge to the individual; group work provides the opportunity for discussion with peers; and provides opportunities for increasing self-esteem and empathic responding; groups also offer a forum for support and sharing of problems which may be a completely new experience for many sex offenders who are generally isolated individuals, often with interpersonal deficits and feelings of inadequacy. Having the experience of being valued, being able to help others, practising social skills and getting to know others in detail can greatly improve an individual's self-esteem and interpersonal functioning. Given that feelings of inadequacy and lack of appropriate relationships may be an important vulnerability factor for many sex offenders, in particular child sex abusers (Thornton, Beech & Marshall, 2004), improvement in these areas is an important element in reducing reoffending.

Throughout the 1990s, most CBT group-work programmes in North America, and the UK, have incorporated such approaches into an integrated package, aiming to target the dynamic risk factors associated with sexual offending (as described in Chapter 6) in order to change sexual arousal, enhance social and empathy skills, restructure offence-supportive attitudes and enhance self-management through the use of relapse prevention techniques (Fisher & Beech, 1999).

However, in the latter half of the 1990s, more sophisticated ideas of tackling the underlying schemas or implicit theories that generate distorted attitudes have been incorporated into treatment (Mann, 1999). While a deeper understanding of the way individuals both commit initial sexual offences and then relapse has been undertaken, with Ward and Hudson (1998b) pointing out the deficits in the original RP model, showing that there are different pathways to offending, with individuals seeking different goals, these being defined as either acquisitive (approach) or inhibitory (avoidant); and that individuals also differ in the regulation of their behaviour. Where some offenders under-regulate their behaviour and so behave in an impulsive, reckless manner; or where they use effective strategies to achieve unacceptable aims, or mis-regulate their behaviours, strategies are used that have an 'ironic' effect, that is, the strategy used to avoid offending actually has the opposite effect.

New methods are being developed to assess these types of problems (see Ward, Polaschek & Beech, 2005) and new methods for treatment targeting specific offence pathways are also starting to be described (Ward, Yates & Long, 2006). Ward and colleagues (that is, Ward & Gannon, 2006) have suggested an alternative to the more traditional approaches to treatment, which is termed the 'Good Lives Model' (GLM).This is concerned with taking a positivistic approach to treatment. Ward and Gannon (2006) note that in the GLM, an individual is hypothesised to commit criminal offences because he lacks the opportunities and/or the capabilities to achieve valued outcomes in personally fulfilling and socially acceptable ways. There are three levels or components to the GLM: (a) a set of general principles and assumptions that specify the values underlying rehabilitation practice and the kind of overall aims for which clinicians should be striving; (b) the implications of these general assumptions for explaining and understanding sexual offending and its functions; (c) the treatment implications of a focus on goals (goods), self-regulation strategies and ecological variables. Although it is too early to evaluate these approaches, they may signal the future for sex offender treatment.

We will now describe current approaches to treatment that rely heavily upon the 'What Works' principles, which underpins current treatment for sexual offenders (Harkins & Beech, 2007).

'WHAT WORKS' AND TREATMENT

Andrews and Bonta (2003) advocate the use of risk, need and responsivity principles in determining the course of treatment for a particular individual. We will now examine these in more detail and how they have been applied in sex offender treatment.

THE RISK PRINCIPLE

There is a growing body of research suggesting that treatment is most effective when administered according to the 'risk principle' (Andrews & Bonta, 2003; Andrews & Dowden, 2006). According to this principle, the most intensive treatment should be offered to the highest (static) risk offenders with little to no treatment being offered to low risk offenders because the latter are less likely to reoffend even without treatment (Harkins & Beech, 2007). Research has demonstrated reductions in recidivism among high-risk offenders only when high intensity treatment is offered. When low-risk offenders were offered intensive treatment, this had either a minimal or negative impact (Andrews & Bonta, 2003). It is of course worth commenting that it is easier to show a real treatment effect in high-risk offenders because their base rate of offending is high, allowing more room for improvement as a result of treatment. The base-rate describes the percentage of (untreated) sexual offenders in a particular population who recidivate after release (see Chapter 3). The difficulty with finding significant results is that if there is a low base-rate of sexual offending, then large sample sizes and long follow-up periods are needed to show that treatment works (Barbaree, 1997).

In order to provide the most effective treatment then, it would seem that treatment should be administered according to static risk level (see Chapter 4), with the most intensive and extensive treatment being offered to the highest risk offenders. Many studies report risk level of the group they are discussing (for example, Looman, Abracen & Nicholaichuk, 2000) or attempt to match comparison groups for risk level (for example, McGrath, Cumming, Livingston & Hoke, 2003), but do not report treatment outcome in terms of risk (Beech, Friendship, Erikson & Hanson, 2002). One exception to this is a study by Friendship, Mann and Beech (2003) who found that significantly lower rates of violent recidivism in the

Medium-Low risk (3% treated vs. 13% untreated) and Medium-High risk (5% treated vs. 13% untreated) categories, as measured by Static-99[1] (Hanson & Thornton, 2000). While, Low risk (2% treated vs. 3% untreated) and High-risk (26% treated vs. 28% untreated) groups showed trends in the expected direction, these were not significant due to the low base-rates in the low risk group and a hypothesised lack of treatment intensity in the high-risk group.

However, while this approach of offering treatment to those who have been measured as being in most need of it, Harkins and Beech (2007) argue that by using assessment methods that include only historical static variables, there is little opportunity for clinicians to provide any meaningful information regarding the impact of treatment on risk level. Therefore, recently, attention has started to turn to the predictive ability of those factors that are fairly stable, but have the potential to change, that is, dynamic risk factors[2] (for example, Beech, et al., 2002; Craig, Browne, Stringer & Beech, 2005; Hanson & Harris, 2000, 2001; Thornton, 2002). The next section of this chapter examines the relationship between dynamic risk and treatment.

THE NEED PRINCIPLE

According to the need principle, treatment should be tailored to address the criminogenic needs of individuals (that is, dynamic risk factors, see Chapter 6) of the offender in question. There is evidence that levels of dynamic (changeable) risk factors are related to recidivism (Beech et al., 2001; Beech & Ford, 2006; Craig, Thornton, Beech & Browne, 2007; Hanson, 2005a). Given the need for clinicians to report an offender's risk for reoffence accurately, it is important that, in addition to the valuable information that static measures of risk provide, dynamic factors are also examined. Thornton (2002), and Hanson and Harris (2000) suggest that stable dynamic risk factors can be encompassed under four overarching domains: (1) sexual interests/sexual self-regulation; (2) distorted attitudes/attitudes tolerant of sexual offending; (3) socio-affective functioning/intimacy deficits; and (4) self-management/self-regulation problems (see Chapter 6 for a discussion of the relationship between these dynamic factors and recidivism). Thornton (2002) identified high levels of problems in Domains 2, 3 and 4 as distinguishing between repeat offenders and those with only one conviction. Pro-offending attitudes (Domain 2) and intimacy deficits (Domain 3) have been noted as commonly occurring among identified dynamic risk predictors (Craissati & Beech, 2003). Hanson and Harris (2000, 2001) identified intimacy deficits, negative social environment, attitudes tolerant of sexual offending, emotional/sexual self-regulation deficits, and general self-regulation deficits as possible dynamic predictors of

---

[1]See Chapter 4 for a description of this measure.
[2]See Chapter 6 for a discussion of these.

recidivism for sex offenders and these domains were found to differentiate recidivists from non-recidivists. Beech and Ward (2004) have discussed the aetiological underpinnings of these domains as they fit into a theoretical framework of offending. It has been argued that the integration of identified risk predictors with theory could potentially result in advances of the treatment of sex offenders by allowing treatment to be varied according to their stable dynamic risk predictor (Ward & Beech, 2004) (see Chapter 8).

In terms of relationships between change and reduced recidivism, evidence is currently fairly scarce, however, Beech et al. (2001) found that those offenders who were not deemed to have made progress in treatment in terms of reducing distorted attitudes (Domain 2) were more likely to be reconvicted than those who did make progress (23% vs. 10%). Marques et al. (2005) found that child molesters who scored low on their 'Got It' scale (which included post-treatment measures of Domain 1 problems – phallometric scores), Domain 2 distorted attitudes problems – as measured by the Justifications, Cognitive Distortions and Immaturity, Child Molest and Rape scales of the Multiphasic Sex Inventory (MSI), Nichols & Molinder (1984) and Domain 4 self-management problems – as measured by clinicians rating the quality of relapse prevention knowledge) reoffended at a significantly lower rate than those who did not. Beech, Fisher and Beckett (1999) found changes within treatment in terms of each of the four dynamic risks and criminogenic need domains: sexual interests (MSI sex deviance admittance), distorted attitudes (cognitive distortions, victim distortions, and MSI Justifications), socio-affective functioning (self-esteem, under-assertiveness, personal distress), and self-management (awareness of risk situations and generation of effective strate-gies). While Ford and Beech (2006) found that none of a residential sample of high risk/highly deviant offenders[3] who had been as responding to treatment (changes across all risk domains) had been reconvicted over a two or five-year follow-up period.

RESPONSIVITY

The responsivity principle dictates that treatment style should be tailored to meet the learning style and abilities of offenders (Andrews & Bonta, 2003). Andrews and Bonta note that when correctional treatment adheres to all three of the risk, need and general responsivity principles, the effect size is for positive outcome is 0.26, if only adhering to two, the mean effect size is 0.18, and if only one of the three principles is adhered to, the effect size is minimal (i.e., 0.02). Responsivity is obviously dependent upon factors such as psychopathy, motivation, as well as the style of

---

[3]See Chapter 6 for a definition of deviance.

treatment offered to the offenders (Beech & Mann, 2002). Hence we will now look at some of these treatment mediators in more detail.

PSYCHOPATHY AND TREATMENT

Psychopathy is a condition marked by interpersonal (for example, grandiosity, pathological lying, manipulativeness), affective (for example, shallow emotions, lack of empathy, guilt or remorse), and behavioural traits (for example, impulsivity, persistent violation of social norms; Hare, 1996). Psychopathy has been widely associated with numerous negative outcomes (see Hare, 1996; Hare, Clarke, Grann & Thornton, 2000; Hart, 1998; Salekin, Rogers & Sewell, 1996). The Psychopathy Checklist, revised (PCL-R; Hare, 2003) is the most common instrument for assessing psychopathy, widely used in both research and clinical settings.

There are a number of studies and reviews discussing the commonly stated position that men scoring high in psychopathy (that is, a PCL-R score more than 25 or 30) generally respond poorly to treatment (for example, Hare et al., 2000; Hobson, Shine & Roberts, 2000). Indeed, there are studies indicating that treatment may even make highly psychopathic sex offenders more likely to recidivate (Looman, Abracen, Serin & Marquis, 2005; Rice, Harris & Cormier, 1992; Seto & Barbaree, 1999). However, upon closer inspection, the studies indicating this are somewhat problematic, making conclusions based upon them contentious. Recent evidence and opinions have called into question the clinical lore surrounding the position that psychopaths are untreatable (for example, D'Silva, Duggan & McCarthy, 2004; Langton, Barbaree, Harkins & Peacock, 2006; Loving, 2002; Salekin, 2002; Stalans, 2005). D'Silva et al. (2004) and Wong (2000) reviewed the extant literature on the treatment of psychopaths and concluded that there is not enough evidence to support the view that men who score high on the PCL-R have a negative response to treatment. Salekin (2002) completed a meta-analysis of 42 psychopathy treatment studies and reported that there is little scientific basis for the belief that psychopaths are untreatable, finding a treatment effect for cognitive-behavioural, psychodynamic and eclectic types of treatment.

An alternative interpretation of the psychopathy treatment outcome studies to date is that perhaps psychopathy presents an obstacle to therapy, but an obstacle that can be overcome. Beech et al. (1999) identified psychopathy as a possible block to successful treatment groups. They noted that one very psychopathic man had a negative impact on the group he attended and that overall this group was not found to be very cohesive and only produced treatment change in 35% of its members (compared to over 60% in other sex offender groups). Psychopaths have been identified as having more criminogenic needs than non-psychopaths, suggesting that psychopathy should perhaps be viewed as a responsivity factor in which the learning styles of psychopaths could be used to guide treatment interventions (Serin, 1995; Simourd & Hoge, 2000; Templeman & Wolversheim, 1979). It may, therefore, be the case that psychopaths present more of a challenge than non-psychopaths, but they are treatable nonetheless.

MOTIVATION

Lack of motivation for treatment has been discussed as an obstacle to successful treatment (Beech & Fisher, 2002; Garland & Dougher, 1991; Kear-Colwell & Pollock, 1997; Miller & Rollnick, 2002; Tierney & McCabe, 2002). Motivation for treatment can be conceptualised in a number of ways (for example, acceptance of accountability for offending, willingness to attend treatment, cognitive distortions regarding offending). It has been applied to sex offenders in terms of Prochaska and DiClemente's (1994) constantly fluctuating stages within the trans theoretical model of change, ranging from lack of acknowledgement of a problem, to beginning to acknowledge a problem and make changes, through to the maintenance of the changes made (for example, Frost & Connelly, 2004; Kear-Colwell & Pollack, 1997). Motivational interviewing is often advocated as an important component in sexual offender treatment (for example, Garland & Dougher, 1991; Kear-Colwell & Pollack, 1997). Much of the discussion of the impact of motivation on treatment effectiveness has been based on clinical experience, rather than empirical studies (Tierney & McCabe, 2002).

Motivation for treatment has also been shown to change within treatment, increasing within institutional treatment for all offender groups (that is, familial child molesters, extra-familial child molesters and sexually aggressive offenders), but dropping for all groups following release into the community (Barrett, Wilson & Long, 2003). For the most part though, these levels remained higher than when they were measured at pre-treatment. Similar increases in motivation within treatment were observed in groups of high and low-risk offenders as well (Stirpe, Wilson & Long, 2001). One study with a small sample size (n=31) demonstrated that overall, sex offenders who were self-motivated to attend treatment (compared to those who participated for other reasons, such as parole eligibility), were not more successful in reducing cognitive distortions by the end of treatment (Terry & Mitchell, 2001). When analysed separately though, those with child victims who were not motivated were significantly less likely to demonstrate a reduction in cognitive distortions, than those with adult victims. As well, recent meta-analysis found that clinical presentation variables, such as low motivation, failed to show a relationship with sexual recidivism (Hanson & Morton-Bourgon, 2004). Given the lack of consistency between the few studies and meta-analyses to date, and clinical opinion, motivation seems to warrant further examination regarding its impact on treatment effectiveness (see Marshall et al., 2005).

THERAPIST STYLE

A number of studies and review papers have identified therapist's characteristics as playing an important role in delivery effective treatment (Marshall, 2005; Marshall & Fernandez et al., 2003; Marshall & Serran, 2004; Marshall & Serran et al., 2003). In a qualitative pilot study of 24 sexual offenders, the offenders reported that, while several techniques were viewed as helpful, they felt the therapists were the most important factor in influencing change (Drapeau, 2005). Marshall & Serran et al. (2003) suggest aggressively confrontational approaches should be avoided and more empathic, respectful type of supportive, with a firm, challenging style, should be employed. This less confrontational approach is also supported by a number of other researchers (for example, Drapeau, 2005; Kear-Colwell & Pollock, 1997; Preston, 2000). This type of approach has also been related to positive group environment (Beech and Fordham, 1997). In addition, empathy, warmth, reward-ingness and directiveness were related to positive indices of change (Marshall & Serran et al., 2003). Harsh confrontation was also adversely related to treatment change (Marshall & Serran et al., 2003).

It is reasonable to consider the amount and type of experience the therapists has. Craig (2005) and Hogue (1995) found that following a training programme related to the treatment of sexual offenders, the participant's attitudes towards sex offenders improved. Particularly, they indicated a greater belief in treatment efficacy as opposed to punishment, believed that they possessed the knowledge required to work with sex offenders, and felt more confident in doing so. This was maintained at six months' follow-up when the participants had had the opportunity to put the training into practice. Nelson, Herlihy and Oesher (2002) found a significant positive correlation between attitudes towards sex offenders and experience working with sex offenders indicating that counsellor's attitudes towards sex offenders became more positive with experience. Also more positive attitudes were associated with having more sex offenders on their caseload. This was also supported in a qualitative study of professional and paraprofessional who have contact with sexual offenders (Lea, Auburn & Kibblewhite, 1999). No correlation between attitudes and amount of specific training in counselling sex offenders, although there was a relationship between attitudes and feeling that training had prepared them for dealing with sex offenders (Nelson et al., 2002). However, another study looking at professionals and paraprofessionals working with sexual offenders did find that those who received training did have more positive attitudes towards sex offenders, although there were still those with experience who also expressed some negative views and stereotypes (Lea et al., 1999).

CURRENT TREATMENT PROVISION IN THE UK: TREATMENT FOR SEXUAL OFFENDERS IN PRISON

A strategy for the treatment of sexual offenders in prison began in 1991 with the implementation of the Sex Offender Treatment Programme (SOTP). This initiative was devised to be a framework for the integrated assessment and treatment of sex offenders (Mann, 1999; Mann & Thornton, 1998). The SOTP is currently running in around 26–28 prisons in England and Wales, with around 1000 men completing treatment every year (Beech & Fisher, 2004). This makes the SOTP the biggest treatment programme in the world at the present time.

Treatment provision for serious[4] sexual offenders in English and Welsh Prison Service consists of the following components: assessment, the Core Programme and the Extended Programme (from Mann, 1999):

ASSESSMENT

Here the offender is assessed for his suitability to undertake a group-work programme. Exclusions are made at this point, on the basis of the following:

– he is in total denial of the offence;
– he is suffering from psychotic illness or was at the time of the offence;
– he has a high score (26 or above) on the Hare Psychopathy Checklist (Hare, 1991). Suggesting that he has psychopathic characteristics, which would suggest that he would not benefit from the group-work programme currently provided for sexual offenders.

As part of the assessment offenders will complete a psychometric test battery and will also be assessed for their level of need using the Structured Assessment of Risk and Need (SARN, Thornton, 2002) in addition to the assessment of actuarial risk, using Risk Matrix-2000 (Thornton et al., 2003).

THE CORE SEX OFFENDER TREATMENT PROGRAMME (SOTP)

If a sexual offender is assessed as being suitable to take part in treatment and does not have learning difficulties[5] he would first undertake the Core SOTP. The

---

[4]We use the term serious here to mean the type of sexual offence that invariably receives a custodial sentence, rather than the type of sexual offence that is seen as less serious by the courts and hence is more likely to receive a community sentence, such offences here typically include: indecent exposure, the making of indecent phone calls or the downloading of child pornography from the internet.

[5]If an offender is assessed as having learning difficulties he would go through an adapted programme specifically designed for those with an IQ 70–80. This has an emphasis on the use of non-verbal material and a reduced empathy component.

goals of this programme are:

- to reduce denial and minimisation;
- to enhance understanding of victims' experiences;
- to develop strategies to avoid reoffending (from Mann, 1999).

When the CORE Programme was introduced in 1991 this was the sum total of treatment a sex offender would receive, which comprised 35 to 40 two hour sessions. This programme was revised and expanded and by late 1994 the 'revised' programme was rolled out generally providing around 160 treatment contact hours. This revised programme has been recently superseded by the 'CORE 2000' programme (Beech & Fisher, 2004). CORE 2000, although essentially covering the same areas as the Revised Programme, now places more emphasis on treatment as a collaborative effort. Here, the primary purposes of the programme are to increase the offender's motivation to avoid reoffending and to develop the self-management skills necessary to achieve this. Cognitive restructuring, modelling and positive reinforcement are seen as central to such treatment. While motivation is developed through undermining the excuses and rationalisations (cognitive distortions) that offenders use to justify their offending, empathy with their victims is increased by creating an emotional and intellectual awareness of the victim's experience of the offence, and by examining the consequences of offending on their own lives.

THE EXTENDED PROGRAMME

If an offender is assessed as having a lot of treatment needs he would also undertake a second stage of treatment, which is termed the EXTENDED Programme. The goals of this programme are (from Mann, 1999) to:

- identify and challenge patterns of dysfunctional thinking;
- to improve the management of emotions;
- to improve relationship and intimacy skills;
- to address deviant fantasy and sexual arousal;
- to understand the links of all of the above to sexual offending.

This programme has again been recently revised and emphasises the importance of learning to manage negative emotions, particularly through the use of positive and calming cognitions rather than behavioural coping strategies, which may not always be available to the offender. The Extended Programme now runs for around 68 two-hour sessions and focuses on the schemas (the underlying core beliefs held by the offender) and the interpersonal skills deficits found in many offenders. Offenders will be offered additional individual work on managing deviant arousal where treatment managers in the various establishments deem this appropriate in places where this programme is run. There are plans to develop a specific programme targeting arousal.

THE ROLLING PROGRAMME

This programme is aimed at offenders with fewer treatment needs than those attending CORE 2000. It covers a number of offence-specific tasks, which offenders have to complete before leaving the programme. Tasks include such things as: completing an offence account, writing a victim apology letter, identifying and challenging distorted thinking, and so on. Tasks are set according to assessed needs and the offender can remain in the programme for as long as required to satisfactorily complete the tasks. Being a rolling programme means that offenders can join and leave the group at any time, which makes it a very flexible programme to run. Treatment typically consists of around 100 hours of treatment.

TREATMENT FOR SEXUAL OFFENDERS IN THE COMMUNITY

In terms of treatment provision in the community, three 'pathfinder programmes' have been accredited by the Joint Prison and Probation Services Accreditation Panel for England and Wales. The three programmes are the West Midlands Programme, the Thames Valley Programme (TV-SOGP) and the Northumbria Programme. Correctional Services Accreditation Panel is made up of a group of experts from both the UK and North America and their task is to accredit treatment programmes, which they consider to be of a suitable standard. Programmes are judged on a range of criteria which meet the 'what works' principles. The 42 probation services in England and Wales are in the process of implementing one of the geographically near programmes. In terms of numbers entering probation-based treatment, this initiative is predicting to treat around 1500 men per year (David Middleton, UK National Probation Directorate, May 2002).

One of the differences between the accredited programmes offered within the prison and probation services is that the probation programmes have to cater for a wide range of offenders with only one programme (exhibitionists, rapists, child abusers) while the prison service is able to offer a range of programmes to suit the needs of different offenders as outlined above. Within the Probation Service limited resources mean that only one programme can be run and thus the programme has to offer a number of modules, which offenders attend according to their needs. There is also the need for flexibility so that offenders can repeat modules as necessary.

As an example of community treatment, the TV-SOGP[6] has four programme blocks, which offenders attend according to their assessed needs. The first block is the *Foundation Block*, which is an intensive two-week block. This is aimed at reducing denial and increasing motivation and responsibility taking for the offending behaviour, identifying and challenging distorted thinking, understanding the links between thoughts, feelings and behaviour and thus recognising the role played by deviant sexual thoughts. It also introduces the idea of relapse prevention, problem solving and simple strategies to control deviant sexual thoughts. The programme then moves to weekly or twice weekly sessions for the remainder of the blocks. The next block being *Victim Empathy* block which aims to help the offender understand the perspective of the victim, the effects of sexual abuse, the behaviour of the victim and the far-reaching consequences of abuse on all those effected. The third block is *Life Skills*, which essentially covers problem solving, coping strategies and interpersonal relationships. The aim of this block is to improve an offender's ability to relate to others and to have more realistic expectations of others. The final block is *Relapse Prevention*, which aims to assist offenders in developing realistic relapse plans and the skills and strategies required to put them into practice. An offender assessed as having many problems would do the entire programme while those with fewer problems, that is, only offence-specific needs would not do *Life Skills*. Offenders who had successfully completed a programme in prison may only attend Relapse Prevention, using it as a form of maintenance in the community. Offenders can repeat blocks as necessary or omit blocks according to need. Hence, those with a high level of problems would typically undertake 200 hours of treatment, while those with fewer problems will only undertake around 100 hours of treatment.

MEASURING TREATMENT EFFECTIVENESS

The effectiveness of sex offender treatment as a whole has been measured in a number of studies (Harkins & Beech, 2007). While the most recent meta-analyses of a number of studies reporting outcome indicate an overall effect for treatment (Hanson et al., 2002; Lösel & Schmucker, 2005), that is, a lower rate of recidivism in those who have undergone treatment compared to those who have not, these observed effect sizes are typically not large. However, there are a number of issues which must be considered when evaluating the effectiveness of sex offender treatment. There are those who feel that nothing but the most rigorous scientific studies can produce meaningful results (e.g., Kenworthy et al., 2004; Rice & Harris, 2003), whereas others feel that given the practical and ethical issues with conducting random assignment studies (that is, is it ethical to withhold treatment from those

---

[6]Described in *The Treatment and Risk Management of Sexual Offenders in Custody and the Community.* HM Prison Service Document, 2003.

who clearly need it in the name of science), and that other quasi-experimental methods can be provide meaningful information (Hanson et al., 2002). Other aspects that must be considered aside from methodological ones include the type of outcome examined (for example, arrests, convictions, official sanctions, and so on) and what is an acceptable length of follow-up (Craig, Browne & Stringer, 2003b).

One means of evaluating effectiveness across various methodologies is the use of meta-analysis. Meta-analytic designs quantitatively combine the results from a number of studies to determine if there is an overall effect amongst the studies as a whole. Meta-analysis is useful because it allows for even small effect sizes to be detected given the large sample size that results from amalgamating a number of studies.

A number of authors have examined the effectiveness of treatment of sex offenders through comprehensive descriptive reviews and meta-analyses (for example, Craig, Browne & Stringer, 2003b; Furby, Weinrott & Blackshaw, 1989; Hall, 1995; Hanson et al., 2002). A review of 42 treatment outcome studies, completed for the most part prior to 1980, concluded that there was no evidence that clinical treatment of sexual offenders successfully reduces recidivism (Furby et al., 1989). Other researchers have reported their belief that the lack of methodologically sound studies does not permit conclusions to be drawn (for example, Quinsey et al., 1993; Rice & Harris, 2003). Meta-analyses of more contemporary treatment programmes than those examined by Furby and colleagues (1989) have yielded more encouraging results (Gallagher et al., 1999; Hall, 1995; Hanson et al., 2002). A review was conducted looking at those sexual offender interventions that were examined using only randomised control studies (Kenworthy et al., 2005). This resulted in only nine studies available to be examined and did not lead to any conclusive results. While the authors did suggest that cognitive-behavioural therapy appeared superior to standard care (Kenworthy et al., 2005), this was based on a study that has recently reported that there were not significant differences in recidivism rates between their groups after all (Marques et al., 2005). In the most recent meta-analysis to date, including a range of methodological designs, the sexual recidivism rate for the treated groups was lower than that of the comparison groups (12.3% versus 16.8% respectively; Hanson et al., 2002). However, even in this recent comprehensive study, only 43 usable studies were available to be included (Hanson et al., 2002). In the most recent meta-analysis to date (Lösel & Schmucker, 2005) found that treated offenders showed 37% less sexual recidivism that untreated controls. This meta-analysis found no differences in outcome between random assignment and other comparative approaches to assess treatment.

In terms of evaluating treatment programme effectiveness, the randomised experiment is considered the gold standard in programme evaluation, and is the design least likely to result in groups that differ in systematic ways. However, this does not always guarantee equivalent groups. Marques, Wiederanders, Day, Nelson and van Ommeren (2005) evaluated the effectiveness of a cognitive-behavioural treatment with sexual offenders in California. The study was a randomised clinical trial that compared the reoffence rates of offenders treated in an inpatient relapse prevention (RP) programme with the rates of offenders in two (untreated) prison control groups. No significant differences were found among the three groups in their rates of sexual or violent reoffending over an eight-year follow-up period. However, closer examination of the RP groups performance revealed that individuals who met the programmes' treatment goals had lower reoffence rates than those who did not. Marques et al.'s study suffered with attrition rates from the RP group which may have impacted on motivation of the group. The RP framework used was adapted from the treatment of addictive behaviours some twenty years ago and may not reflect current thinking on the treatment of sexual offenders.

CONCLUSIONS

Reviews and meta-analytical studies of treatment efficacy have provided conflicting viewpoints. Furby et al. (1989) and Quinsey et al. (1993) previously found no convincing evidence that treatment reduces recidivism, whereas Marshall and Barbaree (1988), Marshall, Eccles and Barbaree (1991), Hanson et al. (2002), and Lösel and Schmucker (2005) have demonstrated positive treatment results in reducing sexual offence recidivism. Methodological differences between treatment studies and recidivism make it difficult to determine how many and which sex offenders will reoffend. However, the meta-analysis by Hall (1995) reported a small but robust treatment effect. Not withstanding methodological criticism (Alexander, 1999), more recent meta-analytical reviews conclude that overall, sex offender treatment resulted in lowering sexual offending, and the typical cognitive-behavioural programme saves more than it costs (Aos, Phipps, Barnoski & Lieb, 2001; Gallagher, Wilson, Hirschfield, Coggeshall & MacKenzie. 1999; Hanson, et al., 2002; Lösel & Schmucker, 2005; Polizzi, MacKenzie & Hickman, 1999).

Although few treatment evaluation studies are not without methodological criticism (Aytes et al., 2001; Hagan & Gust-Brey, 1999; Nicholiachuk et al., 2000; Proulx et al., 1999; Weiss, 1999; Worling & Curwen, 1998/2000), there are a small, but increasing number of studies that demonstrate positive treatment results using sound methodological techniques (randomised samples, matched controls and improved measures (Looman et al., 2000; Marques et al., 1994; 1999; Robinson, 1995).

While sexual offender treatment programmes appear to reduce sexual recidivism, what is not clear is whether this is specific to particular types of sex offenders (adult or adolescent offenders, exhibitionists, child molesters, rapists), which may in turn be limited to specific modalities of treatment (cognitive-behavioural, multisystemic therapy, chemical castration and behavioural therapy). Indeed, a study of adult rapists found that rapists had attacked 7.5 victims, whereas the average number of attacks among child molesters was at least 10 times that number (Abel, Cummingham-Rather, Becker & McHigh, 1983; as cited in Norris, 1992, p. 29). Given the different typological characteristics between child molesters and rapists (Hanson, 2001) it cannot be assumed that treatment programmes are a panacea for all types of sexual offenders.

Treatment efficacy may be better served by exploring which dynamic factors affect recidivism in order to facilitate the forensic practitioner when assessing potential risk of re-offending if released back into the community (Hanson, 1998). Indeed, while there is a need to include dynamic risk factors, deviant sexual interests and appetites appear at the heart of sexual re-offending (see Chapter 6). Research on those dynamic factors associated with the environment, opportunity to offend and changes in criminogenic factors - attitudes, values and beliefs, moods and fantasies that influence offending behaviour, once integrated in treatment programmes, would contribute in reducing the recidivism risks (Mezzo & Gravier, 2001). The integration of environmental triggers on the assessment of risk and treatment need is discussed in Chapters 8 and 11.

One reason why some studies fail to find significant treatment results is that the base rates for sexual re-offending are relatively small. By virtue of the sample, programmes that target lower-risk offenders are likely to have difficulty in demonstrating statistically significant treatment effects in already low rates of recidivism. While the definitive answer to the question 'what works' has yet to be found, what is clearer is that treatment modalities that utilise cognitive-behavioural techniques are more likely to reduce sexual re-offending than any other approach. Treatment studies that continue to adopt well-matched and randomised controls will extend our knowledge beyond that of 'what works?' in reducing recidivism in sexual offenders.

PART IV

Structuring risk assessment

8

Aetiology and Risk

INTRODUCTION

Risk assessment has made great strides in the last few years. However, the lack of clear guidelines of how to integrate current ideas has meant that the very real commonalities between current theorising, clinical expertise and empirical knowledge is only now starting to be recognised (Beech & Ward, 2006). Therefore, the aim of this chapter is to integrate some of those concepts outlined in previous chapters to provide those working in the field with a useful conceptual framework to use in risk assessment and clinical formulation.

CURRENT CONCEPTS IN RISK ASSESSMENT

As noted in Chapter 5, clinicians typically use clinical judgement, actuarial prediction or some combination of these approaches to assess the future risk of a convicted sexual offender. Clinical judgement may, or may not, be rooted in theory depending upon the clinician's knowledge of the field; in the worst case scenario, they may even be based on idiosyncratic judgements by the clinician about which are the most important variables to consider in a report (Beech, Fisher & Thornton, 2003). In contrast the most commonly employed actuarial risk prediction instruments rely almost exclusively on historical or *static* risk factors that cannot change, such as previous convictions for sexual offences, identified lack of long-term intimate relationships and general criminality. These, and other, factors have been identified in various empirical studies reported by the risk assessment developers, that is, Hanson and Thornton (2000) who describe the development and validation of Static-99; Thornton et al. (2003) who describe the development and validation of Risk-Matrix 2000; Quinsey et al. (1998) who describe the Sex Offence Risk

Appraisal Guide (SORAG); Epperson, Kaul and Hesselton (1998) who describe the Minnesota Sex Offender Screening Tools- Revised (MnSOST-R), and the Sexual Violence Risk Scale (SVR-20; Boer et al., 1997) to name but a few of the better known instruments.

However, as noted in Chapter 6, in an attempt to overcome the limitations of purely static actuarial instruments, and to take into account the fact that risk may be reduced by treatment, some researchers have developed classification schemes that additionally incorporate *dynamic* factors, that is, clinical/psychological risk factors that are amenable to change. Probably the most up-to-date thinking in this area, by Thornton (2002) suggests that broadly four *domains* of psychological problems can be identified as being related to the future commission of sexual offences. These are:

(1) *sexual interests* that are broadly deviant, such as arousal to children or to sexualised violence;
(2) *distorted attitudes* that are supportive of sexual assault, such as child abuse supportive beliefs or adversarial sexual attitudes;
(3) a level of *socio-affective functioning* that leads to lack of emotionally intimate relationships with adults and excessive emotional over-identification with children;
(4) *self-management* problems, leading to lifestyle impulsiveness and/or dysfunctional coping as discussed in Chapter 6.

There are several systems around to assess level of stable dynamic risk, probably the best known of these are STABLE (2000, Hanson & Harris, 2000a), the Structured Assessment of Risk and Need (Thornton, 2002; Webster et al., 2006), and the Beech deviancy assessment (Beech, 1998; Mandeville-Norden, Beech & Middleton, 2006). All of these are reviewed in Chapter 6.

Hanson & Harris (2000b) have reported a further innovation in risk prediction with sexual offenders. Here they suggest that any dynamic assessment should consider both stable and acute dynamic factors: *stable* dynamic risk factors are those that tend to be stable over time but are amenable to change, as outlined above; while *acute* dynamic risk factors are those factors which change and fluctuate and appear around the time that an offence takes place. In terms of identifying acute risk factors, Hanson and Harris identified the types of behaviour that indicated increased risk in a group of sex offenders under supervision. Here they interviewed the supervising officers of sex offenders who were under supervision when they committed further sexual offences to find out if there were any overt behaviours that had been noted by the supervisors. The best acute predictors were found to be victim access behaviours, non-cooperation with supervision and anger. Victim access behaviours are any behaviours that gave the offender access to a potential victim. Rejection of supervision included any behaviour that indicated that the offender was attempting to alter the way he related to the supervisor and ranged from being excessively friendly through to hostile and angry, lying, missing appointments and finding reasons not to need further supervision. Shifts in mood, especially becoming hostile and angry were seen as particularly indicative of offending. Hanson and Harris suggest that these behaviours act as warning signs for increased risk and should be monitored by supervisors. Hanson and Harris have developed a comprehensive system for the assessment of acute dynamic risk factors which is known as ACUTE (Hanson & Harris, 2000b) and contains the following seven acute risk factors: victim access; emotional collapse, that is, evidence of severe emotional disturbance/emotional crisis; collapse of social supports; hostility; substance abuse; sexual preoccupations; and rejection of supervision.[1]

RISK ASSESSMENT: WHERE TO NOW?

However, even though the areas of risk assessment can be said to have made great strides in the last few years, in terms of identifying static, stable dynamic and acute dynamic risk factors and that systems have been developed to measure these areas, a lot of this work is essentially atheoretical. That it to say that risk assessment instruments have been developed through the application of statistical analysis of large data sets in order to identify items related to future risk, and the application of meta-analysis to various studies in order to test on an item-by-item basis which factors, static and dynamic, are the best predictors of future risk (for example, Hanson & Bussière, 1998; Hanson & Morton-Bourgon, 2005). Of course this work has been incredibly important to the field, but without a clear conceptual framework, and by taking items in isolation there is very real danger of giving the message to treatment providers that it is only really worth focusing on the items that have shown the clearest relationship to reconviction, that is, deviant sexual interest and general impulsivity/self-management problems. Other areas typically targeted in therapy, but without convincing evidence that they are directly related to recidivism (such as increasing levels of self-esteem, reducing denial and inculcating victim empathy in an offender for example), are no longer regarded as promising treatment targets (Hanson, 2006). Similarly, an argument made in some quarters is that abuse history, which does not appear to have a strong relationship with future risk, should not be something that is dealt with during treatment. We would argue that a theory where only items strongly identified with recidivism is a logical fallacy in that it is not possible to take items that are regarded as putatively associated with risk in isolation. This approach leads to a therapeutic reductionism and does not

---

[1] The final factor in this system is what Hanson and Harris term a 'unique factor' in that some offenders have unique characteristics that represent a real risk factor for that offender.

allow for new approaches to treatment, such as the Good Lives approach (Ward & Brown, 2004).

Risk, we would argue, as those in this field know, is a complex interaction between psychological problems (stable dynamic risk factors) and an individual's history (static risk factors, developmental problems) and current life circumstances (acute/contextual risk factors). Therefore, although self-esteem, for example, may not have a testable relationship with subsequent offending, if an individual's self-esteem is at rock bottom how is that person able to take onboard the messages imparted in therapy and action those in his life? Therefore by not focusing on this area, it is much more likely that treatment will have little, or no, effect. Similarly, a history of sexual abuse, although not having an easily demonstrable association with future offending, can clearly have identifiable negative effect when an individual is in treatment. As such, a history of being sexually abused may lead to treatment dropout, because the issues raised in treatment may remind an individual of his own abuse history. As we know, treatment dropout has been shown to be related to an increased risk of sexual recidivism (Seager, Jellicoe & Dhaliwal, 2004), therefore by not dealing with such a problem there can be increased risk of recidivism.

We think it is now time to take a wider view of risk assessment and begin to stitch together the disparate pieces of the jigsaw. We are not claiming to have the complete answer, but want to give food for thought on how risk fits together within an aetiogical/developmental framework informed by current theories of sexual offending. However, it is fair to say that few have currently provided guidance on how to put these risk factors together. Hanson (2006) has provided one such model that makes some attempt to look at the relationship between stable and acute dynamic risk factors, while Beech and Ward (Beech & Ward, 2004; Ward & Beech, 2004) have probably provided the most comprehensive model, drawing upon theoretical work within the field. Hence, the last part of this chapter will outline the Beech and Ward risk-aetiology framework. However, as this framework is heavily informed by current theorising about sexual offending, the next section briefly outlines some recent theories of sexual offending. It is important to consider these theories as it has been argued that this allows for risk to be embedded in a firmer framework.

THEORIES OF SEXUAL OFFENDING

Ward and Beech (2006) note the importance of theory, in part, is its ability to extend the scope of existing perspectives and to integrate competing or diverse approaches to the study of the relevant phenomena. Ward and Hudson (1998a) have distinguished three levels of theory in sexual offending. *Level I* theories represent comprehensive theories of sexual offending. The aim of these theories is to take account of the core features of sexual offending and to provide a complete account of what causes these phenomena and how they manifest in sexually abusive actions.

Level II theories set out to provide detailed descriptions of the single factors thought to be particularly important in the generation of sexual crimes, and can be said to be theories of psychological mechanisms, that is, the stable dynamic risk domains. *Level III* theories are seen as explaining the *process* of sexual offending. The levels of theory model is meant to help researchers distinguish between different types of theory and ultimately to facilitate their integration through a process of 'theory knitting'. A theory knitting strategy suggests that researchers should seek to integrate the best existing ideas in an area within a new framework (Ward & Hudson, 1998a). This approach has been attempted by Ward and Siegert (2002) within the sexual offending field where the best aspects of current Level 1 theories have been integrated into a comprehensive etiological account of child molestation. While, although beyond the scope of this chapter, Ward and Beech (2006) have taken this approach a stage further through an integration of Level II and Level III theories with ideas from genetics, evolutionary psychology and ecology to clinical observation. However, for the purpose of this chapter we will now consider how Level I theorising can inform and help in the ability to integrate disparate risk factors.

There have been four main multi-factorial theories of sexual offending, Finkelhor's Precondition Theory (1984), Marshall and Barbaree's Integrated Theory (1990), Hall and Hirschman's (1992) Quadripartite Model of child molestation, and Ward and Siegert's 'Pathways model of sexual offending' (2002), we will now consider each of these in turn.

Finkelhor (1984) suggests that four underlying factors have typically been used to explain the occurrence of child sexual abuse. These theories are built around the following claims: sex with children is emotionally satisfying to the offender (emotional congruence); men who offend are sexually aroused by a child (sexual arousal); men have sex with children because they are unable to meet their sexual needs in socially appropriate ways (blockage); and finally, these men become disinhibited and behave in ways contrary to their normal behaviour. He suggests that the first three factors explain why some individuals develop sexual interest in children and the fourth why this interest manifests as sexual deviance (Ward & Beech, 2004).

Marshall and Barbaree's Integrated Theory (1990) proposes that the sexual abuse of children occurs as a consequence of a number of interacting distal and proximal factors. Specifically, this theory suggests that individuals experiencing developmentally adverse events (for example, poor parenting, inconsistent and harsh discipline, physical and sexual abuse) are likely to exhibit distorted internal working models of relationships, particularly with respect to sex and aggression, resulting in poor social and self-regulation skills from an early age. For these individuals, the transition into adolescence is a particularly critical period. It is at this stage that individuals are most receptive to acquiring enduring sexual scripts, preferences, interests and attitudes. Further, the massive increase of sex hormones during this period increases the salience and potency of these sexual cues. According to Marshall and Barbaree, sex and aggression originate from the same neural substrates (for example, hypothalamus, amygdala, septum, and so on.) and are thought to cause qualitatively similar experiences. If an individual comes from an adverse background and, therefore, is already predisposed to behaving in an antisocial manner, the pubertal release of hormones may serve to fuse sex and aggression and to consolidate or enhance already acquired sexually abusive tendencies. As a young adult, the lack of effective social and self-regulation skills makes it more probable that relationships, or attempted relationships, with women will be met by rejection and result in lowered self-esteem, anger and negative attitudes toward females. These powerful negative emotions may fuel the intensity of sexual desires and the development of deviant sexual fantasies. Masturbation to these fantasies will increase their strength and also function as mental rehearsals in which future sexual offences are planned. According to the integrated theory, the above vulnerability factors interact with more transient situational elements such as stress, intoxication, strong negative affect, sexual stimuli, and the presence of a potential victim to impair an individual's ability to control their behaviours, resulting in a sexual offence. The reinforcing effects of deviant sexual activity and the development of cognitive distortions maintain offending. This reinforcement may be positive (for example, sexual arousal, sense of power) or negative (for example, reduction of low mood).

Hall and Hirschman's (1992) Quadripartite Model of child molestation is based on four components: physiological sexual arousal, inaccurate cognitions that justify sexual aggression, affective dyscontrol and personality problems. The first three factors, according to Hall and Hirschman, are considered primarily state and situation dependent (state factors) while personality problems represent enduring vulnerability factors (trait factors). This implies that personality deficits are the source of vulnerabilities to sexually abuse children, which are activated in certain contexts and opportunities, resulting in deviant arousal, affective disturbance and/or distorted thinking. A key idea in the Hall and Hirschman model is that while each of the above factors serve as motivational precursors that increase the probability of offending, usually one factor is prominent for each child molester and constitutes their primary motive. The activation of this primary motivational precursor functions to increase the intensity of the others. This synergistic interaction may in turn propel an individual above the critical threshold for performing a sexually deviant act. Furthermore, various combinations of the above factors are hypothesised to characterise a particular type of sex offender.

Ward and Siegert (2002) have taken a theory knitting approach to these theories in order to develop a more comprehensive pathway theory of child sexual offending that incorporates the strongest elements of each of Finkelhor, Marshall and Barbaree, and Hall and Hirschman. In line with these theories, the Pathways explanation suggests that the clinical phenomena evident among child molesters are generated by four distinct and interacting psychological mechanisms: intimacy and social skill deficits; distorted sexual scripts; emotional dysregulation; and cognitive distortions. Each mechanism depicts a specific offence pathway with different psychological and behavioural profiles, and separate aetiologies and underlying deficits. The number and type of aetiologies will vary depending on a pathway's particular developmental trajectory.

Although each pathway is hypothesised to be associated with a unique set of primary mechanisms and cluster of symptoms or problems, the mechanisms always interact to cause a sexual crime. That is, *every* sexual offence involves emotional, intimacy, cognitive and arousal components, however, each distinct pathway will have at its centre a set of primary dysfunctional mechanisms that impact on the others. The primary causal mechanisms involve other types of mechanisms in order to generate the range of symptoms typically seen in child molesters. But, these additional causal mechanisms may be functioning normally and only exert a dysfunctional effect because of the driving force of the primary set of mechanisms. This is similar to Hall and Hirschman's thesis that one of four factors may be a primary motivational precursor that activates the other elements. However, these authors also suggest that each factor can operate on its own to cause sexual deviance. The Pathways Model, in contrast, argues that *every* sexual offence involves all four sets of mechanisms.

Specifically, the first etiological pathway, *intimacy deficits*, contains individuals who are hypothesised to possess normal sexual scripts and only offend at specific times, for example, if a preferred partner is unavailable or during periods of rejection or sustained emotional loneliness.

The second etiological pathway, *deviant sexual scripts*, contains individuals whose core causal mechanism involves subtle distortions in their sexual scripts, which interact with dysfunctional relationship schemas (where relationships are represented in purely sexual terms).

The third etiological pathway, *emotional dysregulation*, contains individuals who are hypothesised to possess normal sexual scripts but have dysfunctional mechanisms associated with their emotional regulation system (Thompson, 1994).

The fourth etiological pathway, *antisocial cognitions*, contains individuals who have no distortions in their sexual scripts but possess general pro-criminal attitudes and beliefs, and who's offending reflects this general antisocial tendency.

There is also a fifth etiological pathway in this model, *multiple dysfunctional mechanisms*, which describe individuals who have developed deviant sexual scripts, which will activate deviant fantasies and usually reflect a history of sexual abuse or exposure to sexual material or activity at a young age. Coinciding with this will be pronounced flaws in all the other primary psychological mechanisms. They will therefore have dysfunctional implicit theories about children's sexuality and their ability to make informed decisions about sex, inappropriate emotional regulation, intimacy deficits and impaired relationship and attachment mechanisms (Ward, Hudson, Johnson & Marshall, 1997; Ward, Hudson & Keenan, 1998). Thus this group is likely to exhibit a multitude of offence related deficits and constitute 'pure' paedophiles. The predisposition to sexually abuse children is hypothesised to only translate into offending behaviour under certain circumstances, including the presence of a victim (that is, opportunity to offend) and the absence of any conflicting goals. The ultimate aim of deviant behaviour is to achieve pleasure or other primary or secondary goals (for example, a sense of control). Finally, self-esteem will often be high because of this group's entrenched preferences for children as sexual partners and their accompanying beliefs that these interests are legitimate and healthy.

We will now outline Beech and Ward's model of the risk assessment using both the empirical and theoretical ideas outlined above.

AN AETIOLOGICAL MODEL OF RISK

This model draws upon some of the theoretical ideas outlined in the field, by doing this we can hopefully demonstrate the fact that a lot of what has been talked about theoretically, observed clinically, and measured clinically can be potentially pulled together. In the model outlined we have reconfigured some of the concepts outlined in the risk assessment section above, taken some ideas from mainstream psychology and drawn upon theoretical ideas within the field. These ideas were first formulated in an article in Aggression and Violent Behaviour by Beech and Ward (2004), with a shorter version appearing in the ATSA journal shortly after (Ward & Beech, 2004). There have been a few modifications to the original model, as we have now been in a position to get feedback from clinicians on this framework, which we have considered here. However, the model is essentially the same as that originally proposed, and contains the following elements that we think may help us to move towards a more coherent risk assessment framework. Hence, in the model the following has been attempted:

- An integration of developmental factors by consideration of Marshall and Barbaree's theoretical idea that developmental adversity can result in increased vulnerability to sexually abuse a child.
- Show that *stable dynamic* risk factors such as, deviant sexual arousal to children, denotes a psychological vulnerability. While static risk factors, such as previous convictions for the sexual abuse of a child, really act as historical *markers* for stable dynamic risk factors (Mrazek & Haggerty, 1994). Hence both static and dynamic risk factors pick-up on an overall vulnerability factor, one in the here and now, the other at some point in the past.
- Indicate that the distinction between *stable* dynamic and *acute* dynamic risk factors might be better reframed in terms of the more psychologically rigorous

definitions of *trait* risk factors (that is, enduring personality problems) and transient *state* risk factors, that is, the temporary, usually extreme expression of the more enduring stable dynamic risk factors.

- Suggest that acute risk factors, as identified by Hanson and Harris (2000b) such as emotional collapse, collapse of social supports, hostility and substance abuse would be better conceptualised as triggering risk factors.
- And finally argue that states of high risk are due to psychological traits/stable dynamic risk factors being pushed into states of high-risk by an interaction with these triggering risk factors.

The model itself, as shown in Figure 8.1, contains a chain of events from a distal *developmental factors* section, through a vulnerability factors section (as measured

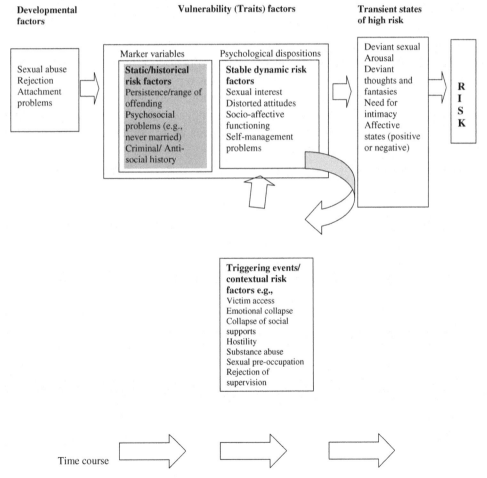

Figure 8.1 An aetiological model of risk

by historical markers of risk and stable dynamic/psychological measures of risk at the time assessment took place), a *triggering factors or contextual events* section, and finally an acute risk factors section at some immediate point in history where an offence is likely to take place.

We will now look at each of the areas shown in the model.

DEVELOPMENTAL FACTORS

The measurement of developmental problems in current risk assessments is rather vague and underspecified, even though theoretically and empirically, a number of variables have been predicted or identified as being clear precursors to sexual abuse, such as the offender has been sexually abused, parental rejection and a history of attachment problems. These developmental variables are technically historical variables, yet the literature on static risk prediction has hardly examined these factors.[2] Craissati (Craissati & Beech, 2005) is one of the few researchers to have considered in detail the relationship between developmental variables and risk assessment. She notes that such variables are implicated in both treatment dropout and compliance in treatment. Specifically, she has reported that: having two or more childhood adaptive difficulties (plus never having been a long-term relationship) correctly identified 87% of poor treatment attendees; while childhood difficulties (coupled with contact with mental health services as an adult) correctly classified 83% of non-compliers in treatment.

DEVELOPMENTAL FACTORS AND THEIR AETIOLOGICAL RELATIONSHIP TO PSYCHOLOGICAL RISK FACTORS

The mechanisms by which developmental variables are related to subsequent risk are far from straightforward, but Watkins and Bentovim (1992) and Beitchman et al. (1992) report that the long-term effects of sexual abuse can clearly be seen as problems in psychological functioning/psychological disorder such as alcohol and drug misuse, disturbed adult sexual functioning, poor social adjustment, and confusion over sexual identity. Craissati, McClurg and Browne (2002), among others, report that parental rejection was found to be highly prevalent amongst the parents of sexual offenders. This experience of childhood rejection is likely to result in problems in regulating affect in intimate relationships. As for childhood attachment problems, Smallbone and Dadds (1998) found that poor paternal attachments predicted sexual coercion in adulthood and that poor relationship

---

[2]Although we would note that a poor relationship with mother, perhaps indicating parental rejection, has been identified as a risk factor for sexual offenders by Hanson and Bussière (1998).

with mother was predictive of general antisocial behaviour. In terms of the link with subsequent vulnerability factors, such as attachment difficulties it could be argued can lead to offenders having difficulties in forming relationships with age appropriate adults. Marshall, Hudson and Hodkinson (1993), for example, noted that attachment difficulties lead adults to seek emotional intimacy through sex, even if they have to force a partner to participate. Therefore, rejection, sexual abuse and attachment problems leading to substance misuse, disturbed sexual functioning, poor social adjustment, confusion over sexual identity, inappropriate attempts to reassert masculinity and recapitulation of the abuse experience, can be seen as being precursors of psychological vulnerabilities to sexually offend. The possible sequelae to such adverse childhood events are dynamic risk problems, that is, intimacy deficits (due to poor attachment), cognitive distortions, self-management problems and deviant arousal. We will now examine these vulnerability factors in more detail.

VULNERABILITY FACTORS

In the second section of our model shown in Figure 1 we note the usefulness of Mrazek and Haggerty's (1994) distinction between those factors that play a *causal* role in offending, and those that act as marker variables of risk. This idea clearly maps onto the static/dynamic risk distinction. Clearly, stable dynamic factors (such as deviant interests and self-management problems) play a causal role in offending, while the so called *static/historical* risk factors identified in risk assessment schedules, such as Static-99 (Hanson & Thornton, 2000) are essentially 'markers' of psychological vulnerability. We will now look at the two aspects of the vulnerability factors section of the model in more detail.

Measurement of vulnerability factors in the here and now – stable dynamic risk factors

Stable dynamic risk factors have been defined by Thornton (2002) as: *sexual interests* (sexual preoccupation, offence related sexual preferences), *distorted attitudes* (generalised belief schemas rather than specific cognitions), level of *socio-affective functioning* (problems here leading to lack of emotionally intimate relationships with adults and an accompanying emotional over- identification with children in child molesters), and *self-management problems* (lifestyle impulsiveness; dysfunctional coping). Here, we would argue that these are in fact psychological traits. Trait theory gives a more theoretical grounding to dynamic risk assessment. Some points useful to consider here are that: traits can only be inferred from behaviour or overt responses which are indicative of deeper causal properties of a person's functioning (Cattell & Kline, 1977) and trait theory suggests that by identifying the level of a particular genetic, physiological, or cognitive trait in an individual, this is likely to help predict a person's future behaviour (Matthews & Deary, 1998). Thus, by conceptualising stable dynamic risk factors as traits, then the temporary state versions of these traits, that is, deviant sexual arousal, deviant thoughts and fantasies, need *for intimacy and control*, and *impulsive_behaviour* emotional regulation problems can be considered as the real acute dynamic risk factors or state aspects of stable dynamic risk factors.

Beech and Ward (2006) also propose that theory has a lot to offer in terms of explaining the etiological underpinning of each of the four risk domains. Space precludes any detailed description of these ideas, however, Table 8.1 shows how theory can be employed to begin to derive and etiological explanation of each of the four risk domains. Here, we have drawn extensively upon Ward and Siegert's (2002) theory knitting approach, which has taken the best of theories, such as those of Marshall and Barbaree (1990), Finkelhor (1984) and Hall and Hirschman (1992).

Table 8.1 Etiological explanation of psychological vulnerability from Ward and Siegert's (2002) Theory of Child Sexual Abuse

Risk Domain	Etiological Explanation
Domain 1: Sexual interests: Child preference	Problems arise from problems in the three other domains below, which, in conjunction with sexual desire (a basic physiological drive), leads to the individual to abuse
Domain 2: Distorted attitudes: Child abuse supportive beliefs	Problems arise out of a set of core schema or implicit theories held by the offender and generate the cognitive distortions that are measured at the surface level. These beliefs will centre on entitlement to sex, whenever, and with whom ever, they want. These beliefs, in conjunction with sexual desire and opportunity, will result in sexual offending
Domain 3: Socio-affective functioning: Emotional congruence with children Lack of emotionally intimate relationships with adults	Problems arise from insecure attachment and subsequent problems establishing intimacy with adults, leading to the children for adult sexual partners. This will result in sexual arousal in the context of a sexual encounter with a child, possibly intimate and 'loving' emotions, and an attempt to create an adult-like relationship with the child.
Domain 4: Self-management Lifestyle impulsiveness Dysfunctional coping	Problems arise from an inability in identifying emotions, modulating negative emotions, or an inability to utilise social supports at times of emotional distress. This inability to effectively manage mood states may result in a loss of control, which, in conjunction with sexual desire, might lead an individual to either become disinhibited or else opportunistically use sex with a child as a soothing strategy to meet his emotional and sexual needs

Measurement of vulnerability factors in the past – static/historical risk factors

In the model we have tried to make more explicit the relationship between static risk and dynamic risk factors under the heading of psychological vulnerabilities. The argument can be most clearly made by mapping static risk factors, described in some of the better known risk schedules, onto the four risk domains described above. This mapping is shown in Table 8.2.

Table 8.2 Static/historical risk markers contained in Static-99, SORAG, MnSOST-R, SVR-20 of developmental problems and dynamic risk domains

	Static-99 markers	SORAG markers	MnSOST-R markers	SVR-20 markers
Developmental variables		Not lived with parents until 16		Victim of child abuse
Domain 1: Sexual Interest	Non contact sexual offences Unrelated victims Stranger victims Male victims Prior sex offences	Male or male + female victims Previous sexual convictions	Multiple acts on single victim Stranger victims Young age of victims Length of sex Offending history Number of Sexual convictions Different age groups of victims	High frequency of sex offences Range of sex offences Escalation in frequency and severity of sex offences
Domain 2: Distorted attitudes				
Doman 3: Socio-affective-functioning	Lack of long-term intimate relationship	Never married		Relationship problems
Domain 4: Self-management	Index non Sexual violence Prior non-sexual violence Prior Sentencing occasions	Violent Criminality Non-violent criminaltiy Failure on Conditional release	Anti-social behaviour as adolescent Discipline history while incarcerated Offender under supervision when offence committed Threat/use of force in offence	Violent non Sexual offences General criminality

Table 8.2 clearly indicates that Static-99, SORAG, Mn-SOST-R and the SVR-20 contain items that are historical risk markers of *sexual interests* and *self-manage-ment* problems indicating that they are proxy measures of the level of these problems in an offender's history. However, Table 8.2 also clearly indicates that these schedules contain no historical items measuring distorted attitudes (although the SVR-20; Boer et al., 1997) does contain a clinical item that indicates that it is important to measure current level of pro-offending attitudes) and few items that tap past level of socio-affective functioning. This is not surprising, as there would not appear to be many historical items that could actually do this. We would note that doing this illustrates how *static* and *dynamic* factors are to some extent two aspects of what we would term psychological vulnerability, with static risk factors identifying strong evidence of [deviant] *sexual interests* and *self-management* problems in an individual's past, and the assessment of the four dynamic risk factors indicating an individual's current levels of problems.

In the next section of the model we will outline how *stable dynamic factors* become transient states of high risk that act as acute precursors to offending.

TRANSIENT STATES OF HIGH RISK

In our model we suggest that underlying traits can be activated to produce transient mental states (Eysenck & Eysenck, 1980) by triggering factors (which we outline in the next section of the model). Table 8.3 illustrates how, if we take each psychological disposition or stable dynamic risk domain, each trait is pushed into a state that acts as a precursor to sexual offending.

It can be seen from Table 8.3, that in the model presented here, deviant sexual arousal, deviant thoughts and fantasies, the need for intimacy/control, and negative or positive emotional states can arise from the core underlying risk domains. In the last section of the model we will consider the triggering or contextual events that produce the transient acute states of risk outlined here.

TRIGGERING FACTORS

Hanson and Harris (2001) identified seven types of *acute risk* factor that indicated increased risk in a group of sexual offenders under supervision. These factors, identified clinically, can be grouped under the following categories: *cognitive* (sexual pre-occupations), *affective* (hostility, emotional collapse), *behavioural* (victim access behaviours, rejection of supervision, substance abuse), *environmental* (collapse of social supports) triggering factors. Hanson and Harris also note that there may well be unique factors to the individual which again can be *environmental* (for example, being made homeless, a specific date or event that causes an emotional response, contact with a specific family member); *cognitive* (being

Table 8.3 Mappings of vulnerability (trait) factors to contextual (state) factors through the operation of triggering factors

Psychological risk domains	Triggering factors operate on the particular disposition in the following way	State risk factors – Acute Dynamic
Domain 1: Sexual interests	Promotes sexual arousal in the probable presence of: distorted sexual attitudes; inter-personal problems; and positive or negative moods states	Deviant sexual arousal
Domain 2: Distorted attitudes (or underlying schemas)	Deviant thoughts/fantasies produced from the core set of schema held by the offender in interaction with specific triggers	Deviant thoughts and fantasies
Domain 3: Socio-affective problems (e.g., for many the paedophilic abusers this would be the lack of emotionally intimate relationships with adults coupled emotional congruence with children)	Inter-personal problems particular to the offender (in many cases underpinned by problematic attachment) activated in times of stress	Need for intimacy/ control
Domain 4: Self-management: Lifestyle impulsiveness; and/or dysfunctional coping	Triggering events produce states of tension	Experiences of negative emotional state if cognitive appraisal is negative or positive feelings if outcome is desired

bothered by intrusive thoughts regarding their own victimisation); or *health problems* which again can be regarded as triggering events.

We suggest in our model that these items would be better conceptualised as triggering thoughts, feelings, behaviours or events that interact with stable dynamic risk factors to generate *states* likely to produce sexual offending behaviours. A revision to our original model is to indicate in Figure 8.1 that there is a clear interaction between these triggering events and the stable dynamic risk factors outlined earlier, with a feedback loop between the psychological vulnerabilities and the triggering risk factors, in that we all to a greater or lesser extent construct our own environments. We will now consider the clinical implications of this model.

CONCLUSIONS

This risk-aetiological model, we think, represents the first explicit attempt to integrate etiological theory with the different types of risk factors. One of our purposes for this was to be useful to clinicians in the field. Here we hope that this work may provide an explanation of why certain types of factors increase an individual's risk of committing a sexual offence in the future. For example, an offender who was sexually abused as a child might have learned to cope with stressful interpersonal events through masturbating, a means of soothing himself. The reliance on sex as a means to control negative mood states constitutes a deficit in emotional and self-regulation and is hypothesised to constitute a vulnerability factor. Following an argument with someone at work the offender might resort to deviant sexual fantasies and masturbation to reduce his feelings of anger and to induce feelings of pleasure. Unfortunately, the resultant high levels of sexual arousal in certain circumstances might increase his changes of sexual offending, particularly if his masturbatory fantasies contain aggressive themes.

We would argue that an advantage in thinking about risk variables in etiological terms is that it encourages clinicians to consider a wider range of marker (risk) variables corresponding to the different types of vulnerability factors when assessing offenders. This enables them to develop case formulations more clearly linked to the different risk domains. In a sense, it could improve the quality of risk assessment and also help to tailor risk assessment procedures to the unique set of causes relevant to individual offenders.

This approach also suggests, perhaps, a novel approach to risk assessment, in that rather than taking a clinically adjusted actuarial approach, it might be worth considering if it is better to start with a dynamic risk assessment and then adjust the level of risk based on the levels of historic risk based on actuarial risk instruments.

Of course it would be wrong not to also assess the framework's weaknesses as they currently stand. Perhaps the most significant of these is that the model has not as yet been subject to empirical testing. Obviously this has to be the next stage of development where it can also be tested against other ideas that this framework may generate.

PART V

Policy and practice

9

Implementing Risk Management Policy

INTRODUCTION

The media attention on national and international cases of the child sexual abuse (CSA) and the implementation of the new Sex Offences Act, 2003 has placed the issue of policing sex offenders into the spotlight of public and political debate. Crucial decisions about the release of violent and/or sex offenders into the community from prison and special hospitals have significant consequences for the police and probation services as these services are responsible for maintaining a local register of cautioned and convicted sex offenders. Resources for the assessment (see Chapter 5 and 6), management, supervision and treatment (see Chapter 7) of these offenders have to be found. In addition, police and probation officers require the time to attend multi-agency meetings to discuss and implement appropriate housing and placement of offenders or to discuss the necessary social and health service interventions that may be required (Gregory & Lees, 1999). New risk management measures, included in the Criminal Justice and Court Services Act 2000, have been introduced to tackle these issues and prioritise the monitoring of dangerous individuals in the community. Although it is unlikely that the risk of re-offending will completely disappear (Fisher & Thornton, 1993), recently introduced legislation and guidelines will go some way to reducing it. A summary of legal provisions since 1991 to combat sex offenders and manage the risk of sexual offending is presented in Table 9.1.

Table 9.1 Legal provisions to combat sex offenders and manage the risk of sexual offending

- **The Criminal Justice Act 1991:** The legislation began to treat sexual offenders differently to other offenders, in relation to *supervision* and Probation Order extensions.
- **The Sex Offenders Act 1997:** This required convicted sex offenders to register their name and address with the Police every 5 years and notify them of any changes of address within 14 days. This helped monitor the movements of those convicted of sexual crimes and established a *sex offender register*. Failure to register is a criminal offence that can result in being sent to prison for up to 5 years.
- **The Police Act 1997:** This legislation extended *access to criminal records* to relevant agencies (e,g., social services) and the release of relevant information on individuals who have, or will have, unsupervised access to children.
- **Crime and Punishment Act 1997:** New powers were introduced for police to take *DNA samples* from offenders convicted of sexual and violent offences.
- **The Crime and Disorder Act 1998:** This legislation introduced *sex offender orders*, whereby the police can apply for an order against any sex offender whose present behaviour in the community gives cause for concern. Amendments were also made to supervision on licence, recall and return to prison (initially introduced in the Criminal Justice Act 1991). This act aimed to increase public protection in combination with *anti-social behaviour orders* that work to prevent physical and sexual harassment.
- **The Crime Sentences Act 1998**: This enabled courts to impose extended period of supervision or *discretionary life sentences* to those individuals who committed a second serious violent or sexual offence.
- **Criminal Justice and Court Services Act 2000:** This legal provision introduced *Multi Agency Public Protection Arrangements (MAPPAs)* for dangerous individuals who commit violent and sexual antisocial acts. Police and probation services (the 'responsible authority') have a duty to cooperate with other agencies to assess and manage the risk posed by dangerous individuals in the community or those released from prison into the community. *Multi Agency Public Protection Panels (MAPPPs)* bring together representatives from education, health service, housing, police, probation and prison services, social services, employment agencies, youth offending teams and other agencies involved in managing offenders in the community. The sex offender's response to 'treatment programmes' in prison and appropriate accommodation and interventions on release into the community are major concerns:
  - *Community and prison treatment programmes for sex offenders*: These group programmes are now well established in the UK. They use cognitive behavioural principles to combat those factors thought to cause and maintain sexual offences against children.
  - *Code of Guidance on Homelessness*: Recently discharged prisoners are eligible for help with accommodation under the guidance of the Local Authorities. Special care and consideration is given to *housing sex offenders*.
  - *Exclusion orders* can be used by the courts as part of the community sentence to prohibit an offender from entering a specified place or area. Like Curfew orders, these can be enforced through electronic monitoring with 'tagging'.

Table 9.1 (*Continued*)

- **The Protection of Children Act 1999:** This introduced a *'disqualification order' to ban sex offenders (and other schedule 1 offenders) from working with children.* This was introduced by the Home Office and the Scottish Office following the Sex Offenders Act 1997, to make it an offence for those convicted of a violent or sexual crime on children to apply for or accept work which would give them access to children. A Criminal Records Bureau was established to ensure all those who work with children have had a *criminal records check*. This followed the recommendations of the Dunblane Inquiry Report by Lord Cullen (1996) for an accredited national body to check the suitability of group leaders and group workers who have unsupervised access to children, especially in relation school clubs, scouts groups and other activities attended by children. Hence, similar legislation was introduced in the *Protection of Children (Scotland) Act 2003*.
- **The Criminal Justice and Police Act 2001:** Enabled the police to *remove computer equipment* from the premises of suspected internet and sex offenders to help in their investigations into the possession of child pornography.
- **The Sex Offences Act 2003:** The law was introduced in May 2004, replacing the old Sexual Offences Act 1956. It proposed harsher sentences for repeat sex offenders and mandatory life sentences are recommended for serious sexual assaults such as rape, even for first time offenders. Rape has been redefined to include penetration of the mouth or anus and a new offence of sexual assault by penetration covers acts involving the insertion of objects or body parts other than the penis. This includes *'marital rape'* between co-habiting or separated intimate partners. Any sexual intercourse with a child aged 12 or younger will now be treated as rape. The offence of *'adult sexual activities with a child'* covers any sexual act that takes place between an adult and a child under the age of 16 regardless of whether it appears to be consensual or not. This would also cover non-contact sexual activities such as inducing children to remove their clothes for adult sexual pleasure, filming or photography. Sexual activities with victims who were abducted subjected to threats or fear of serious harm will be classed as non-consensual. Similarly, victims who are unable to consent due to a learning disability, mental disorder, drugged or rendered unconscious will also be classified as non-consensual sex. The crime of incest has been replaced with the offence *'familial sexual abuse'* to cover sexual offences by co-habitees not related to the child, foster and adoptive parents. An offence of *'abuse of a position of trust'* prohibits contact between adults and children under 18 in schools, colleges and residential care. With regard to the internet, a new offence of *'sexual grooming'* identifies the crime of befriending a child personally or on the internet with the intention of sexual activity. Under the new act, convicted sex offenders now have to register with the police every year instead of every 5 years and the police are able to photograph offenders every time they register. Those individuals on the sex offender register must now report to the police any change of address within 3 days and inform them of any absence from home for more than 6 days. Those people who have only been convicted of sex crimes abroad would also have to comply with the sex offender register. This act also introduced the **sexual offences prevention order (SOPO)** which replaced and combined the earlier sex offender order and restraining order. The SOPO can be applied for by the police on anyone who has a history of sexual convictions and who are demonstrating 'trigger' behaviours as outlined in the sex offender order. The SOPO contains prohibitions on a person's activities in order to protect the public, or identified members of the public, from serious sexual harm. The SOPO also requires registration of the offender if they are not already registered. Failure to comply with the SOPO is a criminal offence.

(*continued*)

Table 9.1 (*Continued*)

- **The Criminal Justice (Scotland) Act 2003**: This gives victims or an eligible family member the right to receive information about the release from prison of an offender, who committed the crime against them, and to receive information from and make representations to the Parole Board for Scotland. Following a pilot study report in 2001 on *victim notification*, victims can ask to be notified when the perpetrator of the violent or sexual act against them is due to be released at the end of their custodial sentence of 4 years or more.
- **The Children Act 2004**: This follows the recommendations of the Victoria Climbie report and builds on the Children Act 1989 and the reform programme entitled 'Every Child Matters: Change for Children'. The overall aim is to encourage integrated planning, commissioning and the delivery of services to improve multi-disciplinary working practices across agencies. There is now a duty to cooperate with guidance provided in 'Working Together to Safeguard Children 2006'. *'Children's Trusts' and 'Local Safeguarding Children Boards'* have since been introduced. The key element of the work is the development of a strategic plan by the local authorities and their partners to safeguard children (aged 0 to 19 years) and promote their health and wellbeing.
- **The Domestic Violence, Crime and Victims Act 2004**: This introduced new powers for the police and courts to deal with violent and sexual offenders in domestic settings and improve the support and protection that victims receive. Common assaults in the home are now an arrestable offence. Aspects of the Family Law Act 1996 that relate to domestic violence now apply to same sex couples and couples who have never lived together or been married. In all cases, a *non-molestation order* can be applied to protect the victim from threats of violence, sexual and physical assaults, abuse and harassment. In addition, an *occupation order* (like an exclusion order) can be applied to remove the abuser and allow the victim to remain safely in the home with her children. Furthermore, a *restraining order* can now be imposed by the courts on conviction or acquittal to protect the victim from abuse and harassment.
- **The Police and Justice Act 2006:** Amended sections of The Protection of Children Act 1978 and the Police and Criminal Evidence Act 1984 to cover the *forfeiture of indecent photographs of children and the misuse of computer equipment* to commit an offence or pervert the course of justice.

CONVICTIONS FOR SEXUAL OFFENCES

The reported level of sexual assault has more than doubled over the last 20 years and the latest Home Office figures show that the police recorded 43,755 serious sexual offences for 2006/07 (Jansson, Povey & Kaiza, 2007). This included rape, sexual assault and sexual activity with children. Therefore, sex offences currently account for about 8 in a 1000 crimes, which is approximately 1% of all recorded crimes. Nearly a third of recorded sex crimes involves rape and 13,780 rapes were reported in 2006/7 (92% to female victims and 8% to male victims). However, just over half of people imprisoned for sex offences have committed rape. In total, sex offenders account for 1 in 13 of people in prison but approximately half of the elderly population in prison (aged 60 and over) have committed a sexual offence. Only 4% of imprisoned sex offenders in custody are juveniles (Greenfield, 1997; Home Office, 1998; Councell & Olagundoye, 2003).

Home Office statistics on the sexual abuse of children are recorded as a subset of 'serious sexual offences'; unlawful sexual intercourse, incest and gross indecency. Research findings (No. 55) from the Home Office Research and Statistics Directorate (Marshall, 1997), showed that at least 110,000 men in 1993 had a conviction for an offence against a child (none of these men were required to register under the 'Sex Offenders Act, 1997' as the 'sex offender register' was not applied retrospectively). Hence, it was estimated that for men born in England and Wales in 1953, seven in every 1,000 had a conviction for sexual offences against a child, by age 40. Most of these men were convicted for an offence with a girl victim (6 in 1000) rather than with a boy victim (1 in 1000). Overall, sexual abuse of children made up the majority of serious sexual offences committed by men under 40 years of age, with at least a third having committed a sexual offence before the age of 18 (Marshall, 1997).

More recently, it has been recognised that at least a third of adult sex offenders began committing sexual assault during their teenage years (Elliott, Browne & Kilcoyne, 1995; Masson & Erooga, 1999) and between 50% and 80% of adult sex offenders acknowledge a sexual interest in children during adolescence (Abel, Osborn & Twigg, 1993). Indeed, official crime statistics for England and Wales illustrate that nearly a quarter of all sexual offences involve perpetrators aged 21 or younger (Home Office, 1998; Masson & Erooga, 1999).

At least two-thirds of sex offenders know their child victim personally, at the time the sex offence is committed (Grubin, 1998). Due to the secretive nature of sexual assaults on children and the problems of obtaining reliable evidence many child sexual assaults go unreported and only a small minority of cases come to the attention of the police. Even a smaller number of cases (approximately 1 in 3) result in the perpetrator being charged and approximately 1 in 10 are convicted (Prior, Glaser & Lynch, 1997). On average men convicted of sexual offences against children claim five or more undetected sexual assaults, for which they were never apprehended or caught (Groth, Hobson & Garry, 1982; Elliott, Browne & Kilcoyne, 1995).

An in depth study of 121 referrals for child sexual abuse (CSA) made in November 1994 (Hamilton, 1997) demonstrated the difficulty of police work with child sexual abuse cases. The sample was approximately 6% of the total number (2,100 in 1994) of CSA referrals to child protection units in the West Midlands Police Area per annum. The study found that in 9 out of 10 referrals there was true cause for concern. Nearly a quarter (24%) of the cases allegedly involved actual or attempted penetration, vaginal and/or anal; 7% involved oral sexual abuse, 60%

involved contact abuse, manipulation and fondling of the child's and/or the offender's genitals and 9% concerned non-contact abuse exhibitionism or obscene photography and video film. However, for 75% of the 108 CSA concern cases there was no further action on behalf of the police and only 17% (approximately 1 in 6 referrals) resulted in a caution or charge of the suspected perpetrator. Eight per cent of these cases were pending further investigations. Over a quarter (27%) of the suspects were already known to the police and had been subject to prior investigations. Eight per cent of perpetrators had been subject to 'no further action' in a prior referral, 4% had been 'cautioned' or 'convicted' and 10% were 'Schedule 1 offenders'.

The low rate of initial conviction and detected recidivism for people who commit sex offences (less than 1 in 5 are reconvicted, Hanson & Bussière, 1998) makes it difficult for any risk assessment tool to be accurate. Under these conditions, there will be a tendency for a high number of false positives (false alarms) where individuals are misclassified as 'dangerous' in order to pick up (or be sensitive to) the majority of high risk offenders (see Chapter 3). To reduce the number of false positives, a higher threshold is required for labelling individuals as dangerous. However, this has a disadvantage of increasing the number of missed cases of truly high risk offenders, such that screening becomes impractical when attempting to identify those most at risk of offending or re-offending.

Such findings demonstrate the need to develop more effective police strategies to prevent and detect the sexual victimisation and repeat victimisation of children. There are obvious limitations to the registration of convicted perpetrators under the Sex Offenders Act, 1997, as this only identifies a small proportion of those individuals who commit such crimes. Thus, there is a necessity to collect and maintain intelligence on alleged sex offenders as well those cautioned or convicted. Under recent legislation, this includes offences concerned with making or possessing indecent photographs of children and using the internet to download such images.

INTERNET OFFENCES

Prior to the existence of the World Wide Web, police seizures of child pornography (under the Obscene Publications Act 1956) would yield a handful of pictures from each offender. With the use of internet, it is not uncommon for an individual suspect to be arrested with thousands of images on his computer. In 2003, an internet sex offender in the English East Midlands was found with approximately 450,000 images of child pornography. In New York, an individual suspect was found with a million such images (Carr, 2003). The possession and/or distribution of child pornography, including images of sex with children, has been a crime since 1988. Between 1988 and 2001, 3,022 individuals were cautioned or charged with child pornography offences. In 2002, a police seizure of information from a group of individuals running a child pornographic website in the United States yielded the names of 6,500 people in the UK who had used credit cards to purchase images of child pornography. This information was passed on to the British police and 'Operation Ore' was launched to apprehend and investigate these alleged sex offenders. This resulted in approximately 2,300 arrests within 12 months (Carr, 2003). Investigating the possession of internet-based child abuse images now accounts for 1 in 10 child sexual abuse cases known to the police (Gallagher et al., 2006).

However, Taylor and Quayle (2003) identify at least six categories of internet sex offences, the last two involving contact sexual abuse:

- downloading and possessing child pornography;
- trading child pornography materials;
- distribution of child pornography materials;
- engagement with internet seduction of children;
- contact offences leading on from internet seduction;
- production of child pornography materials.

The investigation of other types of internet offences accounts for less than 1% of CSA cases dealt with by the police (Gallagher et al., 2006). This is partly because Operation Ore took an immense amount of police resources to investigate internet offences, which was justified on the basis that there was a link between those people who possess and use child pornography and individuals who commit contact sexual offences.

Marshall (1998) reported that a third of child molesters in North America had prior exposure to pornographic materials and Elliott, Browne and Kilcoyne (1995) found that 21% of child molesters in the UK knew how to obtain illicit child pornography and used it prior to their offending. Middleton (2003), using a polygraph examination of child molesters in the UK, found 86% admitted using pornography as a precursor to offending. However, Gallagher, Fraser, Christmann & Hodgson (2006) reported that the proportion of internet offenders who were investigated for the possession of child pornography and were also '*known*' by the police to have sexually abused children was relatively small (approximately 7%).

Therefore, the initial promise of apprehending contact sexual abusers of children through targeting those who possess child pornography has not been realised. It appears that a significant proportion of child molesters use pornography but only a small minority of those who possess images of child pornography may act out their fantasies by sexually abusing children. Indeed, child pornography is not a predictor of risk for sexual reconviction (Hanson & Bussière, 1998, Hanson & Morton-Bourgon, 2005). The question of diagnosable sexual deviance in those who view child pornography has been debated. The assertion that people who use child pornography are likely to be paedophiles is a common reasoning error called 'reversing conditional probabilities'. For example, it may be true that most bank robbers drive fast cars but it does not necessarily follow that people who drive fast cars are likely to be bank robbers. However, to examine this Seto, Cantor and Blanchard (2006) investigated whether being charged with a child pornography offence is a valid diagnostic indicator of paedophilia, as represented by an index of phallometrically assessed sexual arousal to children. The sample of 685 male patients was referred between 1995 and 2004 for a sexological assessment of their sexual interests and behaviour. As a group, child pornography offenders showed greater sexual arousal to children than to adults and differed from groups of sex offenders against children, sex offenders against adults and general sexology patients. The results suggest child pornography offending is a stronger diagnostic indicator of paedophilia than is sexually offending against child victims.

It is essential to identify and convict individuals who encourage sexual crimes against children through the use and possession of child pornography. However, this should not be at the expense or in place of in-depth investigations into alleged contact sex offenders. There needs to be much more effort and resources for the police to identify children who feature in inter child abuse images. Gallagher et al. (2006) observed little progress in relation to this important aspect of police work. There was also little response to internet cases which included communications between offenders on and off line, which glorified or promoted CSA. Proactive police operations to investigate paedophile rings were limited.

POLICING SEXUAL ASSAULT

The role of the police in cases of child maltreatment and sexual assault is the same of that of police in society generally, which is the protection of life (and property), the prevention and detection of crime and the prosecution of offenders against the peace (Ainsworth 1995; 2002; Gregory & Lees, 1999; Thomas, 1994).

The provisions of the Children Act (1989; 2004) allow the police, health and social services to remove a child (a person under 18 years of age) to a place of safety for their protection and well being. In addition, where a crime involving a child victim is suspected the police and social services have a duty to investigate.

The investigative role of the police is to establish whether an offence to a child or adult has occurred and attempt to identify the perpetrator of the offence. When an investigation has resulted in the alleged perpetrator being charged with an offence, the police have a responsibility to report the investigation to the Crown Prosecution Service (CPS) who decides on whether court proceedings should follow.

In addition to their traditional role as detectors and prosecutors of crime, UK Government inter-agency guidelines on 'Working Together to Safeguard Children' (HM Government 1991, 1999; 2006), have enlarged the role of the police in terms of child protection and all investigations into child maltreatment are carried out jointly with social services. Thus, the police make decisions to refer cases of child maltreatment to the CPS in consultation with social services. They consider whether the prosecution is both possible and desirable in terms of the available evidence, whether it is in the best interests of the child, and whether it is in the best interests of the public.

The evidence obtained by the police in cases of child maltreatment and adult sexual assault is often insufficient for criminal proceedings as the 'burden of proof' in a criminal court is 'beyond reasonable doubt'. Nevertheless, the same evidence may be of crucial importance in civil and family court proceedings where judgements are made on the 'balance of probability' in relation to the care of the child.

Nevertheless, the principle role of the police for the prevention and detection of sexual assaults to children and adults remains that of primary investigator and intelligence gatherer.

SPECIALIST UNITS IN THE POLICE SERVICES

A 'Specialist Unit' can be defined as a dedicated office or unit, which specialises and focuses on a specific aspect of police work above all else. To qualify as a 'unit', there must be more than one member of staff and the posts should be permanent rather than transitional (Murphy, 1996).They should be integrated into the organisational structure of the police force (Lloyd & Burman, 1996).

Following the publication of the Report of the Inquiry into Child Abuse in Cleveland 1987 (Butler-Sloss, 1988), the Home Office issued guidelines for police on the special nature of investigations of child abuse. Police forces nationwide were advised to establish specialist units for child protection. There is no universal term for these, but most are referred to as 'Child Protection Teams/Units' (CPUs). These units usually deal with all cases of child maltreatment and sexual abuse within the family. The purpose of the Units is to investigate the majority of allegations or suspicions of child abuse and neglect, jointly with the relevant Social Services Departments and with representatives of other caring agencies (for example; the National Society for the Protection of Cruelty to Children – NSPCC). The police officers and social workers are specially trained to interview and deal with child witnesses (Thomas, 1994), although sexual assaults perpetrated by strangers are usually dealt with by police Criminal Investigation Departments (CID). However, the police usually take the lead in the interview process (Lloyd & Burman, 1996).

However, a Home Office study on the work of child protection units (Browne & Afzal, 1998) found that the majority of CSA suspects were never charged with an offence. In the 47 cases sampled, only 37% of the alleged offenders were charged and a further 9% were 'cautioned'. Nevertheless, this was a considerable improvement on Hamilton's (1997) observation that approximately 1 in 6 (17%) referrals in 1994 resulted in a 'caution' or 'charge' of the suspected perpetrator.

In a study conducted by Plotnikoff and Woolfson (1995), it was found that practical factors can influence whether a case of child sexual assault is dealt with by the police service CPU or the CID; for example, the time of day that an offence was reported. This has implications for the successful investigation and prosecution of a case. Since the UK Government guidelines in the Memorandum of Good Practice (Home Office, 1992), only those officers who have received appropriate training may conduct video taped interviews with a child.

Officers of the Child Protection Units (CPUs) have the responsibility for the dissemination of confidential information to other agencies involved in child protection. The police officers participate in multi-agency child protection case conferences and the Local Safeguarding Children Boards (formally Area Child Protection Committees – ACPCs), that have the statutory responsibility to oversee these activities (Department for Education and Skills, 2007) and may represent other parts of the police service with which they maintain regular contact, such as officers from other specialist units dealing with paedophiles, domestic violence and community safety.

The large urban police services (for example, Metropolitan police, Manchester Police, West Midlands Police) have set up specialist Paedophile Units to investigate all paedophile activities, allegations, organisations, internet activity and circulating child pornography. However, they vary in terms of reference. Smaller police services have dedicated 'Paedophile Intelligence Officers' to facilitate information flow from other local units and police services. The Paedophile Intelligence Officers establish working links with agencies such as the National Child Exploitation and Online Protection (CEOP) Centre, the National Crime Investigation Service (NCIS), Probation, Social Services and Customs.

The Child Exploitation and Online Protection (CEOP) Centre works across the UK and maximises links to tackle child sex abuse nationally and internationally. Part of the Centre's work is to provide internet safety advice for parents and carers. The CEOP website also provides a 'virtual police station' online for people to report child abuse, child pornography and information that may be of help in tracking down and apprehending 'missing child sex offenders'. The 'most wanted' list on the CEOP home page includes face photos (mug shots) of high risk sex offenders who have been placed on the Sex Offenders Register but not complied and are in 'breach of notification requirements' (see Case Study A).

Case Study A: Posted on the web home page of the Child Exploitation and Online Protection Centre (CEOP)

Joshua Karney - *aged 25 to 30, pleaded guilty to indecently assaulting a 15 year old boy he had met at a camping site. He had encouraged the underage boy to drink alcohol (cider) and then sexually assaulted the boy during the night. Karney said he remembered little of the event and was horrified by what happened. He wanted to apologise to the boy. In November 2002, he was given a 15 month prison sentence with a two year extended licence period. He was placed on the Sex Offenders Register for 10 years. On release from prison,*

Karney took a train but failed to arrive at the bail hostel arranged for him. He's been missing ever since and is still on the run. He was born in Ireland but a birth certificate in the name of Joshua Karney for the date on which he says he was born does not exist.

With regard to adult sexual abuse, again, sexual assault by strangers and acquaintances is dealt with by CID and sexual assault within the home by partners and ex-partners by police domestic violence units. In some police forces, the domestic violence units are part of Community Safety Units which also tackle racist and hate crime. In other police forces, they are housed with Child Protection Units to form 'Family Protection Units'. The latter recognises the link between spouse abuse and child maltreatment. Indeed, the link between domestic violence and sexual abuse of children in the family has been well established for over 25 years (Dietz & Craft, 1980; Goddard & Hiller, 1993; Browne & Hamilton, 1999). For example, a study of West Midlands Child Protection Units showed that 46% of child protection files indicated the presence of domestic violence in the family home, yet the rate of overlap of families with files also held by the domestic violence units was 22% (Browne & Hamilton, 1999). Greater collaboration through the establishment of Family Protection Units has the potential to reduce the discrepancy. The same study also found that the severity of maltreatment was greater among families where spousal abuse and child abuse co-occurred. Therefore, the way in which police services structure the units may be important for the detection of crime and the use of proactive approaches to policing sexual assault.

PROACTIVE APPROACHES

The challenge facing police investigations is the complex nature of cases involving sexual assault. Cases can range from one to one acquaintance rape or intra-familial abuse, to gang rape or multi-offender/multi-victim extra-familial sex rings. They can also range from stranger abduction to child prostitution and pornography (Lanning, 1992a, b). Organised paedophile networks and child prostitution and pornography may span not only a specific police area, in which they are initially detected, but also neighbouring areas. Research shows that in order to effectively combat such crime, an effective national intelligence system needs to be established (Hughes, Parker & Gallagher 1996). It is essential that this transcends police boundaries and is easily accessible to investigating officers. The existing systems include both computerised and card index records. The prevailing attitude of some child protection officers in relation to existing national data bases was referred to in the study conducted by Hughes et al. (1996). They found that many officers were unfamiliar with the work of the National Criminal Intelligence Service (NCIS), whilst others regarded it as a waste of time.

No specific guidelines exist on the use of proactive strategies by family and/or child protection units and although individual domestic violence and child protection officers are keen to make use of such methods of investigation, their terms of reference (Butler & Cotterill, 1997), together with the inevitable limitations placed on resources, make such ventures near impossible. To expand further on this, the work of family and child protection units are, by their very nature, dependant on referrals in which the alleged offender is usually known to the child. These referrals therefore come under the umbrella of reactive policing and are victim focused rather than offender focused (Browne & Afzal, 1998). This is reflected in the data bases and information held in these units, which sometimes does not even record details of the alleged offender(s).

The 'Powers of Arrest' granted under the Police and Criminal Evidence Act (PACE, 1984) has been quoted as sufficient for facilitating searches relating to investigations involving child abuse (Home Office, 1988). When evaluated (Browne & Afzal, 1998), it was found that searches were rarely undertaken under such powers. The relevance of conducting searches whilst investigating intra-familial child abuse cases was overshadowed by the myth that paedophiles would necessarily be strangers to the child.

The specialist 'paedophile units' do have terms of reference which include proactive targeting of sex offenders and reliable information gathering is essential (for example, from NCIS packages of intelligence). Paedophile Intelligence Officers act as focal points in other police forces for this purpose and as a contact point for NCIS. The Paedophile units also provide training for the investigation of child pornography on the internet.

Evidence (Linz & Malamuth, 1993) suggests that paedophiles use child pornography and child erotica to fuel their sexual fantasies. Indeed, computers and the internet provide sex offenders and the society at large the access to illicit pornographic material on the World Wide Web. This medium of communication may be exploited by paedophiles and other sex offenders to exchange sexually violent images, child pornography and erotica. This characteristic of sex offenders provides the police with a tool by which to gather evidence against them.

SEARCH WARRANTS

Search warrants serve as an evidence gathering exercise, resulting in the identification of crime, possible victims and associate offenders. Under the Criminal Justice and Police Act 2001, computer equipment can be taken away for further investigation to explore the possible production, possession or distribution of child pornography.

Search warrants are also used to obtain corroborative evidence and incriminating evidence against a suspect, for example;

- Items may be found which corroborate a woman or child's account of abuse, thereby, proving that the victim had been on the said premises, in the said room, and so on.

- If child or sexually violent pornography is discovered, this supports the contention that the suspect has a sexual interest in children or forced sex with adults respectively.
- Diaries may hold the names and address of victims and associate offenders: dates of when meetings took place and in some cases, even accounts of abusive acts perpetrated against women and/or children.

The difficulty in sexual assault cases is that search warrants may not be obtained soon enough, as evidence can be moved or destroyed by an alleged offender relatively quickly (Browne & Afzal, 1998). Physical evidence such as bed sheets, articles of clothing, sexual aids, magazines and ornaments described by a woman or child can disposed of, or hidden, if the alleged offender is aware of a report to social services or to the police. The opportunity for matching a DNA sample is then lost.

PROACTIVE INTELLIGENCE GATHERING

This is more than simply recording information reactively once it has been received, often together with referral information. It entails actively seeking intelligence, for example asking a community safety officer to note down the movements of a suspect on a certain day or noting down what vehicles are used, and so on. Neighbours can also provide useful information on the movements and habits of an alleged offender and who has been seen visiting the suspect's premises. Furthermore, close circuit TV recordings of premises such as clubs, schools and sports centres may be available. This intelligence can be used to justify resources for surveillance activities as part of an ongoing investigation or as a proactive intelligence gathering operation.

TRACKING AND SURVEILLANCE

Surveillance can be either static or mobile and both options are very expensive on police time and resources; hence they are usually reserved for very high risk offenders. A request for the use of surveillance teams to watch a suspect or high risk offender are usually assessed by senior police officers in relation to other policing demands, although surveillance might involve the use of covert cameras or auditory devices being installed at less cost. Satellite tracking and tagging systems to monitor offenders on licence and enforce curfews are controversial but an effective way of managing sex offenders in the community. Undercover operations and covert body recorders may be used with the consent of the senior investigating officer but run the risk of 'entrapment' accusations by the defence lawyers. It should be recognised that in most cases, information on the behaviour and compliance of sex offenders in the community comes from the probation service.

THE PROBATION SERVICE

The role of the Probation Service is to reduce crime through rehabilitatic
reintegration strategies and to ultimately prevent new victims being targeted
Pritchard & Cox, 1997). In addition to risk factors associated with the offend
availability and quality of treatment and supervision by the probation service
significant effect on the probability of recidivism and further offending (McGrath,
1990). The probation service in England and Wales has developed and implemented
nationally accredited community treatment programmes for all sex offenders (see
Chapter 7). These programmes were influenced by the work of Barbaree and
Marshall (1988) in North America, who pioneered sex offender treatment programmes. Barbaree and Marshall (1988), found after two years of treatment,
'treated' sex offenders had a 5% recidivist rate while untreated offenders had a
12.5% recidivist rate. In a follow-up period of 4 years, the treated group showed a
25% re-offending rate while the untreated group rate was as high as 64.3%. Those
who drop out of treatment are also more likely to re-offend than those who complete
a treatment programme (Browne, Foreman & Middleton, 1998). Indeed, Owen and
Steele (1991) found that 25% of incest offenders who dropped out of treatment were
re-convicted for a sexual offence, compared to only 5% of those who completed the
programme. Thus making provisions for treatment is essential.

EFFECTIVENESS OF SEX OFFENDER TREATMENT PROGRAMME IN ENGLAND

Most prison and probation services now run the nationally accredited Sex Offender
Treatment Programme (SOTP) (see Chapter 7). Sex offenders released on license or
those serving community sentences are expected to attend community treatment
programmes. These programmes may be sub-divided into specialist, group sessions,
depending on criminogenic needs such as learning disabilities or sexual victimisation as a child (Allam & Browne, 1998; Allam, Middleton & Browne, 1997).

For example, the West Midlands community sex offender treatment programme
in Birmingham applied cognitive behavioural therapy up to 200 hours with
individuals attending on a weekly basis. The treatment was compulsory and lasted
between 18 months to 2 years. It was evaluated by means of regular psychometric
testing, assessing various components of the therapy and measures of attitudes and
social functioning some of which contained social desirability (faking) scales.
These assessments were adapted from the 'Sex Offender Assessment Pack' used by
the STEP programme for prison sex offenders (Beech et al., 1998). It was hoped that
the offender developed internal mechanisms to help control their behaviour and
reduce their likelihood of further offending. This was achieved by challenging
cognitive distortions and altering the way offenders thought about their sex crimes,

their victims and the consequences of their actions. Towards the end of the treatment programme, participants considered activities that would increase the chances of re-offending and ways to avoid high risk situations and environments ('relapse prevention'). This work was carried out in groups in 8–10 men and supported by regular individual meetings with a probation officer. The probation officer focused on the offenders' attitudes and responses to the treatment programme. Orders and licenses were enforced if the offenders did not comply with the treatment programme (or dropped out) or if there were serious concerns about their behaviour within the group (see Merrington, Hine & Stafford, 2001).

Marques, Wiederanders, Day, Nelson and van Ommeren (2005) evaluated the longitudinal effectiveness of cognitive-behavioural treatment with sexual offenders in California. Although they did not find any significant difference between those who completed the treatment programmes and the control groups in terms of sexual re-offence rates, closer examination of the RP groups performance revealed that individuals who met the programmes treatment goals had lower re-offence rates than those who did not.

An evaluation of sex offenders in the West Midlands who completed the probation services community sex offender group programme demonstrated that treated offenders were half as likely to re-offend as untreated offenders (Allam, 2000; 2001). This was true for child molesters as well as rapists and exhibitionists (see Table 9.2).

Friendship, Mann and Beech (2003) evaluated the national prison-based treatment programme for sexual offenders in England and Wales and found significantly lower rates of sexual and/or violent recidivism in the treated group (4.6%) than the untreated group (8.1%). In terms of sexual recidivism, although the treatment group (2.6%) had slightly lower 2-year sexual reconviction rates than the comparison group (2.8%), these differences were not statistically significant.

The police in collaboration with the probation service closely monitor the progress of sex offenders who attend community treatment programmes. Reports on changes in their attitudes and behaviour are shared in the joint public protection

Table 9.2 A 5-year evaluation of the West Midlands Probation sex offender programme with 150 offenders (adapted from Allam, 2000, 2001)

After 5 years	Treated child molesters n=122	Treated rapists & exhibitionists n=28	Untreated child molesters n=74	Untreated rapists n=31
Reconvicted of a sexual offence	8.2%	15.4%	18.4%	34.6%
Convicted of a violent offence	2.5%	8.3%	10.4%	29.2%
Convicted of other offences	13.1%	25%	27.3%	48.5%

panel meetings which are the core of the police and probation inter-agency cooperation for the management of sex offenders. Any sex offender who drops out of the treatment or breaches their license arrangements is reported by probation to the police.

MULTI-AGENCY MANAGEMENT OF RISK

Multi-Agency Public Protection Arrangements (MAPPA) have been set up across 42 areas of England and Wales in line with the police services, following the implementation of measures contained in the Criminal Justice and Court Services Act (2000) to protect the public from harm. Three category of offenders fall under MAPPA; those who have committed violent and sexual offences, those offenders who are listed on the sex offender register and other offenders considered by the police and probation services to pose a serious risk to the public and others (see Table 9.3). However, for the most dangerous offenders, other measures were included such as new sentences to prevent their release from secure environments if they remain at risk of harming others or themselves (Crime Sentences Act, 1998).

Following the public outcry over the case of Roy Whiting, a convicted paedophile who re-offended and was found guilty of kidnapping and murdering Sarah Payne, aged 8, recent measures have been introduced in the Sex Offences Act 2003, to overhaul and tighten up the Sex Offenders Act 1997 and the Sexual Offences (amendment) Act 2000 (see Table 9.1). In addition, the Sex Offences Act 2003 has updated the concept of sex crimes listed in original Sex Offences Act 1956 to include new offences of sexual grooming and internet offences. Furthermore, it broadens the crime of incest to include cohabitee not related to the child with the offence of 'familial sexual abuse', and tackles sexual abuse by acquaintances with a further offence of 'abuse of position of trust'. Indeed, the offence of 'adult sexual activities with a child' covers any sex act that takes place between a child under the age of

Table 9.3 The total number of sexual, violent and other offenders included within MAPPA 2001/2 (adapted from Bryan & Doyle, 2003)

2001/2	n	%
Registered Sex Offenders (RSOs = 3.5 per 10,000 population)	18,513	39.2
Violent and other sex offenders	27,477	58.2
Other offenders	1,219	2.6
Total MAPPA offenders	**47,209**	**100.0**
RSOs cautioned/convicted for breach of registration requirements	682	3.7
Total Sex Offender Orders granted to RSOs	81	0.4

16 years irrespective of whether the child consented to the sexual activities (see Table 9.1).

The core of the MAPPAs is the joint public protection unit (JPPU) run by the probation and police service in each area. This 'responsible authority' coordinates information and intelligence gathering activities to ensure the effective monitoring and supervision of high risk violent and/or sexual offenders, which were approximately 6% of those convicted of violent and sexual crimes throughout England and Wales ('the critical few'). Furthermore, the public protection unit has a 'duty to cooperate' with a wide range of organisations and agencies associated with education, health, housing, job centres, prisons, social services and youth offending teams to ensure that high risk offenders are managed appropriately in the community. In order to facilitate this, Multi-Agency Public Protection Panels (MAPPPs) meet on a regular basis with a broad range of representatives from the cooperating agencies with specific management tasks (see Table 9.4).

MAPPPs are chaired by a senior member of the police or probation service and provide a forum for an agency to share information in order to assess and manage the risk posed by registered sex offenders and other offenders who are considered to be potentially dangerous. Multi-agency arrangements for public protection often apply a four tier system for dealing with offenders.

1. Low risk offenders: they are dealt with by one agency, usually police or probation and have no current factors to suggest a risk of harm.
2. Medium risk offenders: they are jointly managed by police and probation, supported by information provided by other agencies to develop a risk action plan. They have some identifiable risk factors for harm and the potential to cause harm. However, they are judged unlikely to do so unless there is a change in circumstances, for example, drug or alcohol misuse or failure to take medication.
3. High risk offenders: they are referred to MAPPPs to be assessed, managed and reviewed by all agencies represented on the panel. They have identifiable risk factors for serious harm and the potential to re-offend is high.
4. Very high risk offenders: they are placed in the highest priority by MAPPPs and are assessed, managed and reviewed by all agencies represented on the panel. They have identifiable risk factors that placed them at imminent risk of serious harm and are very likely to re-offend at any time.

RISK ASSESSMENT

Guidelines for the implementation of The Sex Offender Act (1997) from the Home Office (HOC 39/1997) have recommended that interagency meetings consider the

Table 9.4 The work of Multi-Agency Public Protection Panels – MAPPPs
(adapted from Lieb, 2003)

A) How does the panel manage risk?
- Share information on highest risk offenders and determine risk
- Recommend actions to manage risk
- Monitor and implement agreed actions
- Review decisions when circumstances change
- Manage resources

B) What conditions does the panel place on offenders?
- Requirement to live at a specific address and obey a curfew (electronically monitored)
- Prohibition from entering certain localities and making contact with certain people (victims)
- Restrictions on type of employment

C) How does the panel reduce risk to the community?
- Informing professionals
- Informing schools and associations
- Informing the victim
- Restricting the individual's employment
- Rehousing the person
- Visiting the person
- Prompt follow-up in the event of failed visits to the probation officer
- Setting treatment requirements

D) What information is referred to the panel?
- Treatment outcomes from prison programmes
- Assessment of risk from prison psychology departments
- Assessment of risk from probation
- Assessment of risk from RSUs
- Treatment outcomes from RSUs
- Information from the police
- Information from probation

E) How is information on an offender used and how does it influence the assessment of risk?
- Risk assessment tools used
- Personnel carrying out the assessments
- Decision making process
- Weighting of clinical judgement and risk assessment tools in decision making
- Quality of risk assessments used

---

following when developing a risk assessment approach to the targeting of known sex offenders:

- the nature and pattern of previous offences;
- compliance with previous sentences or court orders;
- the probability that a further offence will be committed;
- harm that such behaviour will cause;

- any behaviour that may indicate a likelihood that the perpetrator will re-offend;
- potential objects of harm, for example, children;
- potential consequences of disclosure to offender and their family;
- potential consequences of disclosure in a wider context e.g., Law and Order.

Since these Guidelines were published, the UK National Offender Management Service (NOMS) has standardised an adult Offender Assessment System (OASys). The Youth Justice Board uses ASSET for children and young people under 18 years. These have been developed as a tool to assess risk and identify those offenders who present the greatest danger to the community. Where there is cause for concern, more detailed risk assessments using an actuarial approach are implemented by police and probation officers working in the public protection units, for example Risk Matrix 2000 (Thornton et al., 2002) (see Chapter 5). They are usually categorised as very high, high, medium or low risk and these assessments are reviewed when there are changes and circumstances or patterns of behaviour or new information has been provided relevant to risk management (for example, response to treatment).

DISCLOSURE AND COMMUNITY NOTIFICATION

Information shared between the agencies is confidential and most professionals working with sex offenders recognise the negative impact of personal details being unintentionally 'leaked' or intentionally disclosed to people in the community. As Thomas (2005) notes, by the late 1980s there was pressure to notify the victims when an offender was due for release from prison, if nothing else, to avoid the possibility of the victim bumping into the offender in town. This was highlighted when in 1993 a 14-year-old boy hung himself when he found out that his sexual assailant was being released from prison. An attempt was made to amend to the Criminal Justice and Public Order Act 1994 to make it a statutory requirement to notify victims of release dates. However, this was largely unsuccessful (Thomas, 2005). Thomas (2005) notes before a sex offender is release from prison, several checks are made on the home address where he is proposing to stay. Under new arrangements, information is circulated between prison, probation, police and social services to identify any possible child protection questions arising from the proposed address. These arrangements were primarily for individuals who had offended against children covering all offences, not just sexual offences. These arrangements were revised in 1994 in England and Wales which placed new emphasis on informing the offender that they were classified as a 'Schedule 1 offender'. The notification system to local authorities and GPs remained unchanged. Most professionals working with sex offenders are against the principle of 'Sarah's Law' (or Megan's Law, as it is referred to in the USA). This proposes that the local community should be informed of all sex offenders who reside in their locality. Besides placing the convicted offender at personal risk of retaliation, revenge and vigilante activities, such disclosures will interfere with a re-integration of the offender into society and drive them underground. This makes it difficult for police and probation services to monitor the offender and places them as a risk to the public at large. However, for those high risk sex offenders who do not follow the notification requirements of their registration and 'go on the run', the CEOP website does place their names, profiles and photos on the internet for the public to view.

Using public disclosure and the threat of a prison sentence (up to 5 years) as a deterrent to non-compliance, the notification requirements of the sex offenders register seem to work very well. The Home Office (2002) claimed a National compliance rate of 97% of sex offenders in the community. These individuals initially registered their names and addresses with police and probation and reported any change of address, which helped the joint public protection units keep track of them.

This level of compliance is significantly higher than that observed in a United States survey of agencies dealing with sex offenders; on average nearly a quarter of sex offenders could not be accounted for and only 76% had been registered on the appropriate database (Matravers, 2003). This may be a consequence of Megan's Law, whereby federal legislation mandates the release of information about high risk sex offenders to the community where they reside. This law followed the sexual assault and murder of seven year old Megan Kanka. The sexual murder of Sarah Payne had a number of similarities to the case of Megan, including the call for the same law in the UK. Nevertheless, the current arrangements to protect the public in the UK seem to be working better without such a law.

In some other circumstances, it is necessary to disclose information about the offender's presence in a household or neighbourhood in order to protect victims, families and the public at large. Decisions to disclose information are carefully considered on a case by case basis at a MAPPP meeting. The panel considers the nature of the risk and if all agencies agree, a recommendation is made to the senior officer responsible in the police service who makes the final decision. Under the Children Act 1989; 2004, Social Services are also at liberty to disclose information on Schedule I offenders where they are coming into contact with families and children. This is normally carried out in collaboration with police and probation services.

Case Study B: Example of MAPPA and inter-agency work carried out by the West Midlands Police to manage the risk presented by a man convicted of sex offences (West Midlands Police, 2003).

A sex offender who targets female single parents with children under 16, offences for which he had previously served a prison sentence. Through robust monitoring by police and probation, it became known that he had formed another relationship with a single parent with two children. The police immediately visited the address and took the children into protective custody. Social services were able, under child protection measures, to disclose to the mother details of the offender's convictions. The relationship ended at that point and the offender continued to live in his own flat. Through continued monitoring, the police became aware that he had started to form another relationship with a single mother with young children. An emergency MAPPP meeting was called which recommended disclosure of his previous convictions to the woman. An Assistant Chief Constable of West Midlands Police agreed to this course of action and the relationship was again ended. Because of his persistent behaviour, a Sex Offender Order was obtained from the Court preventing him having any contact with under 16s. Any breach of this order and he will be liable to imprisonment for up to five years.

CONCLUSIONS

Further work needs to be carried out on predictive factors and risk assessment of alleged sex offenders without previous convictions, who represent the majority of suspects who come to the attention of the police and social services. Given the limited resources for proactive strategies in the prevention and detection of sexual assaults, the ability to accurately target those most at risk of perpetrating sexual abuse against women and children is essential for cost effective policing both from a philanthropic viewpoint (safeguarding the public) and from an economic one. The value of proactive approaches to gather intelligence and evidence on alleged sex offenders can not be underestimated, as there is a greater chance of securing a conviction and placing the perpetrator of sex crimes on the sex offender register. This ensures appropriate assessment, management and treatment of the offender and protects the public from harm.

10

Improving Risk Assessment Estimates

INTRODUCTION

As a result of using meta-analytical techniques a number of actuarial sex offender risk assessment measures have been developed and proved to be useful in identifying factors associated with sexual recidivism (see Chapter 5). However, variables considered in the meta-analyses are typically treated as if they were independent of each other. Issues of redundancy (high inter-correlations) and incremental validity are not always addressed. The predictive accuracy of actuarial measures has been widely debated (Grubin, 1999), and it is generally accepted that actuarial risk measures outperform clinical judgement (see Goggin, 1994; Grove et al., 2000; Hanson, Morton & Harris, 2003; Harris, Rice & Cormier, 2002) in regard to *likelihood* that a risk-related event will occur. Actuarial indicators, to date, are not viewed as having anything to say about predictions of severity, duration, or imminence of risk, all of which are important axes of risk assessment. Nor do they claim such predictive powers. Nevertheless, there has been a proliferation of objective, sex offender actuarial risk assessment measures designed to assess the likelihood (reported as a probabilistic estimate) of a convicted sexual offender being reconvicted of a sexual offence within a specified time period. The proliferation of actuarial risk scales is reflected in the number of cross validation studies that have been published. With the advent of actuarial measures, there have been only two studies since 1996 examining the predictive accuracy of the unstructured clinical approach compared with five studies evaluating the empirically guided clinical approaches and 49 published studies investigating actuarial measures (Hanson, 2003). Indeed, there are more than 40 independent tests of the accuracy of the VRAG and approximately 40 replications, involving more than 13,000 cases, of the

Static-99 (Harris, Rice & Quinsey, 2007). However, although recent progress in risk assessment has established the validity of actuarial measures, they are far from delivering what has been expected from them and there continues to be some debate about the application and development of these instruments.

Litwack (2001), Rogers (2000) and Silver and Miller (2002) urge caution over the uncritical acceptance of actuarial measures suggesting that it is difficult to compare clinical determinations and actuarial assessments of dangerousness. Actuarial measures have also been criticised for being atheoretical, that is to say that risk scales have developed meta-analytical studies which have identified a list of risk factors positively associated with recidivism. In contrast, the development of treatment intervention programmes has been informed by theories of sexual offending (see Finkelhor, 1984). Actuarial scales have also been criticised for having limited applicability to diverse groups or populations. Nevertheless, according to Monahan (1996), prediction can be improved with the use of actuarial methods by using criteria that have been empirically validated therefore increasing the validity of the decision-making process.

Common among many sex offender actuarial risk measures are static (historical, non-changeable) risk factors including, prior criminality, prior sexual offences, diagnosis of psychopathy or personality disorder, age at index offence, relationship to the victim, history of substance abuse, relationship and employment problems, paraphilias and deviant sexual interests, all of which have been positively related to sexual reoffending (see Chapter 4). Indeed, 10 out of 12 scales reviewed predominately use static risk factors and 7 do not consider treatment effects (Craig, Browne & Stringer, 2003a). As Hanson, Morton and Harris (2003) argue, much is known about the static factors associated with increased recidivism risk, but less is known about the offender characteristics that need to change in order to reduce risk, or what dynamic risk factors (factors that are amenable to change) increase a person's risk. The aim of this chapter is to consider the application of actuarial measures and whether the inclusion of dynamic factors integrated with existing actuarial scales can improve accuracy in predicting sexual recidivism.

APPLYING ACTUARIAL MEASURES

Before we consider the use and integration of dynamic risk factors with actuarial scales, it is important to explore the extent to which actuarial scales can be generalised to subgroups of sexual offenders. The extent to which actuarial risk measures can be applied to diverse groups or populations has been questioned. Bartosh, Garby, Lewis and Gray (2003) investigated the predictive utility of the Static-99 (Hanson & Thornton, 2000), the Rapid Risk Assessment of Sexual Offence Recidivism (RRASOR; Hanson, 1997), Minnesota Sex Offender Screening Tool-Revised (MnSOST-R, Epperson et al., 1998), and the Sex Offender Risk

Appraisal Guide (SORAG, see Quinsey et al., 1998) in predicting sexual recidivism and found the effectiveness of each instrument varied depending on offender characteristics. The Static-99 and SORAG were both significantly predictive of sexual, violent and any recidivism for extra-familial child molesters. For incest offenders, all four tests were at least moderately predictive of sexual recidivism, whereas the Static-99 and the SORAG were highly predictive of violent or any recidivism. None of the four tests established consistent predictive validity across recidivism categories in regard to rapists or hands-off offenders. Similarly, Craig, Browne and Stringer (2004) consider empirically the application of sex offender risk assessment measures on 139 sex offenders with adult or child victims. Offenders with adult victims obtained significantly higher mean scores using the Risk Matrix 2000-Sexual (RM2000/S; Thornton et al., 2003) and Structured Anchored Clinical Judgment Scale-Min (SACJ-Min; described in Grubin, 1998) than did sex offenders with child victims who obtained significantly higher scores on the RRASOR. Offenders with adult victims were more likely to be considered medium-high to high risk using Static-99 and SACJ-Min respectively, whereas offenders with child victims were more likely to obtained scores in the low to medium-low risk categories using the RM2000/S.

The application of actuarial measures is influenced by base rates, illustrated in Chapter 3. However, these rates only apply to detected recidivism. Indeed, there may be several reasons to believe that detection rates might not be the same for all three groups. Incest offenders, for example, often have control over their victims, which can prevent reporting and may, in part, explain the lower detection rate.

Similarly, compared to non-learning disabled sexual offenders, the base rate for sexual offenders with learning disabilities ranges from 34% at two-years follow-up (Klimecki et al., 1994) compared with 4% within the first year and 21% after four-years (Lindsay et al., 2002). Craig and Hutchinson (2005) compared the rate of sexual reconviction between sexual offenders with learning disabilities and non-learning sexual offenders. They estimate, in some studies, that the sexual recidivism rate of offenders with learning disabilities is 6.8 times and 3.5 times that of non-disabled sexual offenders at 2 years and 4 years follow-up respectively. Sexual offenders with learning disabilities are also at greater risk of reoffending in a shorter time period.

In a sample of 7,724 sexual offenders Harris and Hanson (2002) estimated the five-year recidivism rate was 14%, the 10-year rate was 20%, the 15-year rate was 24% and the 20-year rate was 27%. This is similar to Prentky's finding that first detected incidence of recidivism rose in pretty much linear fashion for 25 years. There are two options to explain how someone could go 20 or 25 years between detected episodes of sex offending. One explanation is that they behaved well for 25 years, and eventually ran out of 'do-right' steam. The second explanation is that they kept doing it until they got caught. Since we never know about undetectable offences, there is of course no scientific way to know which explanation is correct, and for which people.

In an update of the Hanson and Bussière (1998) meta-analysis, Hanson and Morton-Bourgon (2005) reviewed 82 recidivism studies. They reported average rates of 13.7% ($n = 19,267$; 73 studies) for sexual recidivism over an average follow-up of five to six-years. The interpretation of base rates for sexual reconviction need to be viewed with caution. Detected rates often vary depending on whether they are based on official or unofficial sources, and by definitions such as reconviction, recidivism, re-arrest or reoffending (Marshall & Barbaree, 1988). The definition of recidivism (that is, charges, arrests, convictions, behaviours, and so on) also has an important implication when assessing risk. Falshaw, Bates, Patel, Corbett and Friendship (2003) followed 173 sexual offenders for up to six-years and compared differences in offending base rates between official (using the Home Office Offenders Index, OI; and Police National Computer, PNC) and unofficial sources (a community-based sexual offender treatment programme). The sexual recidivism rate was 5.3 times greater than the reconviction rate calculated from the OI, and 1.8 times greater than that calculated from the PNC. Combining these two official sources did not increase the base rate of sexual reconviction above that provided by the PNC alone. Using unofficial data the base rate increased from 6% for sexual 'reconviction', to 7% sexual 'reoffending', to 16% sexual 'recidivism' (high risk sexual offence behaviours). Similarly, Marshall and Barbaree (1988) reported that unofficial sources show 2.4 times more re-offences than official records.

Underreporting of sexual offences and limited clearance rates indicates that re-arrest rates are likely to be lower than actual re-offence rates (see Janus and Meehl, 1997). Clearly, the mechanism of how sexual recidivistic behaviour is being measured has important implications for risk assessment. Indeed, underreporting of sexual offences and limited clearance rates make it likely that re-arrest rates are lower than actual re-offence rates (Janus & Meehl, 1997). Hood et al. (2002) reported that with a base rate of 4% Static-99 over estimated risk 49 times out of 50, and Craissati (2003) found that with a base rate of 2%, Static-99 and Risk Matrix 2000 over predicted risk 29 times out of 30. However, given the difficulties in establishing detected base rates, it follows that it would be hypocritical to accept that the rates reported by Hood et al. and Craissati are correct. Why would anyone assume a base rate of 2% or 4%, which is lower than any reported (that is, detected) base rate among offenders, especially right as detected base rates are lower than actual base rates? Furthermore, by lumping all sexual offences together (that is, non-contact sexual offences, offences against children or adults, or internet-based sex offences) will more likely yield unpredictable results. If we did the same thing for all medical illnesses, we would no doubt find high false-positives and low detection rates.

The variability between risk scales may, in part, be the result of aggregate properties of a category to individuals within that category, discussed in Chapter 3. While actuarial scales have encouraging predictive utility, the actuarial method compares similarities of an individual's profile to the aggregated knowledge of past events of convicted sexual offenders. This can have the effect of reducing the predictive accuracy of the scale when applied to an individual whose characteristics differ from the data cohort. Furthermore, most risk classification instruments designed to provide probabilistic estimates of future behaviour often include factors such as, number of previous criminal convictions, prior sexual convictions and prior non-sexual violence.

It is not clear to what extent actuarial measures translate to other countries where the base rates may be different. Craig, Browne, Stringer and Hogue (in press) reviewed all relevant UK sex offender reconviction follow-up studies. Sixteen UK reconviction studies were identified and divided into incarcerated (8 studies, $N = 5,659$) and non-incarcerated samples (8 studies, $N = 1,274$). For the incarcerated sample (Table 10.1), the UK sexual reconviction rate showed an average of 6.0% up to a two-year follow up (range 1.2 to 10.3%), 7.8% up to a four-year follow-up (range 4.3 to 12%), 19.5% and for six or more years of follow up (range 8.5 to 25%). The UK sexual reconviction rate for the non-incarcerated samples

Table 10.1 UK sexual reconviction rate for incarcerated samples from 8 studies

Author	n	Follow-up (years)	% Mean Sexual Reconviction
Cann, Falshaw & Friendship (2004)	419	2	10.3
		3	15.8
		10	20.0
		21	24.6
Friendship & Thornton (2001)	1,090	4	5.0
Friendship, Mann & Beech (2003)	647(T)	2	4.6 (O) 2.6 (H), 5.5 (MH), 2.7 (ML), 1.9 (L)
	1,910 (U/T)	2	8.1 (O) 2.8 (H), 13.5 (MH), 12.7 (ML), 2.6 (L)
Hanson & Thornton (2000)	531	16	25.0
Hood et al., (2002)	173	2	1.2
	162	4	4.3
	94	6	8.5
Marshall (1994)	402	4	7.0
Thornton & Beech (2002)	174	4	10.9
Thornton & Travers (1991)	313	4	12.0

NOTE:
H = High risk group
L = Low risk group
MH = Medium-high risk group
ML = Medium-low risk group
O = Overall recidivism rate for all risk groups combined
T = Treated
U/T = Untreated

Table 10.2 UK sexual reconviction rate for non-incarcerated samples from 8 studies

Author	n	Follow-up (years)	% Mean Sexual Reconviction
Allam (1999, unpublished)	127	4	1.1
Bates et al. (2004)	183(T)	3.9	5.5
Beckett, Beech et al. (1994)	53	2	4.0
		6	15.0
Craig, Beech & Browne (2006)	85 (SO)	2	7.1
		5	11.8
		10	17.6
	131 (S/V)	2	9.3
		5	14.0
		10	19.8
Craig, Browne et al. (2006)	119	2	6.0
		5	12.0
		10	14.0
Craissati (2003)	310	4	2.0
Craissati, Falla et al. (2002)	178	3	1.3
Falshaw et al (2003)	102	3.9	3.0

NOTE:
SO = Sex offender only sample
S/V = Sex and violent offender samples combined
T = Treated

(Table 10.2) showed an average of 5.7% up to a two-year follow-up (range 4 to 7.1%), 5.9% up to a four-year follow up (range 2 to 5.5%), and 15.5% at six years or more follow up. The trend was for the incarcerated sample to have higher sexual reconviction rates than the non-incarcerated samples. The overall sexual reconviction rate for both samples combined was 5.8% up to a two-year follow up, 6.9% up to four-years of follow up, and 17.4% at six-years or more of follow up. These rates are comparable with that of European and North American follow-up studies. Sjöstedt and Grann (2002) reported a sexual reconviction rate of 6% over a 5.6 year follow-up period ($n = 1258$). In an update of the Hanson and Bussière (1998) meta-analysis, Hanson and Morton (2003) reviewed 46 published and 48 unpublished studies (94 samples). They reported average rates of 13.5% ($n = 23,494$; 83 studies) for sexual recidivism, 14.5% ($n = 7526$; 27 studies) for violent non-sexual recidivism, 25.5% ($n = 13,427$; 34 studies) for any violent recidivism, and 35.5% for any recidivism ($n = 18,167$; 56 studies) over an average follow-up of 5–6 years.

As discussed in Chapter 3, the Area Under the Curve (AUC) of the Receiver Operating Characteristic (ROC) analysis is the preferred indices used when evaluating the predictive accuracy of a risk assessment tool (Harris, 2003). However, as previously discussed in this volume, it is not acceptable to ignore base rates because they are not academically convenient. Indeed, ROC analysis overlooks critical issues. First, this geometry tells us nothing about the individual offender. For this, clinicians must examine such variables as Positive Predictive Power and Negative Predictive Power. While influenced by base rates (that is, reality), estimates can be provided for ranges. ROC indices ignore individual classifications. Second, should every point on a measure be considered a cut point? If so, what is the standard error of measurement, a requirement for all psychological measures and scales (see Standards of Educational and Psychological Testing, 1999). When this is taken into account the moderate numbers (20 to 30% over chance) become further attenuated. The relevance of AUC = 0.75 or 25% over chance can only be considered in light of the base rates. At a small base rate, 25% over chance likely leads to unacceptable levels of false-positives. In truth, using ROC analysis simply hides the base rate problem, it does not solve it. All scales must be formally evaluated. Scales occur whenever items are added or otherwise scored. Different statistics must be used depending on the level of measurement (see Standards of Educational and Psychological Testing, 1999).

IMPROVING ACTUARIAL ESTIMATES

In an attempt to improve actuarial accuracy, several authors have considered additional risk factors such as pro-offending attitudes (Hudson, Wales, Bakker & Ward, 2002) and other dynamic measures (Thornton, 2002; Dempster & Hart, 2002) which have increased predictive accuracy when combined with static risk factors. Beech and colleagues have found the identification and measure of deviancy in child molesters can significantly increase actuarial predictive accuracy (Beech, 1998; Beech, Fisher & Beckett, 1999; Beech, Erikson, Friendship & Ditchfield, 2001; Beech, Friendship, Erikson & Hanson, 2002). Using a range of psychometric measures Beech (1998) was able to distinguish between 'high deviant' and 'low deviant' men. The high deviancy group had higher levels of social inadequacy, personal distress and sexual obsession, minimised their victims and had low levels of denial about offence behaviours and was at greater risk of being reconvicted (see Chapter 6).

However, Harris and Rice (2003) argue that actuarial measures cannot be improved beyond that which has already been demonstrated. They highlight a number of limitations in the use of the ROC analysis that may account for variations in cross validation studies. The ROC statistic can only be applied to binary outcomes (recidivist versus non-recidivist) and cannot interpret continuous scales reflecting the severity or frequency with which recidivism occurs. Harris and Rice also argue that the ROC analysis cannot account for the reliability of the data set (differences in definitions of recidivism), follow-up periods, or variations in offender characteristics as earlier observed questioning the generalisability of actuarial scales across sex offender subgroups. The accuracy of prediction is directly related to the quality of the data. Official reconviction sources only record more serious offences and does not record minor motoring offence and some common assaults, or victim/offence details or the nature, extent and severity of violence during the offence. Indeed, depending upon which definition of sexual recidivism was being used the base rate will vary (Falshaw et al., 2003). Compared to diagnostic tests (such as CT scans for the detection of breast cancer where an AUC of 0.95 is expected), Harris and Rice suggest that a AUC index of 0.90 in reconviction studies represents an upper limit of what can be expected of actuarial measures. Therefore as indices for SORAG (AUC 0.90; Harris & Rice, 2003) and Static (AUC 0.91; Thornton, 2002) approach 0.90, they argue it is unlikely the inclusion of dynamic risk factors will add anything to predictive accuracy due to variance unaccounted for that already exists in the data and analysis techniques.

How dynamic variables are measured has also been scrutinised (see Chapter 6). Indeed, a dynamic factor (measured over at least two occasions) must be shown to add incremental validity when assessed at the pre-release stage and again at follow-up. It is likely that dynamic variables will have undergone several [unobservable] changes during the follow-up period and will be difficult to assess the relative strength and impact these factors have on offending behaviour. It is not surprising then that dynamic factors are seldom identified as risk predictors in long-term follow-up studies. Harris and Rice rightly point out that in order for dynamic predictors to be included in actuarial measures they need to be able to demonstrate an incremental contribution which must be assessed for during a pre-release risk assessment. While they accept that assessing for attitudes, values and beliefs in sexual offenders make for a valuable contribution in developing a formulation of offending behaviour the inclusion of dynamic variables with historical variables would actually decrease predictive accuracy for violent or sexual recidivism (for example, Barbaree et al., 2001).

A number of studies have attempted to improve actuarial estimates by integrating additional risk factors with statistical measures. In a cross-validation study of the Risk Matrix 2000 scales, Craig, Beech and Browne (2006a/b) examined the predictive accuracy of four scales in a sample of 131 sex (n=85) and violent (n=46) offenders followed up for an average of 105 months ($SD = 8.4$ months, range 87 months to 123 months). The Risk Matrix 2000-Sexual and Violent scales (RM2000/S, RM2000/V; Thornton et al., 2003) consistently obtained moderate AUC indices for predicting sexual reconviction over the two (AUC 0.60, 0.66), and five (AUC 0.68, 0.68) years follow-up respectively. Although the RM2000/V obtained moderate predictive accuracy for sexual reconviction, scores for predicting violent reconviction peaked at AUC 0.87 at two years, and 0.86 at five and ten-year follow-up periods. An item analysis of risk items not currently considered by actuarial scales revealed four risk factors positively correlated with sex and violent reconviction: history of foster care, history of substance abuse, history of employment problems/instability, and history of school maladjustment. Rather than being linked to sexual interest *per* se, it was thought that these factors were indicative of psychological vulnerabilities and chaotic lifestyle. Factoring these items with

RM2000/S resulted in a 6.6% increase in predicting sexual reconviction (AUC from 0.60 to 0.71 at two years), and a 2.8% increase in Static-99 (AUC from 0.57 to 0.62). These results share similarities with that of Hanson and Morton-Bourgon's (2005) meta-analysis who found that, amongst other factors such as sexual deviance, any substance abuse and employment instability were significantly associated with sexual recidivism.

In an attempt to further increase the predicative qualities of actuarial measures, researchers have considered the integration of stable and acute dynamic risk factors. Dynamic factors are considered to be enduring factors linked to the likelihood of offending that can change following intervention. Subdivided into *stable* and *acute* factors, stable dynamic risk factors are relatively slowly changing factors including levels of responsibility, cognitive distortions and sexual arousal. In contrast, acute dynamic factors are rapidly changing factors such as substance misuse, isolation and negative emotional states (Hanson & Harris, 2000). In a four-year follow-up study of 310 sexual offenders Craissati (2003) combined dynamic Sexual Risk Behaviour (SRB) factors with actuarial measures. SRB factors included any new offence with a sexual element, the targeting of victims and any behaviour associated with the index offence. For the rapists' sample the AUC increased from 0.71 to 0.85 when considering Static-99 (with risk factors, physical abuse during childhood and a history of two or more childhood disturbances) and Static-99 plus SRB factors. For the child molesters the AUC decreased from 0.78 to 0.68 when considering Static-99 (with risk factors victim of childhood sexual abuse), and Static-99 with SRB factors. It was also found that breach of license conditions or treatment failure was not predicted by offence characteristics.

An alternative approach to structuring risk related information in sexual offenders can be seen in the Structured Risk Assessment (SRA: Thornton, 2002) model discussed in Chapter 6. Thornton and Beech (2002), Craig, Thornton, Beech and Browne (2007), and Craig and Beech (in press) argue that the predictive accuracy of actuarial measures can be improved when combined with measures of stable dynamic risk. These results make persuasive argument that the measure of stable dynamic risk factors offers incremental validity to actuarial scales.

Although they did not examine sexual recidivism, Mills, Kroner and Hemmati (2003) considered the extent to which stable dynamic variables add to static variables in the prediction of violent behaviour in a sample of 209 male offender (violent and non-violent). Using the 54 items from the LSI-R (Andrews & Bonta, 1995) they categorised static factors as those unlikely to change within one year and stable factors as those likely to change within one year. They found that all 22 static risk items were significantly related to violent recidivism compared to 19 out of 32 stable dynamic risk items. When combined into a regression equation they found that the criminogenic stable components relating to family/marital and leisure/reaction added to the prediction of static items in identifying violent and non-violent recidivists respectively.

Collectively, these studies suggest that the integrated use of dynamic indicators, including deviant sexual interest, psychometric approximations of a psychological deviance index, chaotic lifestyle or psychological vulnerabilities, combined with statistical estimates of risk allows for a better prediction of recidivism than that observed in statistical instruments alone. In contrast to Harris and Rice's (2003) observations on the inclusion of dynamic variables with historical factor, these studies demonstrate the assessment of psychological deviance index (as a pre-release measure of stable dynamic variables) has shown to provide incremental predictive value to statistical instruments.

THE MULTIAXIAL RISK APPRAISAL (MARA) MODEL

Research into risk assessment in sex offenders has come a long way in recent years and the advance in our knowledge base has been the genesis for further debate. The current book hopefully highlights both the promise and the peril of actuarial risk assessment for sexual offenders. Yet, although recent progress in risk assessment has established the validity of actuarial measures, there continues to be some debate about the application of these instruments. Factors such as sexual deviance and psychopathy (Barbaree, Langton & Seto, 2002) and treatment related information (Seto, Barbaree & Langton, 2002) significantly impact on risk assessments and recidivism and yet these predictors are not included in some risk instruments. Risk assessment procedures can identify who is likely to be reconvicted and offer time specific probabilistic estimates of likelihood of being reconvicted of a sexual offence (Hanson, 1997; Hanson & Thornton, 2000). This approach standardises the assessment procedure, reduces clinical error (Quinsey et al., 1998) and provides a defensible and transparent decision-making process.

However, given the differences in sexual offender subgroups (that is, in recidivism base rates, victim and offender characteristics, psychopathology and psychosexual traits) we would argue practitioners may be better served by adopting a wider approach to risk assessment by considering both the *nomothetic* approach, that is, searching for general traits of personality (Windelband, 1904), as typically used in risk assessment approaches, as well as, the consideration of the *idiographic* approach (Windelband, 1904) which is about measuring the uniqueness of the individual (that is, through clinical assessment). Given the problems discussed in Chapter 5 about the use and abuse of risk assessment we suggest a multi-axial assessment to risk should be considered.

Not surprisingly, it has been suggested that clinicians should 'adjust' actuarial estimates of risk based on treatment-related information. However, given the limited predictive validity of clinical judgement it makes no sense to adjust measures that have been empirically evaluated and researched (Hart, Laws & Kropp, 2003). Rather, research into actuarially adjusted empirically guided clinical interpretations of dynamic risk factors sounds promising (Hanson, 2003). There is no reason why actuarial risk measures cannot be developed to incorporate both static and dynamic factors of relevance, but until all empirically supported (and sufficiently statistically independent) factors are included in one instrument, then a reason for clinical adjustment will still exist (Doren, 2002). Risk changes over time, place and circumstances and effective management depends on being able to evolve assessments of risk into dynamic systems and the use of static and the variations of dynamic factors is a promising feature in risk prediction. In spite of the extensive research demonstrating the predictive accuracy of actuarial approaches over clinical judgement, actuarial measures are limited. It follows that a more accurate and global assessment of risk will be one that considers actuarial estimates, dynamic changes and psychometric measures. Indeed this is consistent with more recent research where psychometrically assessed deviancy and other dynamic measures increase predictive accuracy when combined with static risk factors (see Chapter 6).

Hence, what we describe here is a multiple pathway approach to risk assessment which we believe encourages a more global approach to risk appraisal. Here, extending the work of Heilbrun (1997) and Sreenivasan et al. (2000), Craig, Browne, Hogue and Stringer (2004) have reported the *Multiaxial Risk Appraisal* (MARA) model, which we would suggest provides an encouraging alternative approach, structures risk-related information. As research continues and more statistically useful dynamic and static variables are incorporated into actuarial instruments, the lack of inclusiveness of the instruments will become less of a concern. We will now describe the MARA in more detail Figure 10.1.

The MARA model essentially describes a multi-axial approach to risk assessment on a nomothetic and idiographic dimension. Risk related information is divided into three domains: risk scales, psychopathology, and empirically guided clinical assessment from which an overall estimate of risk can be derived. This model was developed having considered a number of developments in the risk assessment literature. We will now describe the MARA model in more detail in terms of its nomethetic and ideographic properties.

The nomothetic aspect of the model recognises the utility of actuarial methods in providing estimates of risk within specified time periods. The question here is how many and which actuarial risk measures to use. The use of a single measure has both positive and negative attributes. For example, the use of a single measure promotes consistency in risk appraisal, but there are drawbacks relating to the applicability of that measure to the individual as noted in Chapter 5. When choosing an actuarial measure, the effect of base rates and cohort characteristics also need to be considered (see Chapter 3) and, as far as is possible, closely matched to the offender being assessed. To this extent, a degree of clinical judgement is required when deciding on which actuarial risk scale to use. Beyond the general guideline for the use of actuarial risk instruments a number of other points should be considered. First, as noted in Chapter 5, practitioners should ensure that the assessment

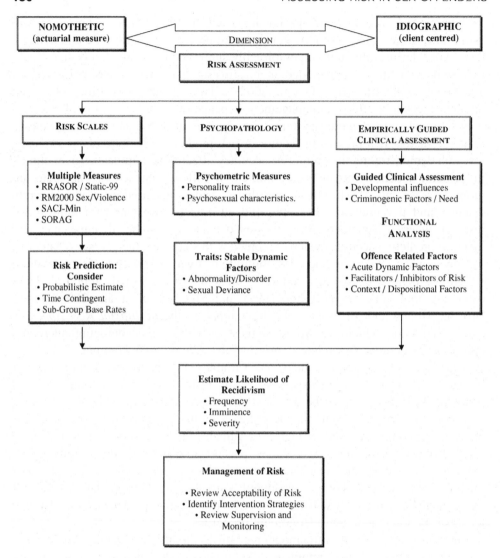

Figure 10.1 Multi-axial Risk Appraisal (MARA)

instruments they use actually have evidence supportive of their use and that they have been designed for use with the relevant subgroup of offenders. Many offender assessment instruments in use today were developed for other populations and they translate poorly to offender groups (Craig, Browne & Stringer, 2004; see also Chapter 5). Second, it is important to recognise that actuarial risk measures only provide probabilistic estimates of risk or likelihood of certain behaviours (as applied to a specific group of offenders used in the construction of the risk measure) will occur in a specified time period. Similarly, the potential multidimensionality of sex offender recidivism is not addressed through the use of any single measure. Accurate multiple-instrument interpretation requires prior knowledge of the degree to which different scales assess each of the multiple aetiological dimensions (Doren, 2002) as discussed in Chapter 8. In examining the dual dimension to sexual offending, Doren (2002) and Roberts, Doren and Thornton (2002) found that the RRASOR tended to correlate with sexual deviance dimensions and deviant profiles using penile plethysmography, whereas Static-99 tended to correlate with the general violence dimension, antisocial personality and PCL-R ratings. We suggest that applying both measures as part of an assessment of risk in sexual offenders will provide a more accurate estimate of sexual deviance and antisociality risk.

As noted in Chapter 5, while actuarial risk assessment measures outperform clinical judgement and offer standardised, defensible decisions, they are fundamentally limited in their utility due to the over-reliance on static risk factors. Although static risk factors are useful for evaluating long-term risk, they say nothing about dynamic changes which may positively or negatively impact on levels of risk. The psychopathology dimension of the MARA model considers the use of psychometric assessment designed to provide information on a number of psychological constructs such as personality, emotional regulation, attitudes, values and beliefs, many of these factors consistent with Thornton's (2002) four deviancy domains described in the Initial Deviancy Assessment (IDA). As discussed in Chapter 6, psychometric measures are effective in assessing the extent of psychological deviance (Beech, 1998; Craig et al., 2007; Thornton & Beech, 2002) and its relationship to sexual reconviction. These measures provide unique psychological information that is otherwise missed by other assessment techniques. However, while psychometric measures provide information on stable or trait factors, subtle changes in employment status, relationships, substance misuse, affective states or parole conditions may also have been missed by psychometric measures designed to measure personality traits or sexual interests. While the use of psychometric measures adds to the risk appraisal along with actuarial risk assessments, the *nomothetic* approach alone is unable to comment on the dispositional and contextual factors. The motivation and criminogenic factors related to offending are not easily accessible from either actuarial or psychometric approaches, which say little of the reasons behind offending. Without an understanding of the processes of offending, it is not possible to determine factors that will facilitate or inhibit offending and in what circumstances an offender's risk of sexual recidivism increases or decreases. The third dimension in the MARA model suggests the use of empirically guided clinical assessment as a method to monitor acute changes in individuals' personal circumstances. This approach is more client centred and utilises measures such as the Sexual Violence Risk-20 (SVR-20; Boer et al., 1997), and the Risk of Sexual Violence Protocol (RSVP; Hart et al., 2003) (see Chapter 5). These scales not only provide information on historical risk but also provide a structured approach to managing acute risk related information such as exposure to destablisers, stress, psychological adjustment, mental disorder, social adjustment and manageability.

The advantage of the MARA approach to risk appraisal over other approaches is that it investigates risk of recidivism from different trajectories. The model is informed by empirical research and allows for a more global assessment risk using actuarial scales, psychometric measures and empirically guided clinical assessments of an individual's change in circumstances.

CONCLUSIONS

There is much about sexual recidivism risk that remains unknown, particularly the assessment and interaction of stable dynamic predictors on recidivism. It is generally agreed that static risk factors provide good indicators of long-term risk. In most cases, the risk factors that are combined to form actuarial scales have been identified from meta-analytical techniques that have included both static and dynamic factors and yet the dynamic factors were not identified as predictive of recidivism. On this basis, it makes no sense to include factors that have not demonstrated incremental validity. However, experts have yet to reach consensus on the best risk factors for predictive accuracy and methods for combining these risk factors into an overall evaluation. For example, Kroner, Mills and Reddon (2005) found that randomly selected factors from four actuarial and clinical based instruments (Violence Risk Appraisal Guide; see Quinsey et al., 1998; Level of Service Inventory-Revised; Andrews & Bonta, 1995; Psychopathy Checklist-Revised; Hare, 1991; General Statistical Information on Recidivism; Nufield, 1982) predicted recidivism as well as the individual scales. Indeed, a review of the relative predictive accuracy of 12 sex offender actuarial risk measures found that most were just as good at predicting general and violent recidivism as they were at predicting sexual recidivism specifically (Craig, Browne & Stringer, 2003a).

Although scale development is theory driven, the application of actuarial scales has been criticised for being atheoretical. As Roberts, Doren and Thornton (2002) point out, 'the development of empirical risk scales has arisen without the benefit of substantial theoretical foundations and examination of the conceptual structure of the instruments' (p. 571). Because of this, construct validity is often nonexistent and counterintuitive findings (for example, the VRAG where murder is a 'better' risk than simple assault) cannot be effectively explained.

One reason why dynamic factors have yet to be included in actuarial measures may lie in the definitions of what dynamic risk factors represent. A model that attempts to redefine 'dynamic' factors and to bridge the gap between empirical risk literature and current theorising has been postulated by Beech and Ward (2004) (see Chapter 8). Having considered some of the major theories that have shaped current assessment and treatment approach for sexual offenders they developed a model of the offence process that incorporates the etiological theories of sexual abuse and risk assessment systems. In the model they consider ideas that developmental adversity can result in vulnerability to sexually abuse a child, descriptions of different offence pathways, stable dynamic or 'psychological vulnerability' factors, and dispositional factors that interact with triggering events (contextual risk factors) to produce acute dynamic risk factors. In describing how these processes interact they redefine stable and acute dynamic risk factors and argue that stable factors should be replaced by 'trait' (that is, dispositional) factors, and acute factors replaced by 'state' (that is, contextual) factors. Actuarial assessments really act as proxies for the above vulnerability factors and function as markers of dispositional sexual behaviours.

Risk assessment schedules should be more specifically related to the psychological dispositions of the offender, considering 'historical markers' of underlying vulnerabilities, and dynamic risk factors which are 'psychological markers' for the same dispositions. Here contextual or acute factors (such as relationship problems or access to the victim) interact with these vulnerabilities to produce acute mental states, for example, deviant sexual desires or intense anger, ultimately leading to recidivism. Seeking to integrate aetiology and risk in sex offenders in a grounded theoretical framework is an area that has been neglected and is a promising feature of future risk assessment systems for sex offenders. This is consistent with Hanson, Morton and Harris (2003) who also suggest that 'many dynamic factors are actually proxies for enduring characteristics that are difficult, if not impossible, to change (for example, intimacy deficits as a symptom of personality disorder)' (p. 163).

It is generally agreed that static factors provide information on who is more likely to re-offend while dynamic variables comment on when a person's risk has changed, once having previously been identified in a pre-release assessment. It would be inappropriate to assess long-term sexual recidivism risk using dynamic factors as it would be expected that such variables will change. Long-term recidivism risk can only accurately be assessed using static factors. However, as Harris and Rice (2003) suggest, dynamic factors are likely to be useful in identifying those individuals who require intense supervision. Trait or psychological dispositional factors assessed at pre-release may also help identify individuals exhibiting characteristics of psychological deviance and whose long-term risk has been assessed as high. The use of dynamic variables would help to inform risk management and supervision strategies. Redefining our understanding of what dynamic risk factors represent may be the genesis for future research into incorporating dynamic or trait-like factors into actuarial systems and is likely to spawn a new generation of risk scales (Mills, 2005). As Hanson (2005b) observes, the tone of the risk assessment literature has changed from the validity of carrying out risk assessments to debating the best method of risk assessment and its application. Further research into the identification, assessment and application of these factors is likely to further advance this debate.

11

Strengths Based Approaches to Risk Assessment

INTRODUCTION

In the preceding chapters we have been considering the areas of concerns or risk factors that sexual offenders have, whether they be static historical factors, such as previous offence histories (sexual and/or violent) or victim type (stranger, male) (see Chapter 4); stable dynamic (for example, deviant interests, pro-offending attitudes, socio-affective problems and self regulation problems (emotional and/or behavioural (see Chapters 6 & 8); or acute/contextual triggering risk factors such as collapse of social supports and/or substance misuse (see Chapter 8). While in Chapter 7 we have examined current treatment approaches that aim to address these risk factors. However, as we have noted in Chapter 7, the broad 'What Works/criminogenic needs approach (Andrews & Bonta, 2003; McGuire, 1995) that targets (static) *risk*, (dynamic) *need*, and *responsivity* factors in treatment is the sole, and most effective way to successfully tackle offending behaviour is starting to be questioned.

Here, probably the primary critic of just using the criminogenic needs approach is Tony Ward (for example, Ward, Mann & Gannon, 2007), who notes that current approaches regarding the identification risk factors and treatment to reduce the level of these risk factors is akin to a pin cushion approach, where 'each risk factor constitutes a pin and treatment focuses on the removal of each risk factor' (p. 88). Therefore what have rarely been considered in this work are the relative strengths that individuals have to prevent themselves reoffending. In the last 10 years there has been a ground swell of interest shown in strengths-based approaches in the caring professions with a particular interest in looking at 'resilience' that is, how people overcome adversity to lead healthy and successful lives (Masten & Reed,

2006). This new paradigm Benard (2006) suggests is a new way of thinking about and working with people that focuses on assets rather than deficits, and working with people rather than doing things to them. Gilgun (1999) notes that strengths-based practice builds upon observations that individuals can overcome substantial risks if they are able to mobilise resources that help them cope with, adapt to, or overcome such problems. Miller, Duncan and Hubble (1997) support the use of strengths-based practice explaining that it not only promotes more comprehensive, balanced and optimistic views of clients and their situations than deficit-based models, but such a positive emphasis is also one of several factors associated with treatment effectiveness. While, O'Callaghan (2002) suggested that interventions with young sexual abusers needs to be informed by factors that promote resilience and positive outcomes.

It is fair to say that the assessment and treatment of sexual offenders might be seen as lagging behind other fields, such as education, prevention and other human services, there are now undoubtedly moves to consider more strength-based approaches. This can mainly be seen in the 'Good Lives' approach to treatment outlined by Ward and colleagues (Ward & Gannon, 2006; Ward et al., 2006; Ward & Stewart, 2003), and in the strengths-based approaches to risk assessment particularly seen in some assessment frameworks developed for adolescents, for example, the Clinical Assessment Package for Risks and Strengths (CASPARS, Gilgun, 1999, 2003, 2006) and the Assessment, Intervention and Moving on (AIM) model (Print, Morrison & Henniker, 2001).

Therefore, the aim of this chapter is to examine these approaches and suggest how they may impact upon our notions of risk assessment discussed in previous chapters. But before we do this we will first give a brief background to strengths-based approaches and positive psychology more generally.

STRENGTHS-BASED APPROACHES AND POSITIVE PSYCHOLOGY

There have been individuals from a number of disciplines who have described the value of individuals leading fulfilling good lives, particularly philosophers such as Keke (1997), who describes the value of focusing on the human effort to create many different forms of 'good lives', particularly noting that a moral stance, on the part of individuals and society, is needed to achieve this. While Rorty (1989) argues that it is authors (for example, George Orwell, Vladimir Nabokov) rather than philosophers, who have been instrumental in shaping ideas about what is fair and just in society, as opposed to cruelty and inhumanity, in what is regarded as a fulfilling positive life. As for psychological ideas it can be said that this idea of focusing on the positives is something that William James was writing about as 'healthy mindedness' more than a century ago (that is, James, 1902). Those who, in psychological terms, can be broadly described as having a humanistic approach have advocated a positive approach to mental health, for example Rogers's (1961) 'fully functioning person' approach and Maslow's (1968) 'self-realizing person' approach.

However, it is really in the last ten years that the idea of focusing on the positive attributes of individuals has become a major part of assessment and treatment in a number of the caring disciplines. In the social work field, for example, Benard (2006) notes that a number of studies are now indicating that positive protective factors or 'resilience' are at least, if not more, important than risk factors in the lives of children and families. About three-quarters of children and young people, even from the most deprived, stressed, dysfunctional families can somehow manage to overcome these obstacles in later life (Rhodes & Brown, 1991), while, even in those children who experience multiple and persistent risks, around half still achieve good developmental outcomes (Rutter, 1987, 1989).[1] Here, resilience is seen as a 'self-righting capacity' for healthy growth and development. Close to the notions of this book, Bremer (2006) notes that 'resilience is a concept that goes hand in hand with risk, for without present risk, or adverse circumstances, there cannot be resilient action or reaction' (p.87).

Criminologists have also been keen to understand the processes by which individuals desist from risky criminal behaviour in order to lead a more fulfilling life. The background to this is that it has been noted for a number of years that for many individuals there is a tendency to drift in and out of criminal activity during their life, rather than crime being a stable life-long trait (Glaser, 1964; Matza, 1964), and that for some, clear voluntary termination of serious criminal participation can be observed (Shover, 1996).

As for explanations of why individuals stop committing offences, criminologists have started to use the term 'desistence', which is the moment that a criminal career terminates (Farrall & Bowling, 1999). Maruna (2001) suggests that desistence from crime is all about an individual carrying out a fundamental and intentional shift in their sense of self and their place in society. The idea, here, is that the individual 'quits crime in the same way as one resigns from a legitimate occupation' (p. 23). As for explanations for why individuals desist, Maruna (2001) suggests that some individuals stop committing crimes or start 'making good' through the process of using 'redemptive scripts'. A redemptive script, according to Maruna is a process by which a person 'rewrite(s) a shameful past into a necessary prelude to a worthy productive life' (p. 87). While the process of making good involves: (1) establishing the 'real me'; (2) having an optimistic perception of self-control over one's destiny; and (3) the desire to be productive and give something back to society.

---

[1] In fact generally, pretty much as per what we know in the sex offender field, factors that indicate a greater risk of future problems generally are: parents divorcing, taken into care, loss of a sibling, attention deficit disorder, developmental delays, delinquency, running away and so forth.

These ideas seem to suggest the importance of an individual's strengths in terms of positive psychological characteristics, such as self-efficacy and an internal locus of control. Bandura (1994) notes that self-efficacy beliefs are said to 'determine how people think, feel and motivate themselves and behave' (p. 71). Bandura further notes that 'self-beliefs of efficacy' play a key role in motivating people, in that because motivation is cognitively generated, they form ideas about what they are capable of, generally make plans to achieve these, and anticipate the possible outcomes of these actions/behaviours. People's beliefs about self-efficacy can be developed through four main sources: *mastery experiences*, that is, being successful at something build's a robust belief in one's own abilities, therefore difficult problems/tasks are there to be accompanied, rather than to be avoided; *vicarious experiences* provided by social models, that is, seeing other people similar to oneself succeed acts as a positive model for one's own possibilities to achieve; *social persuasion* which is seen by Bandura as another avenue to strengthen individual's resolve to succeed; and a *reduction of stress* reactions therefore altering their 'negative emotional proclivities and interpretations of their physical state' (Bandura, 1984, p. 72).

While, the concept of 'locus of control' is described by Colman (2001) as a cognitive style or personality trait characterised by a generalised expectancy about the relationship between behaviour and the subsequent occurrence of punishment or reward. Thus, those with an internal locus of control tend to expect positive reinforcements as a consequence of their own efforts, while people with an external locus of control view rewards or punishments as being due to chance, luck, fate or the actions of powerful others. Therefore, it can be seen that those with an external locus of control are less likely to be successful in undertaking plans and actions leading to positive mastery experiences and reductions in negative affective states and levels of stress.

As for a psychological approach to the idea of experiencing a positive and fulfilling life, Seligman and Csikszentmihaly (2000), in a special issue of the *America Psychologist* on positive psychology[2], argue that the seemingly exclusive focus on pathology in psychology has resulted in a model of the human being that lacks the positive features, which for most make life worth living. They further go on to note that social and behavioural sciences can play an important role in the identification of positive family environments where children can grow up in a nurturing environment, and what factors are important in an individual's life to lead to a sense of well-being.

Therefore, the positive psychology approach attempts to promote human welfare by concentrating on strengths in an individual rather than focusing on deficits (Ward, Polaschek & Beech, 2006). Or to put it more succinctly the application of

---

[2]Including articles on happiness, individual development, subjective well-being, optimism, self-determination theory, adaptive mental mechanisms, emotions and health, wisdom, excellence, creativity, giftedness and positive youth development.

positive psychology is the optimisation of human functioning (Linley & Joseph, 2004). Ward et al. also note that those taking a positive psychology approach suggest (see Snyder & Lopez, 2005, for an overview) that there are a number of basic tenets, as regards human functioning, in particular that human beings are naturally predisposed to seek out things that make them feel good, and that it is the expression of essential human qualities such as love, work, interpersonal skills, aesthetic sensibilities, perseverance, courage, forgiveness, originality, spirituality, talents and wisdom that yields happiness, psychological well-being and fulfilment, that are important to concentrate on work with individuals. Here a number of authors have focused on different aspects of positive psychology, such as: strengths-based approaches (for example, human and environmental); emotion-focused work (for example, resilience, happiness, self-esteem within individuals); cognitive-focused work (for example, creativity, well-being, self efficacy), self-based (for example, the pursuit of authenticity, uniqueness seeking and humility); interpersonal (for example, compassion, empathy and altruism); biological (for example, toughness); and specific adaptive coping approaches (for example, the search for meaning, humour, and spirituality in life). Therefore, even though positive psychology is a fairly new discipline a number of books have already been written on the subject (see Aspinall & Stadinger, 2003; Jospeh & Linley, 2006; Linley & Joseph, 2004; Snyder & Lopez, 2005).

An early description of the application of a positive psychology approach to the treatment of sexual offenders can be found in James Haaven's work with intellectually disabled sexual offenders (Haaven & Coleman, 2000). Here, the distinction is made between the [bad] 'old me' and the 'new [better] me'. The 'old me' is the type of offender who committed sexual offences when his life goals for well-being and fulfilment are pursued in an inappropriate way. The 'new me' involves a new set of plans and goals around the positive approach to the acquisition of an individual's life goals, taking account of an individual's preferences and relative strengths.

Applying positive psychology's aims in the treatment of mainstream sexual offenders has been described by Ward and colleagues (Ward & Fisher, 2006; Ward & Gannon, 2006; Ward, Mann & Gannon, 2006; Ward & Mann, 2004; Ward & Stewart, 2003a, b, c). The Good Lives, it should be noted, although having a lot in common with the positive psychology approach was developed somewhat separately from positive psychology (Ward et al., 2006). We will now examine the Good Lives approach to treatment in more detail, as this may have a lot to offer in terms of reducing the riskiness of sex offenders.

THE 'GOOD LIVES' APPROACH TO SEX OFFENDER TREATMENT

Ward et al. (2006) note that human beings are naturally inclined to seek certain types of experiences or 'human goods' and experience high levels of well being if these goods are obtained. Ward, Mann and Gannon (2007) note that primary goods are defined as 'states of affairs, states of mind, personal characteristics, activities, or experiences that are sought for their own sake and are likely to achieve psychological well-being if achieved' (p. 4). The list of ten 'primary goods' that individuals strive towards can be summarised as follows: (1) *life* (that is, healthy living and a high level of personal functioning); (2) *knowledge* acquisition; (3) *achievements* both in work and play (including the ability to be good at something); (4) *excellence in agency* (that is, being in control and the ability to be able to get things accomplished; (5) *inner peace* (that is, lack of stress and inner tension/emotional dysregulation); (6) *friendship* (including intimate, romantic and family relationships); (7) *community* (that is, involvement with others beyond intimate/family relationships); (8) *spirituality* (in its broadest sense of finding meaning and purpose in life); (9) *happiness*; and (10) *creativity*. All kinds of problems (psychological, social and lifestyle) can emerge when these primary goods are pursued in inappropriate ways. An important point to note here is that Ward does not see the 'goods' that individuals aspire to as necessarily having particular moral values, but they are experiences and/or activities that produce a sense of well-being and will enable an individual to function better if they achieve some/all of the goods listed above.

However, many sexual offenders have not had the opportunity and support to achieve a positive 'good lives' plan in life, due to adverse experiences such as abuse, neglect and poor attachment as children. Typically such experiences have led the offender to have a view of the world that is threatening, and where their level of interpersonal functioning is low, where they feel that they have little control over events, and have distorted views about sexuality leading to deviant sexual urges towards children or non-consenting adults. Because of these problems many sexual offenders lack the skills and capabilities to lead a fulfilling life as an adult (Ward & Stewart, 2003). Therefore sexual offence behaviours are ways of achieving human goods either through a *direct route* where an individual does not have the skills or competencies to achieve these in an appropriate manner; or through an *indirect route* where offending takes place to relieve the negative thoughts and feelings individuals have about their inabilities of achieving human goods. Ward and Mann (2004) note that the absence of certain goods such as excellent in *agency* (that is, a low level of interpersonal functioning), [lack of] *inner peace* (high level of stress and tension), and low level of *relatedness* (low level of intimate/romantic involvement with others) have been strongly related to inappropriate, dysfunctional ways. Therefore, Ward et al. argue obtaining a good life and achieving a sense of well-being should be a key determinant in how sex offenders' treatment is conducted.

However, as has been noted elsewhere in this book, treatment for sexual offenders generally has a narrower focus than this. In fact, the main planks of the 'What Works' approach to the treatment of offenders in general (Andrews & Bonta, 2003) and sexual offenders in particular (see Harkins & Beech, 2007 for a review) is that treatment should be targeted at those who are at the highest risk for reoffending (the *risk principle*), targeted at criminogenic risk factors (that is, dynamic risk factors, see Chapters 6 & 9) (the *need principle*) and that responsivity factors should also be taken into account. Responsivity factors are those that are related to an individual's ability to benefit from treatment (Andrews & Bonta, 2003). According to Andrews and Bonta, treatment should be offered in a manner that is consistent with the learning style of the offender. Therefore, this is a narrow view of a holistic approach to treatment and if responsivity issues are not considered in the treatment of offenders, this could potentially reduce the effectiveness of treatment for sexual offenders (Looman, Dickie & Abracen, 2005; Marshall, Ward et al., 2005; Ward & Stewart, 2003). Or, as Ward et al. (2007) note, the current risk-needs model lacks the 'conceptual resources' to adequately guide therapists and engage offenders as an integrated holistic approach.

The effectiveness of sex offender treatment has been studied and reviewed extensively (Craig, Browne & Stringer, 2003a; Gallagher, Wilson, Hirschfield, Coggeshall & MacKenzie, 1999; Hall, 1995; Hanson et al., 2002; Kenworthy, Adams, Bilby, Brooks-Gordon & Fenton, 2004; Lösel & Schmucker, 2005; Polizzi, Mackenzie & Hickman, 1999; Quinsey, Harris, Rice & Lalumière, 1993; Rice & Harris, 2003). While the most recent meta-analyses indicate an overall effect for treatment (Hanson et al., 2002; Lösel & Schmucker, 2005), these observed effect sizes typically are not large. A number of reasons why this may be the case have been noted by Harkins and Beech (2007).

Specifically, there is evidence that individuals at different risk levels have differential responses to treatment (Andrews & Dowden, 2006; Friendship, Mann & Beech, 2003); and that levels of need (dynamic risk factors) are differentially related to recidivism as discussed in Chapter 6 (Craig, Thornton, Beech & Browne, 2007; Hanson & Harris, 2001; Thornton, 2002). It has also been suggested that a number of intra-personal characteristics affect responsivity such as: level of psychopathy, motivation to change and locus of control (Harkins & Beech, 2007).[3] The factors can be loosely viewed as relative presence or absence of strengths. Therefore, according to Ward et al. the treatment of sexual offenders should be the combination of both the 'What Works' principles (Andrews & Bonta, 2003, see Chapter 7) in order to reduce risk, as well as applying Good Lives principles in order to enhance the strengths of the individual being worked with.

We will now examine work that has looked at strengths and resilience factors in the assessment of young people who sexually offend. But before we do that we will briefly look at current risk assessment instruments for young people.

---

[3]Harkins and Beech (2007) also note that other factors influence the process of treatment by influencing men in group therapy (which is the treatment of choice in many CBT approaches), for example, the therapeutic climate of treatment, the mix of men in treatment groups, and not unsurprisingly therapist characteristics (Beech & Fordham, 1997; Beech & Hamilton-Giachristis, 2005; Marshall, 2005).

ASSESSING RISK IN YOUNG PEOPLE

Bremer (2006) notes that assessing risk factors defines areas of weakness or 'concerns' (Print, Morrison & Henniker, 2001). Meanwhile, identifying protective factors helps to builds strengths. As for the assessment of young people's level of problems, currently there are only a few empirically-based risk assessment schedules available for juvenile sexual offenders: the Juvenile Sexual Offence Recidivism Risk Assessment Tool-II (JSORRAT-II, Epperson, Ralston, Fowers & DeWitt, 2006); the Estimate of Risk of Adolescent Sexual Offender Recidivism (ERASOR, Worling & Curwen in Calder, 2001), and the Juvenile Sex Offender Assessment Protocol (JSOAP, Prentky, Harris, Frizzell & Righthand, 2000).

The JSORRAT is designed as a risk assessment tool for sexual offenders between the ages of 12 and 18, and contains 12 items that can be broadly regarded as static risk factors, that is, number of adjudications for sexual offences; number of adjudications for non-sexual offences; offences committed in public places; number of victims; length of sexual offending history; under court ordered supervision at the time of offending; was deception/grooming involved in commission of offences; has the offender been involved in treatment, and if so what was the outcome; was the offender sexually abused; was the offender physically abused; special needs history; discipline problems in school. Therefore the JSORRAT can be broadly seen as tapping deficits/concerns about the young person.

The ERASOR is designed to assess risk in 12 to 18-year-old sexual offenders. Items assess *static* variables (for example, offences against males victims, offences against strangers, diverse sexual assault behaviours, indiscriminate choice of victim), *dynamic* variables (for example, sexual interests, attitudes and behaviours and psych-social functioning), [problematic] *family/environmental functioning* (such as high-stress family situation, lack of parental support, and an environment that supports the opportunities to re-offend), and attitude towards *treatment* (for example, no realistic relapse prevention strategies, non-completion of treatment). Therefore this assessment can very much be seen to focus on concerns rather than strengths, although lack of high-stress family situations, parental support, and an environment that does not support the opportunities to re-offend, can be seen as tapping into family and environmental support networks.

The JSOAP is designed to assess risk in 12 to 20-year-old sexual offenders. Items in the JSOAP cover four factors. The first factor, *Sexual Drive/Preoccupation*, contains static risk items specifically related to sexual assaultative behaviour such as prior charges for sexual offences and duration of sexual offence history and therefore can be seen to be broadly related to Thornton's (2002) Domain 1 Sexual Interests set of stable dynamic risk factors (see Chapter 6). The second factor, *Impulsive/Antisocial Behaviour*, contains a set of general static risk items, such as caregiver consistency, history of expressed anger, conduct disorder and multiple types of offences, and therefore can be seen to be broadly related to Thornton's

(2002) Domain 4 Self-Management set of stable dynamic risk factors (see Chapter 6). The third factor, *Intervention*, contains items such as accepting responsibility for offending, internal motivation to change, and an understanding of the sexual assault cycle. Therefore this factor can be seen as tapping more into an intrapersonal strengths factor. The final factor, *Community Stability/Adjustment* contains items such as stability of current living situation, stability of school, evidence of support systems and quality of peer relationships. This factor can be seen somewhat as measuring family and community support for the young person. Broadly speaking the JSOAP can be seen as having a mix of risk and strength related items.

ASSESSING STRENGTHS AND RESILIENCE FACTORS IN YOUNG PEOPLE WHO SEXUALLY OFFEND

Bremer (2006) notes that resilience is a concept that 'refers to the ability of the child to maintain positive growth and socially appropriate behaviour in the face of adverse circumstances'. Bremer goes on further to note that resilience is often viewed as a mediator when risks such as those within the individual (developmental problems), within the family (violence), or in the community (anti-social peers) are present. Bremer also notes that building blocks of resiliency are protective factors (or strengths), which are those elements of personality, family function and community environment that mediate adverse circumstances.

The incorporation of strengths and resilience factors in clinical assessments of young people is supported by research that has shown these factors can have a significant impact on the likelihood of general recidivism (Hoge, Andrews & Leschied, 1996) but is only now starting to be examined in sexual offender work. The Department of Health (DoH, 2000), in the UK also identified the importance of the inclusion of resilience in assessments of young people and their families and recognised the following as significant positive factors for adolescents: (1) supportive relationships with at least one parent; (2) supportive relationships with siblings and grandparents; (3) a committed non-parental adult who takes a strong interest in the young person and serves as an ongoing mentor and role model; (4) a capacity to develop and reflect on a coherent story about what has happened and is happening to them; (5) talents and interest; (5) positive experiences in school; (6) positive friendships; (7) the capacity to think ahead and plan their lives.

Gilgun (1999) has developed a Clinical Assessment Package for Risks and Strengths (CASPARS) that provides equal weighting to child and family strengths and risks rather than focusing solely on deficits in the general assessment of young people. In her research on adult sex offenders Gilgun (1990) identified that having a confidant was a significant factor in reducing recidivism and that the presence of healthy peer, family and community relationships were also positively significant. Since then Gilgun (2003) has gone on to look at how assets, protective factors and qualities associated with resilience can be used when individuals have risks of sexually harmful behaviours.

Bremer (2001) has developed the Protective Factors Scale (PFS) which can be employed to assess the level of intervention young sexual abusers. Here she argues that accessing positive factors that promote resiliency is important in attempting to engage young people in treatment. The PFS consists of 10 items covering personal development (general behaviour, school attendance, social and emotional adjustment), sexuality (harmful sexual behaviour, personal boundaries, sexual preferences) and environmental support (caregiver stability, family style and cooperation).

In the UK the AIM (Assessment, Intervention and Moving on) model (Print et al., 2001) is starting to be widely employed and examines strengths and concerns in young people. The original AIM model was introduced in 2001 across Greater Manchester. Four domains were considered in relation to the young person: *offence specific*; *development*, *family/carers*; and *environmental*. The assessment information was organised around two continua: strengths and concerns. An evaluation of the initial assessment model by Griffin and Beech (2004) on the basis of this report AIM2 has been developed. This again assesses concerns and strengths factors but has been specifically attempted to link, and expand, the approach to the risk-aetiology model developed by Beech and Ward (Beech & Ward, 2004; Ward & Beech, 2004) described in Chapter 8. Hence, the AIM2 model groups the *concerns* and *strengths* factors around developmental issues, sexually and non-sexually harmful behaviours, developmental issues, family and environmental factors. Preliminary unpublished analysis of the items looking at the relationship to recidivism of the items included in AIM2 on 70 young people suggests that two fairly robust measures of strengths and concerns could be identified. The *concerns* scale consists of eight items: abused a stranger, threatened or used violence during sexual offending, any general convictions, cold callous attitude in sex offending, impulsive behaviours, emotional regulation problems, maintains contact with pro-criminal peers. The *strengths* scale also consists of eight items: healthy physical development, above average intelligence, positive talents/interests, positive attitude from significant adults in the young person's life, positive emotional coping from significant adults in the young person's life, at least emotional confidant, positive evaluations from work/education staff, positive relationships towards staff.

Both the *concerns* scale (AUC = 0.93, p < 0.00001, CL = 0.88 to 0.99) and the *strengths* scale (AUC = 0.95, p < 0.000001, CL = 0.90 to 1.04) made an independent contribution to risk prediction. However, interestingly, in the analysis it was the strengths factor that was a better predictor of level of risk than the concerns factor, with a high score acting as a protective factor even if an individual had a high score on the concerns scale, suggesting the amelioration of risk if an individual has good internal resources, and positive support and a good relationship with potential adult role models.

This work is of course of a preliminary nature but suggests that, for young people, the importance of strengths cannot be underestimated. Of course, the question that remains unanswered at the present time is the extent to which strengths factors are important in adults and this is an area of research that has only just begun to be explored. In the last section of this chapter we will look at some work that suggest the importance of the strengths-based approach in the assessment generally, and inculcation of motivation and an internal locus of control in adult sexual offenders.

APPLYING A STRENGTHS BASED APPROACH IN WORK WITH ADULT OFFENDERS

A COLLABORATIVE APPROACH TO RISK ASSESSMENT

In Chapter 5 we have provided an extensive outline of current approaches to risk assessment, while in Chapter 10 the Multi-Axial approach is outlined, the implications of a more strengths-based approach suggests that there is more of a focus on assessment as a collaborative process than in previous approaches (see Beech, 2001) and that the client's best interests are served by this process (Sihngler & Mann, 2006).

A more positive application of the risk assessment approach in sexual offenders has been reported by Shingler and Mann who note the importance of this collaborative approach as client's invariably know themselves better than any assessor will necessarily know and that the assessment process must be approached in a genuine way. Therefore, given these ideas Shingler and Mann suggest the following approach should be taken in a collaborative approach to risk assessment: (1) sensitively introducing and explaining the assessment process and how the report based on the assessment will be used and how it can [potentially] benefit the client; (2) listening to the client in an open minded way; (3) dealing with perhaps initial negative reactions in the assessment process; (4) the results of static and dynamic assessments must be discussed openly, with the client being asked to comment upon these results; (5) if the client shows an awareness of the highlighted problems he should be complimented, if not the assessment should be presented in such a way as to help the client understand how he ended up in his current situation. This approach is important in order to provide starting point for potential subsequent work on his treatment needs (that is, dynamic risk factors); (6) the subsequent report written on the basis of the previous points should be explained in such a way that the client understand the concepts outlined in the report; (7) the client should then be asked to comment upon the relevance of particular treatment needs identified in the report; (8) if the client disagrees with the identification of treatment needs he should be asked to explain why this is the case, and if his comments seem to be correct the report should be modified accordingly.

As to the specifics of assessing an individual's potential strengths, Ward et al. suggest that for each human good, individuals should be asked questions around the following key points: (1) what does the [good] mean to you? (2) how important is this to you, has your view of its importance changed over time? (3) how have you gone about achieving this [good] in your life, what strategies have worked best or worst? (4) would you like to have more of this in your life? (5) what do you think has prevented you achieving this [good] in your life? (6) where do you see yourself in one year, five year, ten years time? Ward et al. suggest that these questions allow for the assessment of what an individual sees as a good life, as well as under-standing what the individual's strategies have been in the past, and can be in the future for realising primary goods. And that an assessment can be made about the scope of the individuals' desire for human goods, whether these have been pursued through inappropriate means, are conflicting goals in operation, and do individuals currently have the abilities to formulate and carry out a Good Lives plan?

PROMOTING SELF EFFICACY IN THERAPEUTIC INTERVENTIONS

As noted earlier, an individual's beliefs about self-efficacy can be developed through four main sources: *mastery experiences*; *vicarious experiences*, *social persuasion*; and reductions in *stress levels*. Of course these are aspects of individuals' lives that can be addressed using a Good Lives approach where strengths are built upon. Here, Ward et al. (2007) suggest that the major aim of interventions with sexual offenders should be to 'equip the offenders with the skills, values, attitudes, and resources necessary to lead a different kind of life, one that is personally meaningful and satisfying and does not involve inflicting harm on children or adults' (p. 6).

Therefore, the aim of interventions with sexual offenders is to get them to lead meaningful, non-offending lives in order to move an offender's level of interperso-nal functioning to a more optimal level. Ward et al. also note that such an approach should be both about promoting goods as well as reducing risk, therefore therapy should accentuate the positives rather than getting clients to focus on the negatives in their lives, part of this ethos would be an avoidance of terms like 'dynamic risk factors' risk and 'relapse prevention', these perhaps being replaced with terms such as 'treatment need' and 'self management'.

Ward et al. also suggest a major part of getting therapy right would be to achieve the correct mix of promoting positive goods in the future lives of sexual offenders (*approach goals*), while also still working with offenders to recognise and deal with future risk situations, behaviours and thoughts and feelings (*avoidance goals*). As Ward et al. note this may be a delicate balancing act in that just promoting well-being may produce a more socially skilled/happy offender; on the other hand just managing risk without promoting the individual's well-being could lead to aversive manage-ment of risk factors (that is, telling offenders that this is what they cannot do anymore) leading to the individual feeling disengaged and hostile from the therapeutic process.[4] Hence, Ward et al. suggest that taking a Good Lives approach here can be helpful to therapists in that those in therapy can be clearly seen as 'human agents' and that their offending is understandable in the light of the pursuit of human goods.

ASSESSING AN INDIVIDUALS LOCUS OF CONTROL

Another strength to be assessed in sex offender work is a person's locus of control. Untreated sexual offenders tend to have an external locus of control (for example, Fisher, Beech & Browne, 1998), and therefore regard things that happen as being due to others. Such individuals are less likely to benefit from treatment unless they can be encouraged to take responsibility for their behaviour and become more internally controlled (Fisher et al., 1998). This would seem to link strongly to denial in that unless the individual is able to admit the offence behaviour and detail the processes, which led to the offence, he is not in a position to take responsibility for his actions.

Offenders can be encouraged to take responsibility and develop a more internal locus of control in a number of ways. Functional analysis of the offence (using decision chains, Ward, Louden, Hudson & Marshall, 1995) can be used to identify the thoughts that preceded the behaviour and the decisions made which led to the offence. Distorted thinking, which has been used to excuse or blame others, can be highlighted and the offender helped to challenge such thinking and relapse prevention provides the offender with a number of strategies he can use to avoid offending in the future. In addition, use of frameworks of offending, such as the Finkelhor (1984) four-stage model can provide a very helpful good illustration to many offenders of the process of offending to which they can relate. This helps them to acknowledge that offending does not 'just happen' but rather is an active process in which they made the decision to act as they did, whether this process was over a long time period or happened very quickly. Locus of control will perhaps also affect all of the areas targeted in treatment; empirical evidence suggests that locus of control is strongly related to level of denial and a positive treatment outcome in therapy in terms of reductions of offence related attitudes (Fisher et al., 1998).

BUILDING MOTIVATION IN SEXUAL OFFENDERS

Probably the best known of the current approaches in terms of building upon strengths has been the inculcation of motivation to not offend again. As for level of motivation, it is likely that most offenders have an ambivalent attitude towards changing their offending behaviour. Many will have enjoyed the offence, but not the

---

[4]See Mann (2000) for suggestions about managing resistance and rebellion in relapse prevention work. In this approach there is also a strong emphasis on motivating offenders and creating a sound therapeutic alliance and establishing positive group norms in therapy.

negative consequences for themselves. Others may be reluctant to change because they have little else in their lives. Some may be unmotivated to change because they do not believe they have the ability to do so and may be very fearful of what change will involve. By demonstrating that change is possible, that there are alternatives to offending, and by understanding that an abuse-free 'good life' will ultimately be more rewarding than continuing to offend, it is possible to develop a motivation to change in offenders.

Motivation has been discussed as a factor in successful treatment (Beech & Fisher, 2002; Garland & Dougher, 1991; Looman, Dickie & Abracen, 2005; Tierney & McCabe, 2002), where motivation has also been considered in terms of Prochaska and DiClemente's (1982) transtheoretical model of change by a number of authors (for example, Kear-Colwell & Pollack, 1997; Miller & Rollnick, 2002), motivation here being seen as ranging from lack of acknowledgement of a problem, to beginning to acknowledge a problem and make changes, through to the maintenance of the changes brought about in treatment.

Although much of the discussion of the impact of motivation on treatment effectiveness has been based on clinical experience, rather than empirical studies (Harkins & Beech, 2007), Beech and Fisher (2002), for example, note that unless an individual is motivated to use what he has learned in therapy he will not apply his newly acquired skills and knowledge to changing his lifestyle and therefore his likelihood of recidivism will not be reduced. Hence a more positive approach to treatment should focus on enhancing skills, instilling pro-social attitudes, and increasing the client's self-worth, rather than approaching treatment from negative or avoidance terms, to maximise treatment benefits (Fernandez, 2006; Marshall, Ward et al., 2005; Ward & Stewart, 2003). In fact, using a more positive goal-oriented approach (as opposed to avoidance type treatment goals), Mann, Webster, Schofield and Marshall (2004) found that therapists perceived the sexual offenders in the treatment groups to be more genuinely motivated to live life without offending by the end of treatment.

Harkins and Beech (2007) note that a number of studies and review papers have identified therapist's characteristics as playing an important role in delivering effective treatment (for example, Marshall, 2005; Marshall, Fernandez et al., 2003; Marshall & Serran, 2004; Marshall, Serran, et al., 2003). Marshall, Fernandez and colleagues (2003) identified variables influencing treatment effectiveness in general, positing the likely role these variables play in sex offender treatment. Specifically, they discussed the importance of factors such as the therapist's style, how the client perceives the therapist, and the therapeutic alliance itself.[5] Evidence for the usefulness of this approach has been reported by Drapeau

---

[5]This is a term typically used in psychoanalysis which describes the implicit cooperative compact between a therapist and patient where the therapists undertakes to interpretations and the patient undertakes to obey the fundamental rule of psychoanalysis and try to understand the analyst's interpretations (Colman, 2001).

(2005). The establishment of group norms is something that Beech and Fordham (1987) discussed 10 years ago.

CONCLUSIONS

The aim of this chapter has been to look at some of the strengths-based work that is starting to be used in work with sex offenders in order to see whether this may have its uses in terms of risk assessment with sexual offenders. However, strengths approaches are certainly starting to be employed in adolescent sexual offender work, and there is some evidence that the presence of strengths, and/or strong social support networks would appear to go someway to explain why some high-risk individuals adolescents do not commit further sexual offences no current risk assessment schedules for adults would appear to examine strengths. And by extension an argument can be made that there are strengths elements of personality and community environment/social support that can mediate adverse circumstances in adult sexual offenders. Therefore, it should certainly be the case that therapeutic interventions should work on improving individual's motivation, self-efficacy and locus of control, for example. However, initiatives such the Circles of Support and Accountability (CSA) would seem to be a useful way to provide community support. CSA was developed in Canada with the support of the Mennonite Church and the Corrections Service to provide high-risk sexual offenders support on being discharged into the community by providing them with a group of volunteers, operating under a 'covenant' agreed with them (Eldridge & Findlater, in press). The aim of CSA is to provide both practical and emotional support to the offender as he aims to maintain an offence-free life (for example, Wilson, Huculak & McWhinnie, 2002) and may have a strong part to play in providing a positive community environment to build self efficacy in offenders who are strongly motivated to desist from offending.

References

Abel, G. G., Becker, J. V. & Cunninghan-Rathner, J. (1984). Complications, consent and cognitions in sex between children and adults. *International Journal of Law and Psychiatry, 7,* 89–103.

Abel, G. G., Blanchard, G. T. & Becker, J. (1978). An integrated treatment program for rapists. In R. Rada, (ed.), *Clinical Aspects of the Rapist.* (pp. 161–214). New York: Grune and Stratton.

Abel, G. G., Gore, D. K., Holland, C. L., Camp, N., Becker, J. & Rathner, J. (1989). The measurement of the cognitive distortions of child molesters. *Annals of Sex Research, 2,* 135–153.

Abel, G. G., Huffman, J., Warberg, B. & Holland, C. L. (1998). Visual reaction time plethysmography as measures of sexual interest in child molesters. *Sexual Abuse: A Journal of Research and Treatment, 10,* 81–95.

Abel, G. G., Lawry, S. S., Karlstrom, E. M., Osborn, C. A. & Gillespie, C. F. (1994). Screening tests for pedophilia. *Criminal Justice and Behavior, 21,* 155–131.

Abel, G., Osborn, C. & Twigg, D. (1993). Sexual assault through the life span: Adult offenders with juvenile histories. In H. E. Barbaree, W. L. Marshall, and S. M. Hudson (eds.), *The Juvenile Sex Offender* (pp. 104–117). New York: Guildford.

Abel, G. & Rouleau, J. (1990). The nature and extent of sexual assault. In W. L. Marshall, D. R. Laws & H. E. Barbaree (eds.), *Handbook of Sexual Assault: Issues, Theories and Treatment of the Offender.* New York: Plenum.

Ahlmeyer, S., Heil, P. & English, K. (2000). The impact of polygraphy on admissions of victims and offences in adult sexual offenders. *Sexual Abuse: A Journal of Research and Treatment, 12,* 123–138.

Ainsworth, P. B. (1995). *Psychology and Policing in a Changing World.* Chichester: Wiley.

Ainsworth, P. B. (2002). *Psychology and Policing.* Cullompton, Devon: Willan Publishing.

Ainsworth, P. B. (2000). *Psychology and Crime: Myths and Reality.* Edinburgh: Pearson Education Ltd.

Alaska Department of Corrections (1996). *Sex Offender Treatment Programs: Initial Recidivism Study.* Alaska Justice Statistical Analysis Unit Justice Centre, University of Alaska-Anchorage.

Alexander, M. A. (1999). Sexual offender treatment efficacy revisited. *Sexual Abuse: A Journal of Research and Treatment, 11,* 2, 101–116.

Allam, J. (2001). *Effective practice in work with sex offenders: A reconviction study comparing treated and non-treated offenders.* Report to the West Midland Probation Service. Birmingham: West Midlands Probation.

Allam, J. (2000). *Community based treatment for child sex offenders: An evaluation.* Unpublished PhD thesis. Birmingham: University of Birmingham.

Allam, J. (1999). *Effective practice in work with sex offenders: A re-conviction study comparing treated and untreated offenders.* West Midlands Probation Service, Sex Offender Unit. 826 Bristol Road, Selly Oak, Birmingham,[xxx1] B29 6NA, UK.

Allam, J. & Browne, K. D. (1998). Evaluating community-based treatment programmes for sexual abusers of children. *Child Abuse Review, 7,* 13–29.

Allam, J., Middleton, D. & Browne, K.D. (1997). Different clients, different needs? Practice issues in community-based treatment for sex offenders. *Criminal Behaviour and Mental Health, 7,* 69–84.

American Educational Research Association (2000). *Standards for Educational and Psychological Testing 1999.* Washington, DC: author.

Andrews, D. A. & Bonta, J. (1994). *The Psychology of Criminal Conduct.* Cincinnati, OH: Anderson.

Andrews, D. A. & Bonta, J. (1995). *Manual for the Level of Service Inventory-Revised.* Toronto, Ontario: Multi-Health Systems, Inc.

Andrews, D. A. & Bonta, J. (2003). *The Psychology of Criminal Conduct,* 3rd edition. Cincinnati, OH: Anderson.

Andrews, D. A. & Bonta, J. (2006). *The Psychology of Criminal Conduct,* 4th edition. Cincinnati, OH: Anderson.

Andrews, D. A. & Dowden, C. (2006). Risk principle of case classification in correctional treatment. *International Journal of Offender Therapy and Comparative Criminology, 50,* 88–100.

Aos, S., Phipps, P., Barnoski, R. & Lieb, R. (2001). *The comparative costs and benefits to reduce crime.* Washington State Institute for Public Policy. Document Number: 01-05-1201. Available from: http://www.wa.gov/wsipp

Aspinall, L. G. & Staudinger, U. M. (2003). *A Psychology of Human Strengths: Fundamental Questions and Future Directions for Positive Psychology.* Washington, DC: American Psychological Association.

Aytes, K. E., Olsen, S. S., Takrajsek, T., Murray, P. & Ireson, R. (2001). Cognitive behavioral treatment for sexual offenders: An examination of recidivism. *Sexual Abuse: A Journal of Research and Treatment, 13,* 4, 223–231.

Bagley, C. & Pritchard, C. (2000). Criminality and violence in intra- and extra-familial Child abusers in a 2-year cohort of convicted perpetrators. *Child Abuse* Review, *9,* 264–274.

Baker, A. W., & Duncan, S. P. (1985). Child sexual abuse: a study of prevalence in Britain. *Child Abuse and Neglect, 8,* 457–467.

Bakker, L., Hudson, S., Wales, D. & Riley, D. (1998). *Evaluating the Kia Marama Treatment Program for New Zealand Sex Offenders against Children.* Psychological Service, Department of Corrections, PO Box 25-146, Christchurch, New Zealand.

Bandura, A. (1977). *Social Learning Theory.* Englewood Cliff, NJ: Prentice-Hall.

Bandura, A. (1994). Self-efficacy. In V. S. Ramachaudran (ed.), *Encyclopedia of Human Behavior,* volume 4 (pp. 71–81). New York: Academic Press.

Barbaree, H. E. (1997). Evaluating treatment efficacy with sexual offenders: The insensitivity of recidivism studies to treatment effects. *Sexual Abuse: A Journal of Research and Treatment, 9,* 111–128.

Barbaree, H. E., Blanchard, R. & Langton, C. M. (2003). The development of sexual aggression through the lifespan: The effect of age on sexual arousal and recidivism among sex offenders. In R. A. Prentky, E. S. Janus, & M. C. Seto. (eds.), *Understanding and Managing Sexually Coercive Behavior,* New York: Annals of the New York Academy of Sciences, 989, 59–71).

Barbaree, H. E., Langton, C. M., & Seto, M. C. (2002). *Does psychopathy of deviant sexual arousal add to the predictive validity of actuarial risk assessment?* Paper presented at the 21st Annual Conference for the Association for the Treatment of Sexual Abusers, October 2–5, Montreal, Quebec Canada.

Barbaree, H. E. & Marshall, W. L. (1988). Deviant sexual arousal, offence history and demographic variables as predictors of reoffense among child molesters. *Behavioral Sciences and the Law, 6,* 267–280.

Barbaree, H. E., Seto, M. C. & Langton, C. M. (2001a, November). *Psychopathy, treatment behavior, and sex offender recidivism: An extended follow-up.* Paper presented at the 20th Annual Conference of the Association for the Treatment of Sexual Abusers, San Antonio, Texas.

Barbaree, H. E., Seto, M. C., Langton, C. M. & Peacock, E. J. (2001b). Evaluating the predictive accuracy of six risk assessment instruments for adult sex offenders. *Criminal Justice and Behavior, 28*, 4, 490–521.

Barratt, E. S. (1994). Impulsiveness and aggression. In J. Monahan, & H. J. Steadman (eds.), *Violence and Mental Disorder: Developments in Risk Assessment* (pp. 21–79). Chicago, IL: University of Chicago.

Bartol, C. R. & Bartol, A. M. (1987). History of forensic psychology. In I. B. Weiner & A. K. Hess (eds.) *Handbook of Forensic Psychology.* New York: John Wiley & Sons.

Bartosh, D. L., Garby, T., Lewis, D. & Gray, S. (2003). Differences in the predictive validity of actuarial risk assessments in relation to sex offender type. *International Journal of Offender Therapy and Comparative Criminology, 47*, 422–438.

Beck, A. T., Freeman, A. & Associates (1990). *Cognitive Therapy of Personality Disorders.* New York: Guilford Press.

Beckett, R. C. (1987). *The Children and Sex Questionnaire.* Available from Richard Beckett, Room FF39, The Oxford Clinic, Littlemore Health Centre, Sandford Rd., Littlemore, Oxford, England.

Beckett, R. C., Beech, A. R., Fisher, D. & Fordham, A. S. (1994). *Community-based treatment for sex offenders: An evaluation of seven treatment programs:* Home Office Occasional Report. Available from the Information and Publications Group, Room 201, Home Office, 50 Queen Anne's Gate, London, SW1H 9AT, England.

Beech, A. R. (1998). A psychometric typology of child abusers. *International Journal of Offender Therapy and Comparative Criminology, 42*, 319–339.

Beech, A. R. (2001). Case material and interview. In C. Hollin (ed.), *Handbook of Offender Assessment and Treatment* (pp. 123–138). Chichester: Wiley.

Beech, A.R., Erikson, M., Friendship, C. & Ditchfield, J. (2001). A six year follow-up of men going through representative probation based sex offender treatment programmes. *Home Office Research Findings, 144.* Available electronically from: http://www.homeoffice.gov.uk/rds/pdfs/r144.pdf

Beech, A, R. & Fisher, D. D. (2002). The rehabilitation of child sex offenders. *Australian Psychologist, 37*, 206–215.

Beech, A. R. & Fisher, D. D. (2004). Treatment of sexual offenders in prison and probation settings. In H. Kemshall & G. McIvor (eds.), *Research Highlights in Social Work: Sex Offenders: Managing the Risk* (pp. 137–164). Jessica Kingsley Publications.

Beech, A. R., Fisher, D. & Beckett, R. C. (1999). *Step 3: An evaluation of the prison sex offender treatment programme.* London: HMSO. UK Home Office Occasional Report. Home Office Publications Unit, 50, Queen Anne's Gate, London, SW1 9AT, England. Available electronically from www.homeoffice.gov.uk/rds/pdfs/occ-step3.pdf

Beech, A., Fisher, D., Beckett, R. & Fordham, A. (1996). Treating sex offenders in the Community. *Home Office Research and Statistics Directorate: Research Bulletin, 38*, 21–25. London: Home Office. Available form: Research, Development and Statistics Directorate, 50 Queen Anne's Gate, London, SW1H 9AT.

Beech, A., Fisher, D., Beckett, R. & Scott-Fordham, A. (1998). An evaluation of the prison sex offender treatment programme. *Home Office Research and Statistics Directorate Research Findings, 79*, 1–4. London: Home Office. Available form: Research, Development and Statistics Directorate, 50 Queen Anne's Gate, London, SW1H 9AT.

Beech, A. R., Fisher, D. D. & Thornton, D. (2003). Risk assessment of sex offenders. *Professional Psychology: Research and Practice, 34*, 339–352.

Beech, A. R., Fisher, D. & Ward, T. (2005). Sexual murderers' implicit theories. *Journal of Interpersonal Violence, 20*, 1366–1389.

Beech, A. R. & Ford, H. (2006). The relationship between risk, deviance, treatment outcome and sexual reconviction in a sample of child sexual abusers completing residential treatment for their offending. *Psychology, Crime and the Law, 12*, 6, 685–701.

Beech, A. R. & Fordham, A. S. (1997). Therapeutic climate of sexual offender treatment programs. *Sexual Abuse: A Journal of Research and Treatment, 9*, 219–237.

Beech, A. R., Friendship, C., Erikson, M. & Hanson, R. K. (2002). The relationship between static and dynamic risk factors and reconviction in a sample of U.K. child abusers. *Sexual Abuse: A Journal of Research and Treatment, 14*, 2, 155–167.

Beech, A. R. & Hamilton-Giachritsis, C. E. (2005). Relationship between therapeutic climate and treatment outcome in group-based sexual offender treatment programs. *Sexual Abuse: A Journal of Research and Treatment, 17*, 127–140.

Beech, A. R. & Mann, R. E. (2002). Recent developments in the treatment of sexual offenders. In J. McGuire (ed.), *Offender Rehabilitation and Treatment: Effective Programs and Policies to Reduce Re-offending* (pp. 259–288). Chichester: Wiley.

Beech, A. R., Oliver, C., Fisher, D. & Beckett, R. C. (2006). *STEP 4: The Sex Offender Treatment Programme in prison: Addressing the needs of rapists and sexual murderers.* Birmingham: University of Birmingham. Available electronically from www.hmprisonservice.gov.uk/assets/documents/100013DBStep_4_SOTP_report_2005.pdf

Beech, A. R. & Ward, T. (2004). The integration of etiology and risk in sexual offenders: A theoretical framework. *Aggression and Violent Behavior, 10*, 31–63.

Beech, A. R. & Ward, T. (2006). Risk assessment in the 21st Century. *ATSA Forum.* Online in-house journal of the Association for the Treatment of Sexual Abusers (ATSA).

Beech, A. R., Ward, T. & Fisher, D. (2006). The identification of sexual and violent motivations in men who assault women: Implications for treatment. *Journal of Interpersonal Violence, 21*, 1635–1653.

Belanger, N. & Earls, C. (1996). Sex offender recidivism prediction. *Forum on Corrections Research, 8*, 22–24.

Benard, B. (2006). Using strengths-based practice to tap resilience of families. In D. Saleeby, *Strengths Perspective in Social Work Practice* (pp. 197–220). Boston, MA: Allyn and Bacon.

Bickley, J. & Beech, A. R. (2001). Classifying child abusers: Its relevance to theory and clinical practice. *International Journal of Offender Therapy and Comparative Criminology, 45*, 51–69.

Bickley, J. & Beech, A. R. (2002). An empirical investigation of the Ward and Hudson self-regulation model of the sexual offence process with child abusers. *Journal of Interpersonal Violence, 17*, 371–393.

Beitchman, J., Zucker, K., Hood, J., DaCosta, G., Akman, D. & Cassavia, E. (1992). A review of the long-term effects of child sexual abuse. *Child Abuse and Neglect, 16*, 101–118.

Blackburn, R. (1982). *The Special Hospital Assessment of Personality and Socialization (SHAPS).* Park Lane Hospital. Unpublished manuscript. Available from School of Psychology, University of Liverpool, Liverpool, UK.

Blackburn, R. & Fawcett, D. J. (1999). *Manual for the antisocial personality questionnaire (APQ):* An inventory for assessing personality deviation in offenders. *European Journal of Psychological Assessment, 15*, 14–24.

Blau, G. M. & Gullotta, T. P. (1996). *Adolescent Dysfunctional Behaviour: Causes, Interventions, and Preventions.* London: Sage.

Belanger, N. & Earls, C. (1996). Sex offender recidivism prediction. *Forum Corrections Research, 8*, 2, 22–24.

Boer, D. P. (2006). Assessment of risk manageability for individuals with developmental and intellectual limitations who offend (ARMIDILO). Paper presented at the 9th Conference of the International Association for the Treatment of Sexual Offenders (IATSO). Hamburg, Germany, September 2006.

Boer, D. P., Hart, S. D., Kropp, P. R. & Webster, C. D. (1997). *Manual for the Sexual Violence Risk-20 professional guidelines for assessing risk of sexual violence.* Canada: Mental Health, Law, and Policy Institute, Simon Frazer University, Vancouver, BC.

Boer, D. P., Tough, S. & Haaven, J. (2004). Assessment of risk manageability of intellectually disabled sex offenders. *Journal of Applied Research in Intellectual Disabilities, 17*, 275–283.

Bonta, J. & Hanson, R. K. (1994). *Gauging the risk for violence: Measurement, impact and strategies for change.* (User Report No. 1994-09). Ottawa, Canada: Department of the Solicitor General of Canada. Also available electronically at: http://ww2.psepc-sppcc.gc.ca/publications/corrections/199409_e.asp.

Bonta, J. & Hanson, R. K. (1995). *Violent recidivism of men released from prison.* Paper presented at the 103rd annual convention of the American Psychological Association: New York. August, 1995.

Bonta, J., Law, M. & Hanson, K. (1996). The prediction of criminal and violent recidivism among mentally disordered offenders: A meta-analysis. *Psychological Bulletin, 123*, 2, 123–142.

Borum, R. (1996). Improving the clinical practice of violence risk assessment: Technology, guidelines and training. *American Psychologist, 51*, 945–956.

Bowlby, J. (1973). *Attachment and Loss: Vol 2. Separation: Anxiety and Anger.* New York. Basic Books.

Bowlby, J. (1988). Developmental psychiatry comes of age. *American Journal of Psychiatry. 145*, 1–10.

Bremer, J. (2006). Building resilience: An ally in assessment and treatment. In D. S. Prescott (ed.), *Risk Assessment of Youth Who Have Sexually Abused: Theory, controversy, and emerging issues* (pp. 222–238). Oklahoma City, OK: Wood'n'Barnes.

Briere, J. (1992). *Child Abuse Trauma.* Beverley Hills: Sage.

Broadhurst, R. G. & Maller, R. A. (1992). The recidivism of sex offenders in the Western Australian prison population. *British Journal of Criminology, 32*, 1, 54–77.

Brown, S. (2005). *Treating Sex Offenders: An introduction to sex offender treatment programmes.* Cullompton, Devon: Willan.

Browne, K. D. (1994). Child sexual abuse. In J. Archer (ed.), *Male Violence* (pp. 210–232). London: Routledge.

Browne, K. D. & Afzal, S. (1998) *Police operations against child sexual abuse: prevention and detection.* Report to the Home Office Police Research Group Crime Detection and Prevention Series. London: Home Office.

Browne, K. D., Foreman L. & Middleton, D. (1998). Predicting treatment dropout in sex offenders. *Child Abuse Review, 7*, 402–419.

Browne, K. D., Foreman, L. & Middleton, D. (1998). Predicting treatment drop out in sex offenders. *Child Abuse Review, 7*, 6, 410–428.

Browne, K. D. & Hamilton C. E. (1999). Police recognition of links between spouse abuse and child abuse. *Child Maltreatment, 4*, 136–147.

Browne, K. D. & Herbert, M. (1997). *Preventing Family Violence.* Chichester: Wiley.

Brownmiller, S. (1975). *Against Our Will: Men, Women and Rape.* NY: Martin Secker & Warburg.

Bryan, T. & Doyle, P. (2003). Developing multi-agency public protection arrangements. In A. Matravers (ed.) *Sex Offenders in the Community: Managing and reducing the risks.* (pp. 189–206). Cullompton, Devon: Willan.

Budin, L. & Johnson, C. (1989). Sex abuse prevention programs: Offenders' attitudes about their efficacy. *Child Abuse and Neglect, 13*, 77–87.

Bumby, K. (1996). Assessing the cognitive distortions of child molesters and rapists: Development and validation of the RAPE and MOLEST scales. *Sexual Abuse: A Journal of Research and Treatment, 8*, 37–54.

Butchart, A., Harvey, A. P, Mian, M. & Furniss, T. (2006). *Preventing child maltreatment: A guide to taking action and generating evidence.* World Health Organisation and International Society for Prevention of Child Abuse and Neglect, 2006. Geneva.

Butler, A. J. P. & Cotterill K. (1997). *Child protection units: Survey of terms of reference, exchange of information between agencies & proactive initiatives against sex offenders'*. ACPO Crime Committee.

Butler-Sloss, E. (1988) *'Report of the inquiry into child abuse in Cleveland 1987'* CM 412, London: Home Office ACPO Crime Committee.

Burt, M. (1980). Cultural myths and support for rape. *Journal of Personality and Social Psychology, 39*, 217–230.

Caan, J., Falshaw, L. & Friendship, C. (2004). Sexual offenders discharged from prison in England and Wales: A 21 year reconviction study. *Legal and Criminological Psychology, 9*, 1–10.

Cadoret, R. J., Troughton, E., Merchant, L. M. & Whitters, A. (1990). Early life psychosocial events and adult affective symptoms. In L. Robins & M. Rutter (eds.), *Straight and Devious Pathways from Childhood to Adulthood*. (pp. 300–313). New York: Cambridge University Press.

Cannon, C. K. & Quinsey, V. L. (1995). The likelihood of violent behavior: Predictions, postdictions, and hindsight bias. *Canadian Journal of Behavioural Science, 27*, 92–106.

Caprara, G. V. (1986). Indications of aggression: The dissipation-rumination scale. *Personality and Individual Differences, 7*, 763–769.

Carr, J. (2003). *Child Abuse, Child Pornography and the Internet*. London: National Children's Homes.

Caspi, A., Elder, G. H., & Herbener, E. S. (1993). Childhood personality and the prediction of life-course patterns. In, L. Robin. & M. Rutter (eds.), *Straight and Devious Pathways from Childhood to Adulthood*. (pp. 13–35). New York: Cambridge University Press.

Cawson, P., Wattam, C., Brooker, S. & Kelly, G. (2000). *Child maltreatment in the United Kingdom: A study of prevalence of child abuse and neglect*. London: NSPCC.

Cattell, R. B. & Kline, P. (1977). *The Scientific Analysis of Personality and Motivation*. New York: Academic Books.

Check, J. V. P. (1984). The hostility towards women scale. Unpublished doctoral dissertation. University of Manitoba, Canada.

Chess, S. & Thomas, A. (1993). Continuities and discontinuities in temperament. In L. Robins & M. Rutter (eds.), *Straight and Devious Pathways from Childhood to Adulthood*, (pp. 205–220). New York: Cambridge University Press.

Christenson, J. & Blake, R. (1990). The grooming process in father-daughter incest. In A. Horton, B. L. Johnson., L. M. Raundy & D. Williams (eds.) *The Incest Perpetrator.* (pp. 88–98). Beverly Hill, CA: Sage.

Cohen, J. (1969). *Statistical Power Analysis for the Behavioral Sciences*. New York: Academic Press.

Cohen, J. (1988). *Statistical Power Analysis for the Behavioral Sciences*. 2nd edn. Hillsdale, NJ: Erlbaum.

Cohen, L. J. (1981). Can human irrationality be experimentally demonstrated? *Behavioral and Brain Sciences, 4*, 317–331.

Cohen, M. L., Seghorn, T. & Calmas, W. (1969). Sociometric study of sex offenders. *Journal of Abnormal Psychology, 94*, 249–255.

Coid, J., Petruckevitch, A., Feder, G., Chung, W. S., Richardson, J. & Moorey, S. (2001). Relation between childhood sexual and physical abuse and risk of revictimisation in women: A cross-sectional survey. *Lancet, 358*, 450–454.

Conte, J., & Smith, T. (1989). What sexual offenders tell us about prevention strategies. *Child Abuse and Neglect, 13*, 293–301.

Colman, A. M. (2001). *Dictionary of psychology*. Oxford: Oxford University Press.

Cooper, A. (2002). *Sex and the Internet: A guidebook for clinicians*. New York: Bruner Routledge.

Cooper, A., Demonico, D. L. & Burg, R. (2000). Cybersex users, abusers, and compulsives: New findings and implications. *Sexual Addictions and Compulsivity, 7*, 5–29.

Corbett, C., Patel, V., Erickson, M. & Friendship, C. (2003). The violent reconvictions of sexual offenders. *Journal of Sexual Aggression, 9*, 31–39.

Cote, G. & Hodgins, S. (1990). Co-occurring mental disorders among criminal offenders. *Bulletin of the American Academy of Psychiatry and the Law, 18*, 271–281.

Councell, R. & Olagundoye, J. (2003). The prison population in 2001: A statistical review. *Home Office Research Findings, 195*. London: Home Office.

Cox, D. J. & MacMahon, B. (1978). Incidence of male exhibitionism in the United States as reported by victimised female college students. *National Journal of Law and Psychiatry, 1*, 453–457.

Craig, L. A. (2005). The impact of training on the attitudes toward sex offenders. *Journal of Sexual Aggression, 11*, 197–207.

Craig, L. A. (2007). The effect of age on sexual and violent reconviction. Manuscript submitted for publication.

Craig. L. A. & Beech, A. R. (in press). Psychometric assessment of sexual offenders. In: A. R. Beech, L. A. Craig. & K. D. Browne (eds.), *Assessment and Treatment of Sexual Offenders: A Handbook*. Wiley & Son.

Craig. L. A., Beech, A. R. & Browne, K. D. (2006a). Cross validation of the Risk Matrix 2000 Sexual and Violent scales. *Journal of Interpersonal Violence, 21*, 5, 612–633.

Craig, L. A., Beech, A. R. & Browne, K. D. (2006b). Evaluating the predictive accuracy of sex offender risk assessment measures on UK Samples: A cross-validation of the risk matrix 2000 scales. *Sex Offender Treatment, 1*, 1–16. Available from www.sexual-offender-treatment.org/19.0.html

Craig, L. A., Browne, K. D., Beech, A. R. & Stringer, I. (2004). Personality characteristics associated with reconviction in sex and violent offenders. *Journal of Forensic Psychiatry and Psychology, 15*, 3, 532–551.

Craig, L. A., Browne, K. D., Beech, A. R. & Stringer, I. (2006a). Psychosexual characteristics of sexual offenders and the relationship to reconviction. *Psychology, Crime and Law, 12*, 231–244.

Craig, L. A., Browne, K. D., Beech, A. R. & Stringer, I. (2006b). Personality characteristics and recidivism rates in sex, violent and general offenders. *Criminal Behaviour and Mental Health, 16*, 183–194.

Craig, L. A., Browne, K. D., Hogue, T. E., & Stringer, I. (2004). New directions in assessing risk for sex offenders. In: G. Macpherson & L. Jones (eds.). *Risk Assessment and Management: Issues in Forensic Psychology*. (pp. 81–99). Leicester, The British Psychological Society.

Craig, L. A., Browne, K. D. & Stringer, I. (2003a). Risk scales and factors predictive of sexual offence recidivism. *Trauma, Violence, and Abuse: A Review Journal, 4*, 1, 45–68.

Craig, L. A., Browne, K. D. & Stringer, I. (2003b). Treatment and sexual offence recidivism. *Trauma, Violence, and Abuse, 4*, 1, 70–89.

Craig, L. A., Browne, K. D. & Stringer, I. (2004). Comparing sex offender risk assessment measures on a UK sample. *International Journal of Offender Therapy and Comparative Criminology, 48*, 7–27.

Craig, L. A., Browne, K. D., Stringer, I. & Beech, A. (2004). Limitations in actuarial risk assessment of sexual offenders: A methodological note. *The British Journal of Forensic Practice, 6*, 16–32.

Craig, L. A., Browne, K. D., Stringer, I. & Beech, A. (2005). Sexual recidivism: A review of dynamic and actuarial predictors. *Journal of Sexual Aggression, 11*, 65–84.

Craig, L. A., Browne, K. D., Stringer, I. & Hogue, T. E. (in press). Assessing risk in sexual offenders. *Child Abuse and Neglect*.

Craig, L. A. & Hutchinson, R. (2005). Sexual offenders with learning disabilities: Risk, recidivism and treatment. *Journal of Sexual Aggression, 11*, 3, 289–304.

Craig, L. A., Thornton, D., Beech, A. & Browne, K. D. (2007). The relationship of statistical and psychological risk markers to sexual reconviction in child molesters. *Criminal Justice and Behavior, 34*, 3, 314–329.

Craissati, J. (2003). *Adjusting standard assessment and treatment models to meet the needs of sex offenders in the community*. Paper presented at the 12th Annual Conference of the Division of Forensic Psychology, 26th–28th March 2003. Churchill College Cambridge.

Craissati, J. & Beech, A. R. (2003). A review of dynamic variables and their relationship to reconviction. *Journal of Sexual Aggression, 9*, 41–56.

Craissati, J. & Beech, A. R. (2005). Risk prediction and failure in a complete urban sample of sex offenders. *Journal of Forensic Psychiatry and Psychology*, 16, 24–40.

Craissati, J., McClurg, G. & Browne, K. D. (2002). Characteristics of perpetrators of child sexual abuse who have been sexually victimized as children. *Sexual Abuse: A Journal of Research and Treatment, 14,* 225–240.

Cramer, D. & Howitt, D. (2004). *The Sage Dictionary of Statistics*. London: Sage.

Creighton S. J. (2002) Recognising changes in incidence and prevalence. In: K. D. Browne, H. Hanks, Stratton P, Hamilton C. E. (eds.). *Early Prediction and Prevention of Child Abuse. A handbook* (pp. 5–22). Chichester. Wiley.

Cybulska, B. (2007). Sexual assault: key issues. *Journal of the Royal Society of Medicine. 100,* 1–4.

Davis, G. E. & Leitenberg, H. (1987) Adolescent Sex Offenders, *Psychological Bulletin, 101,* 417–427.

Dempster, R. J. & Hart, S. D. (2002). The relative utility of fixed and variables risk factors in discriminating sexual recidivists and non-recidivists. *Sexual Abuse: A Journal of Research and Treatment, 14,* 121–138.

Department for Children, Schools and Families (2007). *Referrals, assessments and children and young people who are the subject of a child protection plan or are on child protection registers, England – year ending 31 March 2007*. London: National Statistics.

Department for Education and Skills (2007). *Local safeguarding children board: A review of progress.* London: The Stationery Office.

Department of Health (2000). *Assessing children in need and their families: Practice guidance.* London: HMSO.

Dicara, L. V. (1970). Learning in the autonomous nervous system. *Scientific American, 222,* 30–39.

Dietz, C. A. & Craft, J. L. (1980). Family dynamics of incest: A new perspective. *Social Case Work, 61,* 602–609.

Dingwall, R. (1989). Some problems about predicting child abuse and neglect. In O. Stevenson (ed.), *Child Abuse: Public Policy and Professional Practice.* (pp. 28–53). Hemel Hempstead: Harvester Wheatsheaf.

Dobash, R.P., Carnie, J. & Waterhouse, L. (1994). Child sexual abusers: Recognition and response. In L. Waterhouse (ed.), *Child Abuse and Child Abusers: Protection and prevention* (pp. 113–135). London. Jessica Kingsley Publications.

Dolan. M. & Doyle. M. (2000). Violence risk prediction – Clinical and actuarial measures and the role of the Psychopathy Checklist. *British Journal of Psychiatry, 177,* 303–311.

Doren, D. M. (2001). *The relative value of the RRASOR and Static-99 in assessing sexual recidivism risk within the context of U. S. A. sex offender civil commitment statutes.* Unpublished manuscript available from author at, Sand Ridge Secure Treatment Center – Evaluation Unit, Mendota M.H.I Annex 301, Troy Drive Madison, WI 53704.

Doren, D. M. (2002). *Evaluating Sex Offenders: A manual for civil commitments and beyond.* California. Sage.

Doren, D. M. (2006). What do we know about the effect of aging in recidivism risk for sexual offenders. *Sexual Abuse: A Journal of Research and Treatment, 18,* 137–158.

Doren, D. (2007). A critique of Hart, Michie, and Cooke' (2007). The precision of actuarial risk instruments. Unpublished manuscript: Available from the author at Sand Ridge Secure Treatment Center – Evaluation Unit, Mendota M.H.I Annex 301, Troy Drive Madison, WI 53704.

Doren, D. M. & Epperson, D. L. (2001). Great analysis, but problematic assumptions: A critique of Janus and Meehl (1997). *Sexual Abuse: A Journal of Research and Treatment, 13,* 1, 45–51.

Doren, D. M. & Roberts C. F. (1998). *The proper use and interpretation of actuarial instruments in assessing recidivism risk.* Paper presented at the 17th Annual Research and Treatment Conference of the Association for Treatment of Sexual Abusers, Vancouver, British Columbia, October, 1998.

Drapeau, M. (2005). Research on the processes involved in treating sexual offenders. *Sexual Abuse: A Journal of Research and Treatment, 17*, 117–125.

D'Silva, K., Duggan, C. & McCarthy, L. (2004). Does treatment really make psychopaths worse? A review of the evidence. *Journal of Personality Disorders, 18*, 163–177.

Eldridge, H. (1998). *Therapist Guide for Maintaining Change: Relapse Prevention for Adult perpetrators of Child Sexual Abuse*. Thousand Oaks, CA: Sage.

Eldridge, H. & Findlater, D. (in press). A community residential treatment approach for child sex abusers: Lucy Faithfull Foundation's Wolvercote clinic. In A. R. Beech, L. Craig. & K. D. Browne (eds.). *Assessment and Treatment of Sexual Offenders: A handbook*. Chichester: Wiley.

Ellis, A. (1977). The basic clinical theory of rational emotive therapy. In A. Ellis & R. Grieger (eds.). *Handbook of Rational-Emotive Therapy* (pp. 3–34). New York: Springer.

Elliott, M., Browne, K. D. & Kilcoyne, J. (1995). Child sexual abuse prevention: What offenders tell us, *Child Abuse and Neglect, 19*, 579–594.

Emde, R. N. & Harmon, R. J. (1984). *Continuities and discontinuities in development*. London. Plenum Press.

English, K. (1999, June). *Adult sex offender risk assessment screening instrument: Progress Report* 1.a. Denver, CO: Colorado Division of Criminal Justice.

Epperson, D. L., Kaul, J. D. & Hesselton, D. (1998). *Final Report on the Development of the Minnesota Sex Offender Screening Tool-Revised (MnSOST-R)*. Paper presented at the 17th Annual Conference of the Association for the Treatment of Sexual Abusers, Vancouver, Canada, October 1998.

Epperson, D. L., Kaul, J. D., Hout, S. J., Hesselton, D., Alexander, W. & Goldman, R. (2000). *Cross validation of the Minnesota Sex Offender Screening Tool-Revised (MnSOST-R)*. Paper presented at the 19th Annual Conference of the Association for the Treatment of Sexual Abusers, San Diego, California, November, 2000.

Epperson, D. L., Ralston, C., Fowers, D., & DeWitt, J. (2006). Juvenile Sexual Offenses Recidivism Rate Assessment Tool-II (J-SORAT). In D. S. Prescott (ed.). *Risk Assessment of Youth who have Sexually Abused: Theory, controversy, and emerging issues* (pp. 222–238). Oklahoma City, OK: Wood'n'Barnes.

Erickson, M. & Friendship, C. (2002). A typology of child abduction events. *Legal and Criminological Psychology, 7*, 115–120.

Eron, L. D. (1987). The development of aggressive behavior from the perspective of a developing behaviorism. *American Psychologist, 42*, 435–442.

Evans, I. M. (1985). Building systems models as a strategy for target behavior selection in clinical assessment. *Behavioral Assessment, 7*, 21–32.

Eysenck, M. W. & Eysenck, H. J. (1980). Mischel and the concept of personality. *British Journal of Psychology, 71*, 191–204.

Faller, K. C. (1990). *Understanding child sexual maltreatment*. Beverley Hills, CA: Sage.

Falshaw, L. (2002). Assessing reconviction, re-offending and recidivism in a sample of UK sexual offenders. Paper presented at the Eleventh Annual Conference of the Division of Forensic Psychology, Manchester, April 2002.

Falshaw, L., Bastes, A., Patel, V., Corbett, C. & Friendship, C. (2003). Assessing reconviction, reoffending and recidivism in a sample of UK sexual offenders. *Legal and Criminological Psychology, 8*, 207–215.

Farrall, S. & Bowling, B. (1999). Structuration, human development and desistence from crime. *British Journal of Criminology, 39*, 253–268.

Felitti, V. J., Anda, R. F., Nordenberg, D., Williamson, D. F., Spitz, A. M., Edwards, V., Koss, M. P. & Marks, J. S. (1998). Relationship of childhood abuse and household dysfunction to many of the leading causes of death in adults: The Adverse Childhood Experience (ACE) study. *American Journal of Preventive Medicine, 14*, 245–258.

Fergusson, D. M. & Lynskey, M. T. (1998). Conduct problems in childhood and psychosocial outcomes in young adulthood: A prospective study. *Journal of Emotional and Behavioral Disorders, 6*, 2–18.

Fergusson, D. M. & Mullen, P. E. (1999). *Childhood Sexual Abuse: An evidence based perspective. Volume 40*, Developmental Clinical Psychology and Psychiatry. London: Sage.

Fernandez, Y. M. (2006). Focusing on the positive and avoiding negativity in sexual offender treatment. In W. L. Marshall, Y. M. Fernandez, L. E. Marshall and G. E. Serran (eds.), *Sexual Offender Treatment: Controversial issues* (pp. 187–197). Chichester: Wiley.

Finkelhor, D. (1984). *Child Sexual Abuse: New theory and research.* New York: Free Press.

Finkelhor, D. & Yllo, K. (1985). *License to Rape: Sexual abuse of wives.* New York: Holt, Rinehart & Winston.

Finkelhor, D. & Associates (1986). *A Sourcebook on Child Sexual Abuse*, Beverley Hills, CA: Sage.

Finkelhor D. (1994). The international epidemiology of child sexual abuse. *Child Abuse and Neglect, 18*, 409–418.

Finkelhor, D., Hotaling, G., Lewis, I. A. & Smith, C. (1990). Sexual abuse in a national survey of adult men and women: Prevalence, characteristics and risk factors. *Child Abuse and Neglect, 14*, 19–28.

Finkelhor, D. & Jones, L. M. (2006). Why have child maltreatment and child victimization declined? *Journal of Social Issues, 62*, 685–716.

Finkelhor, D., Ormrod, R. K., Turner, H. A. & Hamby, S. L. (2005). The victimization of children and youth: A comprehensive, national survey. *Child Maltreatment, 10*, 5–25.

Firestone, P., Bradford, J. M., McCoy, M., Greenberg, D. M., Larose, M. R. & Curry, S. (1999). Prediction of recidivism in incest offenders. *Journal of Interpersonal Violence, 14*, 511–531.

Fisher, D. & Beech, A. R. (1999). Current practice in Britain with sexual offenders. *Journal of Interpersonal Violence, 14*, 233–249.

Fisher, D. D. & Beech (2004). Adult male sexual offenders. In H. Kemshall, and G. McIvor (eds.), *Research Highlights in Social Work: Sex offenders: Managing the risk.* (pp. 25–48). London: Jessica Kingsley Publications.

Fisher, D., Beech, A. R. & Browne, K. D. (1998). Locus of control and its relationship to treatment change in child molesters. *Legal and Criminological Psychology, 3*, 1–12.

Fisher, D., Beech, A. R. & Browne, K. D. (1999). Comparison of sex offenders to non-sex offenders on selected psychological measures. *International Journal of Offender Therapy and Comparative Criminology, 43*, 473–491.

Fisher, D., Beech, A. R. & Browne, K. D. (2000). The effectiveness of relapse prevention training in a group of incarcerated child molesters. *Psychology, Crime and Law, 6*, 181–195.

Fisher, D. & Beech, A. R. (2004). Adult male sexual offenders. In H. Kemshall and G. McIvor (eds.), *Research Highlights in Social Work: Sex ffenders: Managing the risk* (pp. 25–48). London: Jessica Kingsley Publications.

Fisher, D. & Mair, G. (1998). A review of classification schemes for sex offenders. *Home Office Research Findings, 78.* London: Home Office. Home Office Publications Unit, 50, Queen Anne's Gate, London, SW1 9AT, England.

Fisher, D. & Thornton, D. (1993). Assessing risk of re-offending in sexual offenders. *Journal of Mental Health, 2*, pp. 105–117.

Fitch, Z. H. (1962). Men convicted of sexual offences against children: A descriptive follow-up study. *British Journal of Criminology, 3*, 1, 18–37.

Ford, P., Pritchard, C. & Cox, M. (1997). Consumer opinions of the probation service: Advice, assistance, befriending and the reduction of crime. *The Howard Journal, 36*, 1, 42–61.

Foss, C. (2003). *Internet offenders: An examination of emotional loneliness and offending characteristics.* Birmingham: University of Birmingham, Centre for Forensic and Family Psychology, Unpublished M.Sc. Dissertation.

Friendship, C., Beech, A. R. & Browne, K. D. (2002). Reconviction as an outcome measure in research: A methodological note. *British Journal of Criminology, 42*, 442–444.

Friendship, C. & Corbett, C. (2003). *The violent reconvictions of sexual offenders*. Paper presented at the 12th Annual Conference of the Division of Forensic Psychology, Churchill College Cambridge, March 2003.

Friendship, C., Mann, R. E. & Beech, A. R. (2003). Evaluation of a national prison-based treatment program for sexual offenders in England and Wales. *Journal of Interpersonal Violence, 18*, 744–759.

Friendship, C. & Thornton, D. (2001). Sexual reconviction for sexual offenders discharged from prison in England and Wales. *British Journal of Criminology, 41*, 2, 285–292.

Frisbie, L. V. (1969). Another look at sex offenders in California. *California Mental Hygiene Research Monograph, 12*. Sacramento, CA: State of California Department of Mental Hygiene.

Frisbie, L. V. & Dondis, E. H. (1965). Recidivism among treated sex offenders. *California Mental Health Research Monograph, 5*. Sacramento, CA: State of California Department of Mental Hygiene.

Frost, A. & Connelly, M. (2004). Reflexivity, reflection, and the change process in offender work. *Sexual Abuse: A Journal of Research and Treatment, 16*, 365–380.

Furby, L., Weinrott, M. R. & Blackshaw, L. (1989). Sex offender recidivism: A review. *Psychological Bulletin, 105*, 3–30.

Gallagher, B., Fraser, C., Christmann, K. & Hodgson, B. (2006). *International and Internet child sexual abuse and exploitation: Nuffield Foundation Research Project Report*. Huddersfield: University of Huddersfield, Centre for Applied Childhood Studies.

Gallagher, C. A., Wilson, D. B., Hirschfield, P., Coggeshall, M. B. & MacKenzie, D. L. (1999) A quantitative review of the effects of sex offender treatment on sexual re-offending. *Corrections Management Quarterly, 3*, 4, 19–29.

Garland, R. J. & Dougher, M. J. (1991). Motivation intervention in the treatment of sex offenders. In W. Miller and S. Rollnick (eds.), *Motivational Interviewing: Preparing people to change addictive behavio.* (pp. 303–313). New York: Guilford.

Gebhard, P. H., Gagnon, J. H., Pomeroy, W. B. & Christenson, C. V., (1965). *Sex Offenders: An analysis of types*. London: Heinemann.

Gendreau, P. & Ross, R. R. (1979). Effective correctional treatment: Bibliography for cynics. *Crime and Delinquency, 25*, 463–489.

Gerhold, C. K., Browne, K. D. & Beckett, R. (2007). Predicting recidivism in adolescent sexual offenders. *Aggression and Violent Behavior, 12*, 427–438.

Gilgun, J. F. (1990). Factors mediating the effects of childhood maltreatment. In M. Hunter (ed.) *The Sexually Abused Male: Prevalence, impact and treatment* (pp. 177–190). Lexington, MA: Lexington Books.

Gilgun, J. F. (1999). CASPARS: Clinical assessment instruments that measure strengths and risks in children and families. In M. C. Calder (ed.), *Working with Young People who Sexually Abuse: New pieces of the jigsaw puzzle* (pp. 48–58). Lyme Regis: Russell House Publishing.

Gilgun, J. F. (2003). Working with young people who have sexual behaviour problems: Lessons from risk and resilience. Presented at G-MAP Conference *Working holistically with young people who sexually harm*. Bolton, UK, June 2003.

Gilgun, J. (2006). Children and adolescents with problematic sexual behaviours: Lessons from research on resilience. In R. Longo and D. Prescott (eds.), *Current Perspectives: working with sexually aggressive youth and youth with sexual behavior problems.* (pp. 383–394). Holyoke, MA: Neari Press.

Ginsberg, J. L. D., Mann, R. E., Rotgers, F. & Weekes, J. R. (2002). Motivational interviewing with criminal justice populations. In W. Miller & S. Rollnick (eds.), *Motivational Interviewing: Preparing people to change* (pp. 333–346). New York: Guilford.

Gittelson, N.L. Eacott, S.E. & Mehta, B.M. (1978). Victims of indecent exposure. *British Journal of Psychiatry, 132*, 61–66.

Glaser, D. (1964). *Effectiveness of a prison and parole system.* Indianapolis, IN: Bobbs-Merrill.

Glasgow, D., Horne, L., Calam, R. & Cox., A. (1994). Evidence, incidence, gender and age in sexual abuse of children perpetrated by children: Towards a developmental analysis of child sexual abuse. *Child Abuse Review, 3,* 196–210.

Glasgow, D., Osbourne, A. & Croxon, J. (2003). An assessment tool for investigating paedophile sexual interest using viewing time: An application of single case research methodology. *British Journal of Learning Disabilities, 31,* 96–102.

Goddard, C. & Hiller, P. (1993). Child sexual abuse: Assault in a violent context. *Australian Journal of Social Issues, 28,* 20–33.

Goggin, C. E. (1994). *Clinical versus actuarial prediction: A Meta-Analysis.* Unpublished manuscript, University of New Brunswick, St. John, New Brunswick.

Goldiamond, I. (1974). Toward a constructional approach to social problems: Ethical and constitutional issues raised by applied behavior analysis. *Behaviorism, 2,* 1–84.

Gordon, A. & Nicholaichuk, T. (1996). Applying the risk principle to the treatment of sexual offender. *Forum on Corrections Research, 8,* 36–38.

Gough, H. G. (1987). *California Psychological Inventory: Administrator's Guide.* Palo Alto, CA: Consulting Psychologists Press.

Gray, N. S., Brown, A. S., MacCulloch, M. J., Smith, J. & Snowden, R. J. (2005). An implicit test of the associations between children and sex in pedophiles. *Journal of Abnormal Psychology, 114,* 304–308.

Greenberg, D. M. (1998). Sexual recidivism in sex offenders. *Canadian Journal of Psychiatry-Review Canadienne De Psychiatrie, 43,* 459–465.

Greenfield, L. (1997). *Sex Offenses and Offenders: An analysis of data of rape and sexual assault.* Washington, DC: Bureau of Justice Statistics, US Department of Justice.

Gregory, J. & Lees, S. (1999). *Policing Sexual Assault.* London: Routledge.

Gresswell, D. M. & Hollin, C. R. (1992). Toward a new methodology of making sense of case material: An illustrative case involving attempted multiple murder. *Criminal Behaviour and Mental Health, 2,* 329–341.

Gretton, H. M., McBride, M., Hare, R. D., O'Shaughnessy, R. & Kumka, G. (2001). Psychopathy and recidivism in adolescent sex offenders. *Criminal Justice and Behavior, 28,* 4, 427–449.

Griffin, H. M. & Beech, A. (2004). An evaluation of the AIM framework for the assessment of adolescents who display sexually harmful behaviour. Available electronically from www.youth-justice-board.gov.uk

Griffin, H. M. & Beech, A. (in press). An evaluation of the Initial Assessment Tool (IAT) for the assessment of young people who have sexually abused, held in juvenile secure accommodation. London: Youth Justice Board.

Groth, A. N. (1978). Patterns of sexual assault against children and adolescents. In A. W. Burgess, A. N. Groth, L. L. Holstrom & S. M. Groi, (eds.), *Sexual Assault of Children and Adolescents* (pp. 3–24). Boston: Heath.

Groth, A. N. (1979). *Man Who Rape: The psychology of the offender.* New York: Plenum.

Groth, A. N., Burgess, A. W. & Holmstrom, L. L. (1977). Rape, power, anger and sexuality. *American Journal of Psychiatry, 134,* 1239–1248.

Groth, A. N., Hobson, W. & Garry, T. (1982). The child sexual molester: clinical observations. In J. Conte & D. Shore (eds.), *Social Work and Child Sexual Abuse,* New York: Haworth Press.

Groth, A. N., Longo, R. E. & McFadin, J. B. (1982). Undetected recidivism among rapists and child molesters. *Crime and Delinquency, 28,* 450–458.

Grove, W. M. & Meehl, P. E. (1996) Comparative efficiency of informal (subjective, impressionistic) and formal (mechanical, algorithmic) prediction procedures: The clinical–statistical controversy. *Psychology, Public Policy, and Law, 2,* 293–323.

Grove, W. M., Zald, D. H., Lebow, B. S., Snitz, B. E. & Nelson, C. (2000). Clinical versus mechanical prediction: A meta-analysis. *Psychological Assessment, 12*, 1, 19–30.

Grubin, D. (1997). Inferring predictors of risk sex offenders. *International Review of Psychiatry, 9*, 225–231.

Grubin, D. (1998). *Sex Offending Against Children: Understanding the risk. Police Research Series Paper 99.* Home Office, Policing and Reducing Crime Unit, Research, Development and Statistics Directorate, 50 Queen Anne's Gate, London, SW1H 9AT. Also available electronically at: http://www.homeoffice.gov.uk/rds/prgpdfs/fprs99.pdf.

Grubin, D. (1999). Actuarial and clinical assessment of risk in sex offenders. *Journal of Interpersonal Violence, 14*, 331–343.

Grubin, D. & Gunn, J. (1990). *The Imprisoned Rapist and Rape.* London: Department of Forensic Psychiatry, Institute of Psychiatry.

Grubin, D. & Wingate, S. (1996). Sexual offence recidivism: Prediction versus understanding. *Criminal Behaviour and Mental Health, 6*, 349–359.

Haaven, J. L. & Coleman, E. M. (2000). Treatment of the developmentally disabled sex offender. In D. R. Laws, S. M. Hudson & T. Ward (eds.), *Remaking Relapse Prevention with Sex Offenders: A sourcebook* (pp. 369–388). Thousand Oaks, CA: Sage.

Hagen, M. A. (1997). *Whores of the Court: The fraud of psychiatric testimony and the rape of American justice.* New York: Regan/Harper Collins.

Hagan, M. P. & Gust-Brey, K. L. (1999). A ten year longitudinal study of adolescent rapists upon return to the community. *International Journal of Offender Therapy and Comparative Criminology, 43*, 448–458.

Hall, G. C. N. (1995). Sexual offender recidivism revisited: A meta-analysis of recent treatment studies. *Journal of Consulting and Clinical Psychology, 63*, 802–809.

Hall, G, C. N. & Hirschman, R. (1991). Towards a theory of sexual aggression: A quadripartite model. *Journal of Consulting and Clinical Psychology, 55*, 111–112.

Hall, G. C. N., & Hirschman, R. (1992). Sexual aggression against children: A conceptual perspective of etiology. *Criminal Justice and Behavior, 19*, 8–23.

Hamilton, C. E. (1997) *Repeat Victimisation of Children.* Unpublished PhD Thesis, School of Psychology, University of Birmingham.

Hamilton, C. E. & Browne, K. D. (1998). The repeat victimisation of children: Should the concept be revised. *Aggression and Violent Behavior, 3*, 1, 47–60.

Hamilton C. E. & Browne, K. D. (1999). Recurrent abuse during childhood: A survey of referrals to police child protection units. *Child Maltreatment, 4*, 275–286.

Hanson, R. K. (1997*). The Development of a Brief Actuarial Risk Scale for Sexual Offence Recidivism.* (User Report No. 1997-04). Ottawa: Department of the Solicitor General of Canada. Available electronically from http://www.sgc.gc.ca/epub/corr/e199704/e 199704.htm

Hanson. R. K. (1998). What do we know about sex offender risk assessment? *Psychology, Public Policy and Law, 4*, 50–72.

Hanson, R. K. (2001a). *Age and Sexual Recidivism: A comparison of rapists and child molesters.* (Cat No.: JS42-96/2001). Department of the Solicitor General of Canada. Also available electronically at: http://www.sgc.gc.ca/EPub/Corr/eAge200101/eAge200101.htm

Hanson, R. K. (2001b). Sex offender risk assessment. In C. Hollin (Ed.), *Handbook of Offender Assessment and Treatment* (pp. 85–96). Chichester: Wiley.

Hanson, R. K. (2002). Recidivism and age: Follow-up data from 4,673 sexual offenders. *Journal of Interpersonal Violence, 17*, 1046–1062.

Hanson, R. K. (2003). Stable and acute risk factors in community supervision. Paper presented at the 13th Annual National Organisation for the Treatment of Abusers Conference, Heriot-Watt University, Edinburgh, September 2003.

Hanson, R. K. (2005a). Twenty years of progress in violence risk assessment. *Journal of Interpersonal Violence, 2*, 212–217.

Hanson, R. K. (2005b). The assessment of criminogenic needs of sexual offenders by community supervision officers: Reliability and validity. Paper presented at the Annual Conference of the Canadian Psychological Association, Montreal, Canada, June 2005.

Hanson, R. K. (2006a). Does Static-99 predict recidivism among older sexual offenders. *Sexual Abuse: A Journal of Research and Treatment, 18*, 4, 343–356.

Hanson, R. K. (2006b). What works: The principles of effective interventions with offenders. Paper presented at the 25th Annual Conference of the Association for the Treatment of Sexual Abusers, Chicago, IL, September 2006.

Hanson, R. K. & Bussière, M. T. (1996). *Predictors of Sexual Offender Recidivism: A meta-analysis.* (User Report No. 1996-04). Ottawa: Department of the Solicitor General of Canada. Also available electronically at: http://www.sgc.gc.ca/epub/corr/e199604/e199604.htm

Hanson, R. K. & Bussière, M. T. (1998). Predicting relapse: A meta-analysis of sexual offender recidivism studies. *Journal of Consulting and Clinical Psychology, 66*, 2, 348–362.

Hanson, R. K., Gizzarrelli, R. & Scott, H. (1994). The attitudes of incest offenders: Sexual entitlement and acceptance with children. *Criminal Justice and Behavior, 21*, 187–202.

Hanson, R. K., Gordon, A., Harris, A. J. R., Marques, J. K., Murphy, W., Quinsey, V. L. & Seto, M. C. (2002). First report of the collaborative outcome data project on the effectiveness of psychological treatment for sex offenders. *Sexual Abuse: A Journal of Research and Treatment, 14*, 2, 169–194.

Hanson. R. K., & Harris. A. (1998). *Dynamic Predictors of Sexual Recidivism.* Corrections Research Ottawa: Department of the Solicitor General Canada. Also available electronically at: http://www.sgc.gc.ca/epub/corr/e199801b/e199801b.htm

Hanson, R. K. & Harris, A. J. R. (2000a). *STABLE-2000.* Unpublished manuscript. Department of the Solicitor General Canada. Available from the authors at: Andrew.Harris@PSEPC-SPPCC.GC.CA

Hanson, R. K. & Harris, A. J. R. (2000b). *ACUTE-2000.* Unpublished manuscript. Department of the Solicitor General Canada. Available from the authors: at Andrew.Harris@PSEPC-SPPCC.GC.CA www.sgc.gc.ca/epub/corr/e200001a/e200001b/e200001b.htm

Hanson. R. K. & Harris. A. J. R. (2000c). Where should we intervene? Dynamic predictors of sexual offense recidivism. *Criminal Justice and Behavior, 27*, 1, 6–35.

Hanson. R. K. & Harris. A. (2001). A structured approach to evaluating change among sexual offenders. *Sexual Abuse: A Journal or Research and Treatment, 13*, 105–122.

Hanson, R. K., Morton, K. E. & Harris, A. J. R. (2003). Sexual offender recidivism risk: What we know and what we need to know. In R. A. Prentky, E. S. Janus & M. C. Seto. (eds.), *Understanding and Managing Sexually Coercive Behavior, New York Annals of the New York Academy of Sciences, 989*, 154–166.

Hanson, R. K. & Morton-Bourgon, K. E. (2004). *Predictors of Sexual Recidivism: An updated meta-analysis.* Corrections User Report No. 2004-02: Public Safety and Emergency Preparedness, Ottawa, Canada. Available from: http://www.psepc-sppcc.gc.ca/publications/corrections/pdf/200402_e.pdf

Hanson, R. K. & Morton-Bourgon, K. E. (2005). The characteristics of persistent sexual offenders: A meta-analysis of recidivism studies. *Journal of Consulting and Clinical Psychology, 73*, 1154–1163.

Hanson, R. K. & Scott, H. (1995). Assessing perspective-taking among sexual offenders, non-sexual criminal and non-offenders. *Sexual Abuse: A Journal of Research and Treatment, 7*, 259–277.

Hanson, R. K., Scott, H. & Steffy, R. A. (1995). A comparison of child molesters and non-sexual criminals: Risk predictors and long-term recidivism. *Journal of Research in Crime and Delinquency, 32*, 3, 325–337.

Hanson, R. K., Steffy, R. A. & Gauthier, R. (1993). Long term recidivism of child molesters. *Journal of Consulting and Clinical Psychology, 61*, 646–652.

Hanson, R. K. & Thornton, D. (2000). Improving risk assessment for sex offenders: A comparison of three actuarial scales. *Law and Human Behavior, 24,* 1, 119–136. (A description of Static-99 can also be found on the Public Safety Canada website: Hanson, R., & Thornon, D. (1999). Static 99: Improving actuarial risk assessments for sex offenders. Available at: http://ww2.ps-sp.gc.ca/publications/Corrections/199902_e.pdf

Hare, R. D. (1991). *Manual for the Revised Psychopathy Checklist.* Toronto, Canada: Multi-Health Systems.

Hare, R. D. (1996). Psychopathy: A clinical construct whose time has come. *Criminal Justice and Behavior, 23,* 25–54.

Hare, R. D. (2002). *Psychopathy and dangerousness: From risk assessment to risk reduction.* Paper presented at the National Organisation for the Treatment of Abusers: Annual Conference; The Challenge of Dangerous, Lancaster University, UK, September 2002.

Hare, R. D. (2003). *The Hare Psychopathy Checklist-Revised (PCL-R) (2nd edn.).* Toronto, Canada: Multi-Health Systems.

Hare, R. D., Clarke, D., Grann, M. & Thornton, D. (2000). Psychopathy and the predictive validity of the PCL-R: An international perspective. *Behavioral Sciences and the Law, 18,* 623–645.

Hare, R., Forth, A., Kosson, D. & Hare, R. (2003). *Psychopathy Checklist: Youth Version (PCL:YV).* Toronto, Canada: MultiHealth Systems, Inc.

Harkins, L. & Beech, A.R. (2007). Measurement of the effectiveness of sex offender treatment. *Aggression and Violent Behavior, 12,* 1, 36–44.

Harris, A. J. R. & Hanson, R. K. (2003). The Dynamic Supervision Project: Improving the community supervision of sex offenders. *Corrections Today, 65,* 62–64.

Harris, G. T. (2003). Men in his category have a 50% likelihood, but which half is he in? *Sexual Abuse: A Journal of Research and Treatment, 15,* 389–392.

Harris, G. T. & Rice, M. E. (1992). Reducing violence in institutions: Maintaining behavior change. In R. D. Peters, R. J. McMahon & V. L. Quinsey (eds.), *Aggression and Violence Throughout the Life Span* (pp. 261-282). Newbury Park, CA: Sage.

Harris, G. T., & Rice, M. E. (2003). Actuarial assessment of risk among sex offenders. In R. A. Prentky, E. S. Janus. & M. C. Seto (eds.), *Sexually Coercive Behavior: Understanding and management. Annals of the New York Academy of Sciences, 989,* 198–210.

Harris, G. T. & Rice, M. E. (2007). Adjusting actuarial violence risk assessments based on aging or the passage of time. *Criminal Justice and Behavior, 34,* 267–313.

Harris, G. T. & Rice, M. E. (in press). Characterizing the value of actuarial violence risk assessment. *Criminal Justice and Behavior.*

Harris, G. T., Rice, M. E. & Cormier, C. A. (2002). Prospective replication of the violent risk appraisal guide in predicting violent recidivism among forensic patients. *Law and Human Behavior, 26,* 4, 377–394.

Harris, G. T., Rice, M. E. & Quinsey, V. L. (2007). Abandoning evidence-based risk appraisal in forensic practice: Comments on Hart et al. *British Journal of Psychiatry, 15 August,* 2007 Electronic letters sent to the journal available from: http://bjp.rcpsych.org/cgi/eletters/190/49/s60#5674

Harris, G. T., Rice, M. E., Quinsey, V. L., Earls, C. & Chaplin, T. C. (1992). Maximizing the discriminant validity of phallometric assessment data. *Psychological Assessment, 4,* 502–511.

Harris G. T., Rice, M. E. & Quinsey, V. L. (1998). Appraisal and management of risk in sexual aggressors: Implications for Criminal Justice Policy. *Psychology, Public Policy and Law, 4,* 73–115.

Hart, S., Laws, D. R. & Kropp, P. R. (2003). The promise and the peril of sex offender risk assessment. In T. Ward., D. R. Laws. & S. M. Hudson (eds.), *Sexual Deviance: Issues and controversies* (pp. 207–225). Thousand Oaks, CA: Sage Publications.

Hart, S. D., Michie, C. & Cooke, D. J. (2007). Precision of actuarial risk assessment instruments: Evaluating the 'margins of error' of group v. individual predictions of violence. *British Journal of Psychiatry, 190* (suppl. 49), 60–65.

Hart, S. D., Webster, C. D. & Menzies, R. L. (1993). A note on portraying the accuracy of violence predictions. *Law and Human Behavior, 17,* 695–700.

Hartwell, L. L. (2001). Sex Offender Risk Appraisal Guide: Validity and utility for Hawaii sex offender risk assessments. Unpublished Clinical Research Project, American School of Professional Psychology, Hawaii Campus.

Hathaway, S. R. & McKinley, J.C. (1943). *The Minnesota Multiphasic Personality Inventory (MMPI).* Minneapolis: University of Minnesota Press.

Hazelwood, R. R. & Burgess, A. W. (1987). *Practical Aspects of Rape Investigation: A multi-disciplinary approach.* New York: Elsevier.

Hedges, L. V. & Olkin, I. (1985). *Statistical Methods for Meta-analysis.* New York: Academic Press.

Heilbrun, K. (1997). Prediction versus control methods relevant to risk assessment: The importance of legal decision-making context. *Law and Human Behavior, 21,* 347–359.

Herbert, M. (1987). *Behavioural Treatment of Problem Children: A practice manual.* London. Academic Press.

Herman, J. & Hirschman, L. (1981). Families at risk for father-daughter incest. *American Journal of Psychiatry, 138,* 7, 967–970.

HM Government (2006). *Working together to safeguard children: A guide to inter-agency working to safeguard and promote the welfare of children.* London: The Stationery Office.

Hobson, J., Shine, J., & Roberts, R. (2000). How do psychopaths behave in a prison therapeutic community? *Psychology, Crime and Law, 6,* 139–154.

Hoge, R. D., Andrews, D. A. & Leschied, A. W. (1996). An investigation of risk and protective factors in a sample of youthful offenders. *Journal of Child Psychology and Psychiatry, 37,* 419–424.

Hogue, T. E. (1993). Attitudes towards prisoners and sexual offenders. In N. C. Clark & G. Stephenson (eds.), *Division of clinical and legal psychology occasional papers: Sexual offenders.* Leicester, UK: British Psychological Society.

Hogue, T. E. (1995). Training multi-disciplinary teams to work with sex offenders: Effects on staff attitudes. *Psychology, Crime and Law, 1,* 227–235.

Holmes, T. H. & Rahe, R. H. (1967). The social adjustment rating scale. *Journal of Psychosomatic Research, 11,* 213–218.

Home Office, Departments of Health, Education & Science, Welsh Office (1991) *Working together under the Children Act 1989: A guide to arrangements for interagency co-operation for the protection of children from abuse* London: HMSO.

Home Office (1992). *Memorandum of good practice on video interviewing of child witnesses.* London: HMSO.

Home Office (1998). *Criminal statistics for England and Wales, 1997.* London: Home Office.

Home Office (1988). *The investigation of child abuse,* Circular 52/1988. London: Home Office.

Home Office (2005). Statistics of mentally disordered offenders in England and Wales 2004. *Home Office Statistical Bulletin.* 22/05. London: Home Office.

Hood, R., Shute, S., Feilzer, M. & Wilcox, A. (2002). Sex offenders emerging from long-term imprisonment: A study of their long-term reconviction rates and of parole board members' judgements of their risk. *British Journal of Criminology, 42,* 2, 371–394.

Howells, K. (1981). Adult sexual interest in children: considerations relevant to theories of etiology. In M. Cook and K. Howells (eds.), *Adult Sexual Interest in Children* (pp. 55–94). London: Academic Press.

Howitt, D. (1997). *Paedophiles and Sexual Offences Against Children.* Chichester: Jphn Wiley & Sons.

Hudson, S. M., Wales, D. S., Bakker, L. & Ward, T. (2002). Dynamic risk factors: The Kia Marama evaluation. *Sexual Abuse: A Journal of Research and Treatment, 14,* 2, 103–119.

Hudson, S. & Ward, T. (1997). Rape: Psychopathology and theory. In D. R. Laws & W. O'Donohue (eds.), *Sexual Deviance: Theory, assessment and treatment.* (pp. 332–355). New York: Guilford.

Hughes, B., Parker, H. & Gallagher, G. (1996). *Policing Child Sexual Abuse: The view from police practitioners*: London: Home Office, Police Research Group.

Huot, S. (1997). *Community based sex offender program evaluation project*. St. Paul, MN: Minnesota Department of Corrections: 1997 Report to the Legislature,

Jansson, K., Povey, D. & Kaiza, P. (2007). Violent and sexual crime. In S. Nicholas, C. Kershaw and A. Walker (eds.), *Crime in England and Wales 2006/07 (4th edition* (pp. 49–65). London: Home Office.

Janus, E. A. & Meehl, P. E. (1997). Assessing the legal standard for predictions of dangerousness in sex offender commitment proceedings. *Psychology, Public Policy and Law. 3*, 33–64.

Jehu, D. (1988). *Beyond Sexual Abuse: Therapy with women who were childhood victims*, Chichester: Wiley.

John Jay College of Criminal Justice (2004). *The nature and scope of the problem of sexual abuse of minors by Catholic priests and deacons in the United States*. Report to the United States Conference of Catholic Bishops. New York: John Jay College of Criminal Justice.

Jones, L. M., Finkelhor, D. & Kopiec, K. (2001). Why is sexual abuse declining? A survey of state child protection administration. *Child Abuse and Neglect, 25*, 1139–1158.

Jones, L. M., Finkelhor, D. & Halter, S. (2006). Child maltreatment trends in the 1990s. Why does neglect differ from sexual and physical abuse? *Child Maltreatment, 11*, 107–120.

Joseph, S. & Linley, P. A. (2006). *Positive Therapy: A meta-theory for positive psychological practice*. London: Routledge.

Kear-Colwell, J. & Pollock, P. (1997). Motivation or confrontation: Which approach to use with child sex offenders? *Criminal Justice and Behavior, 24*, 20–33.

Kekes. J. (1997). *Moral Wisdom and Good Lives*. Ithaca, NY: Cornell University Press.

Kelly, L., Lovett, J. & Regan, L. A. (2005). *A Gap or a Chasm: Attribution in reported rape cases. Home Office Research Study, 293*. London: Home Office.

Keltner, A. A., Marshall, P. G. & Marshall, W. L. (1981). Measurement and correlation of assertiveness and social fear in a prison population. *Corrective and Social Psychiatry, 27*, 41–47.

Kenworthy, T., Adams, C. E., Bilby, C., Brooks-Gordon, B. & Fenton, M. (2004). Psychological interventions for those who have sexually offended or are at risk of offending. *Cochrane database of systematic reviews, 4*, 1–50. Art. No.: CD004858. DOI: 10.1002/ 14651858. CD004858.

Kiehl, K. A., Hare, R. D., McDonald, J. J. & Brink, J. (1999). Semantic and affective processing in psychopaths: An event-related potential (ERP) study. *Psychophysiology, 36*, 765–774.

Klimecki, M., Jenkinson, J. & Wilson, L. (1994). A study of recidivism among offenders with an intellectual disability. *Journal of Intellectual and Developmental Disability, 19*, 3, 209–219.

Knight, R. A., Carter, D. L. & Prentky, R. A. (1989). A system for the classification of child molesters: Reliability and application. *Journal of Interpersonal Violence, 4*, 3–23.

Knight, R. A. & Prentky, R. A. (1990). Classifying sexual offenders: The development and corroboration of taxonomic models. In W. L. Marshall, D. R. Laws & H. E. Barbaree (eds.), *The Handbook of Sexual Assault: Issues, theories, and treatment of the offender* (pp. 23–52). New York: Academic Press.

Knight, R. A. & Thornton, D. (2007). Evaluating and improving risk assessment schemes for sexual recidivism: A long-term follow-up of convicted sexual offenders. Available electronically from: http://www.ncjrs.gov/pdffilesl/nij/grants/217618.pdf

Koehler, J. J. (1996). The base rate fallacy reconsidered: Descriptive, normative, and methodological challenges. *Behavioral and Brain Sciences, 19*, 1–17.

Lalumière, M. L. & Harris, G. T. (1998). Common questions regarding the use of phallometric testing with sexual offenders. *Sexual Abuse: A Journal of Research and Treatment, 10*, 3, 227–237.

Lalumière, M. L. & Quinsey, V. L. (1994). The discriminability of rapists from non-sex-offenders using phallometric measures: A meta-analysis. *Criminal Justice and Behavior, 21*, 150–175.

Lanagan, P. A., Schmitt, E. L. & Durose, M. R. (2003). *Recidivism of sex offenders released from prison in 1994*. Washington, DC: US Department of Justice, Office of Justice Programs, Bureau of Justice Statistics.

Lang, P. (1970). Stimulus control, responses control and the desensitisation of fear. In D. Lewis (ed.), *Learning Approaches to Therapeutic Behavior.* Chicago, IL: Aldine.

Lang, R. & Frenzel, R. (1988). How sex offenders lure children. *Annals of Sex Research, 1,* 303–317.

Långström, N. & Grann, M. (2000). Risk for criminal recidivism among young sex offenders. *Journal of Interpersonal Violence, 15,* 8, 855–871.

Långström, N., Sjostedt, G. & Grann, M. (2004). Psychiatric disorders and recidivism in sex offenders. *Sexual Abuse: A Journal of Research and Treatment, 16,* 139–150.

Langton, C. M., Barbaree, H. E., Harkins, L. & Peacock, E. J. (2006). Sexual offenders' response to treatment and its association with recidivism as a function of psychopathy. *Sexual Abuse: A Journal of Research and Treatment, 18,* 99–120.

Langton, C. M., Barbaree, H. E., Seto, M. C., Peacock, E. J., Harkins, L. & Hansen, K. T. (2007). Actuarial assessment of risk for reoffense among adult sex offenders: Evaluating the predictive accuracy of the Static-2002 and five other instruments. *Criminal Justice and Behavior, 34,* 37–59.

Lanning, K. (1992a). *Child Molesters: A behavioural analysis.* Arlington, VA: National Center for Missing and Exploited Children.

Lanning, K. (1992b). *Child Sex Rings: A behavioural analysis.* Arlington, VA: National Center for Missing and Exploited Children.

Lanning, K. (1996) Criminal investigation of suspected child abuse on Section 1: Criminal investigation of sexual victimisation of children. In J. N. Briere, L. Berliner, J. Bulkley, C. Jenny. & T. Reid (eds.), *The APSAC Handbook on Child Maltreatment, American professional society on the abuse of children* (pp. 247–263). Beverley Hills, CA: Sage.

Laws, D. R. (2003). Penile plethysmography: Will we ever get it right? In T. Ward, D. R. Laws. & S. M. Hudson, *Sexual Deviance: Issues and controversies* (pp. 82–102). Thousand Oaks, CA: Sage.

Laws, D. R. & Marshall, W. L. (2003). A brief history of behavioral and cognitive behavioral approaches to sexual offenders: Part 1. Early developments, *Sexual Abuse: A Journal of Research and Treatment, 15,* 75–92.

Lazarus, R. S. & Folkman, S. (1984). *Stress, Appraisal, and Coping.* New York. Springer.

Lea, S., Auburn, T. & Kibblewhite, K. (1999). Working with sex offenders: The perceptions, and experiences of professionals and paraprofessionals. *International Journal of Offender Therapy and Comparative Criminology, 43,* 103–119.

Lee-Evans, J. M. (1994) Background to behaviour analysis. In M. McMurran & J. Hodge (eds.), *The Assessment of Criminal Behaviour of Clients in Secure Setting.* (pp. 6–34). London. Jessica Kingsley Publishers.

Lees, S. (1996). *Carnal Knowledge: Rape on trial.* London: Hamish Hamilton.

Leventhal, J. M. (1988). Can child maltreatment be predicted during the peri-natal period: Evidence of longitudinal cohort studies. *Journal of Reproductive and Infant Psychology, 6,* 139–161.

Levine, E. M. & Kanin, E.J. (1987). Sexual violence among dates and acquaintances: trends and their implications for marriage and family. *Journal of Family Violence, 2,* 55–65.

Leue, A., Borchard, B. & Hoyer, J. (2004). Mental disorders in a forensic sample of sexual offenders. *European Psychiatry, 19,* 123–130.

Lieb, R. (2003). Joined-up worrying: The Multi-Agency Public Protection Panels. In A. Matravers (ed.), *Sex Offenders in the Community: Managing and reducing the risks* (pp. 207–218). Cullompton, Devon: Willan.

Lindsay, W. R., Smith, A. H. W., Law, J., Quinn, L., Anderson, A., Smith, A., Overend, T. & Allan, R. (2002). A treatment service for sex offenders and abusers with learning disability: Characteristics of referral and evaluation. *Journal of Applied Research in Learning Disabilities, 15,* 166–174.

Linehan, M. M. (1993). *Cognitive-behavioural Treatment of Borderline Personality Disorder.* New York: Guilford Press.

Linley, P. A. & Joseph, S. (2004). *Positive Psychology in Practice.* Chichester: Wiley.

Linz, D. & Malamuth, N. (1993). *Pornography.* London: Sage.

Litwack, T. R. (2001). Actuarial versus clinical assessments of dangerousness. *Psychology, Public Policy and Law, 7, 2,* 409–443.

Lloyd, S. & Burman, M. (1996). Specialist Police Units & the Joint Investigation of Child Abuse, *Child Abuse Review, 5,* 4–17.

Lloyd, C., Mair, G. & Hough, M. (1994). *Explaining Reconviction Rates: A critical Analysis,* London: Home Office. Home Office Publications Unit, 50, Queen Anne's Gate, London, SW1 9AT, England.

Looman, J. (2006). Comparison of two risk assessment instruments for sexual offenders. *Sexual Abuse: A Journal of Research and Treatment, 18,* 193–206.

Looman, J., Abracen, J. & Nicholiachuk, T. P. (2000). Recidivism among treated sexual offenders and matched controls: Data from the regional treatment centre (Ontario). *Journal of Interpersonal Violence, 15,* 279–290.

Looman, J., Abracen, J., Serin, R. & Marquis, P. (2005). Psychopathy, treatment change and recidivism in high risk high need sexual offenders. *Journal of Interpersonal Violence, 20,* 549–568.

Looman, J., Dickie, I. & Abracen, J. (2005). Responsivity in the treatment of sexual offenders. *Trauma, Violence, and Abuse, 6,* 330–353.

Lorenz, K. (1966). *On Aggression.* London: Metheun.

Lösel, F. & Schmucker, M. (2005). The effectiveness of treatment for sexual offenders: A comprehensive meta-analysis. *Journal of Experimental Criminology, 1,* 117–146.

Loving, J. L. (2002). Treatment planning with the Psychopathy Checklist–Revised (PCL-R). *International Journal of Offender Therapy and Comparative Criminology, 46,* 281–293.

Malamuth, N. (2001). Pornography. In N. J. Smelser & P. B. Baltes (ed.). *International Encyclopedia of Social and Behavioral Sciences,* 17 (pp. 11816–11821). Elsevier: Amsterdam, New York.

Malamuth, N. M. & Brown, L. M. (1994). Sexually aggressive men's perception of women's communication: Testing three explanations. *Journal of Personality and Social Psychology, 67,* 699–712.

Malamuth, N. M. (1996). The confluence model of sexual aggression. In D. M. Buss. & N. M. Malamuth (eds.), *Sex, Power, Conflict: Evolutionary and feminist perspectives* (pp. 269–295). NY: Oxford University Press.

Malcolm, P. B., Andrews, D. A. & Quinsey, V. L. (1993). Discriminant and predictive validity of phallometrically measured sexual age and gender preferences. *Journal of Interpersonal Violence, 8,* 486–501.

Mandeville-Norden, R., Beech, A. R. & Middleton, D. (2006). The development of the Sex Offender Psychometric Scoring System (SOPSSys) for use in the Probation Service. *Probation Journal, 53,* 89–94.

Mann, R. E. (1999). The sex offender treatment programme, HM Prison Service England and Wales. In S. Hofling., D. Drewes & I. Epple-Waigel (eds.), *Auftrag prevention: Offensive gegen sexuellen kindesmibbrauch* (pp. 346-352). Munich: Atwerb-verlag KG Publikation.

Mann, R. E. (2000). Managing resistance and rebellion in relapse prevention. In D. R. Laws, S. H. Hudson & T. Ward (eds.), *Remaking Relapse Prevention* (pp. 187–200). London: Sage.

Mann, R. E., Ginseberg, J. I. D. & Weekes, J. R. (2002). Motivational interviewing with offenders. In M. McMurran (ed.), *Motivating Offenders to Change: A guide to enhancing engagement in therapy* (pp. 87–102). Chichester: Wiley.

Mann, R. E. & Thornton, D. (1998). The evolution of a multisite sexual offender treatment program. In W. L. Marshall., Y. M. Fernanadez., S. M. Hudson & T. Ward, (eds.), *Sourcebook of Treatment Programs for Sexual Offenders* (pp. 47–58). New York: Plenum.

Marlatt, G. A. & Gordon, J. R. (1985). *Relapse Prevention: Maintenance Strategies in the Treatment of Addictive Behaviors.* New York: Guilford Press.

Marques, J. K. (1982). *Relapse prevention: A self-control model for the treatment of sex offenders.* Paper presented at the 7th Annual Forensic Mental Health Conference, Asilomar, CA, March 1982.

Marques, J. K. (1999). How to answer the question: Does sex offender treatment work? *Journal of Interpersonal Violence, 14*, 4, 437–451.

Marques, J. K., Day, D. M., Nelson, C. & West, M. A. (1994). Effects of cognitive behavioural treatment on sex offenders' recidivism: Preliminary results of a longitudinal study. *Criminal Justice and Behaviour, 21*, 28–54.

Marques, J. K., Wiederanders, M., Day, D. M., Nelson, C. & van Ommeren, A. (2005). Effects of a relapse prevention program on sexual recidivism: Final results from California's Sex Offender Treatment and Evaluation Program (SOTEP). *Sexual Abuse: A Journal of Research and Treatment, 17*, 79–107.

Marshall, P. (1994). Reconviction of imprisoned sexual offenders. *Home Office Research Bulletin, 36*, 23–29.

Marshall, P. (1997). The prevalence of convictions for sexual offending. *Home Office Research and Statistics Directorate Research Findings, 55*. London: Home Office.

Marshall, W. L. (1988). The use of sexually explicit stimuli by rapists, child molesters and non-offenders. *Journal of Sex Research, 25*, 267–288.

Marshall, W. L. (2000). Adult sexual offenders against women. In C.R. Hollin (ed.). *Handbook of Offender Assessment and Treatment* (pp. 333–348). Chichester. John Wiley & Son.

Marshall, W. L. (2005). Therapist style in sexual offender treatment: Influence on indices of change. *Sexual Abuse: A Journal of Research and Treatment, 17*, 109–116.

Marshall, W. L. & Barbaree, H. E. (1988). The long-term evaluation of a behavioral treatment program for child molesters. *Behavior, Research and Therapy, 6*, 499–511.

Marshall, W. L. & Barbaree, H. E. (1990). An integrated theory of the etiology of sexual offending. In W. L. Marshall, D. R. Laws and H. E. Barbaree (eds.), *Handbook of Sexual Assault: Issues, theories, and treatment of the offender* (pp. 257–275). New York: Plenum.

Marshall. W. L., Eccles, A. & Barbaree, H. E. (1991). The treatment of exhibitionists: A focus on sexual deviance versus cognitive and relationship features. *Behavior Research and Therapy, 29*, 2, 129–135.

Marshall, W. L., Fernandez, Y. M., Serran, G. A., Mulloy, R., Thornton, D., Mann, R. E., & Anderson, D. (2003). Process variables in the treatment of sexual offenders: A review of the relevant literature. *Aggression and Violent Behavior, 8*, 205–234.

Marshall, W. L., Hudson, S. M. & Hodkinson, S. (1993). The importance of attachment bonds in the development of juvenile sex offending. In H. E. Barbaree, W. L. Marshall & S. M. Hudson (eds.), *The Juvenile Sex Offender* (pp. 164–181). New York: Guildford Press.

Marshall, W. L., Jones, R., Ward, T., Johnston, P., & Barbaree, H. E. (1991). Treatment outcome with sex offenders. *Psychology Review, 11*, 465–485.

Marshall, W. L. & Serran, G. A. (2004). The role of the therapist in offender treatment. *Psychology, Crime, and Law, 10*, 309–320.

Marshall, W. L., Serran, G. A., Fernandez, Y. M., Mulloy, R., Mann, R. E. & Thornton, D. (2003). Therapist characteristics in the treatment of sexual offenders: Tentative data on their relationship with indices of behavior change. *Journal of Sexual Aggression, 9*, 25–30.

Marshall, W. L., Ward, T. Mann, R. E., Moulden, H., Fernandez, Y. M., Serran, G. & Marshall, L. E. (2005). Working positively with sexual offenders: Maximizing the effectiveness of treatment. *Journal of Interpersonal Violence, 20*, 1096–1114.

Martin, E.K., Taft, C.T. & Resick, P.A. (2007). A review of marital rape. *Aggression and Violent Behavior, 12*, 329–347.

Martinson, R. (1974). What works? Questions and answers about prison reform. *The Public Interest, 35*, 22–54.

Maruna, S. (2001). *Making Good: How ex-offenders reform and rebuild their lives.* Washington, DC: American Psychological Association.

Mash, E. J. & Hunsley, J. (1990). Behavior assessment: A contemporary approach. In A. S. Bellack, M. Hersen & A. E. Kazdin (eds.), *International Handbook of Behavior Modification and Theory* (pp. 87–106). New York: Plenum Press.

Maslow, A. H. (1968). *Towards a Psychology of Being.* New York: Van Nostrand.

Masson, H. & Erooga, M. (1999). *Children and Young People who Sexually Abuse Others.* London: Routledge.

Masten, A. S. & Reed, M-G. J. (2005). Resilience in development. In C. R. Snyder & A. J. Lopez (eds.), *The Handbook of Positive Psychology* (pp. 74–88). Oxford: Oxford University Press.

Matravers, A. (2003). Setting some boundaries: rethinking responses to sex offenders. In A. Matravers (ed.), *Sex Offenders in the Community: Managing and reducing the risks.* (pp. 1–29). Cullompton, Devon: Willan.

Matthews, G. & Deary, I. J. (1998). *Personality Traits.* Cambridge: Cambridge University Press.

Matza, D. (1964). *Delinquency and Drift.* New York: Wiley.

MacDonald, J. M. (1973). *Indecent Exposure.* Springfield, IL: Charles C. Thomas.

McDonald, W. R. and Associates (2005). *Child Maltreatment 2003: Reports from the States to the National Child Abuse and Neglect Data System.* Washington, DC: US Department of Health and Human Services, Children's Bureau.

McElroy, S. L., Soutullo, C. A., Taylor, P., Nelson, E. B., Beckman, D. A., Brusman, L. A., Ombaba, J. M., Strakowski, S. M. & Keck, P. E. Jr. (1999). Psychiatric features of 36 men convicted sexual offences. *Journal of Clinical Psychiatry, 60*: 414–420.

McGrath, R. J. (1990). Assessment of sexual aggression: Practical clinical interviewing strategies. *Journal of Interpersonal Violence, 5*, 507–519.

McGrath, R. J., Hoke, S. E. & Vojtisek, J. E. (1998). Cognitive-behavioral treatment of sex offenders. *Criminal Justice and Behavior, 25*, 203–225.

McGuire, J. (1995). *What Works: Reducing offending – Guidelines from research and practice.* Chichester: Wiley.

McGuire, T. J. (2000). Correctional institution based sex offender treatment: A lapse behavior study. *Behavioral Sciences and the Law, 18*, 57–71.

McGuire, J. (2000). Explanations of criminal behavior. In J. McGuire, T. Mason & A. O'Kane (eds.), *Behavior, Crime and Legal Processes: A guide for legal practitioners* (pp. 135–159). Chichester: Wiley.

McGuire, R. J., Carlisle, J. M. & Young, B. G. (1965). Sexual deviations as conditioned behavior: A hypothesis. *Behavior Research and Therapy, 2*, 185–190.

Maguire, M., Kemshall, H., Noaks, L. & Wincup, E. (2001). Risk management of sexual and violent offenders: The work of public protection panels. *Police Research Series Paper 139.* London: Home Office.

McNeil, D. E., Sandberg, D. A. & Binder, R. L (1998). The relationship between confidence and accuracy in clinical assessment of psychiatric patients' potential for violence. *Law and Human Behavior, 22*, 655–669.

Meehl, P. E. & Rosen, A. (1955). Antecedent probability and the efficiency of psychometric signs, patterns or cutting scores. *Psychological Bulletin, 52*, 194–216.

Merrington, S., Hine, J. & Stafford, E. (2001). *A Handbook for Evaluating Probation Work with Offenders.* London: Home Office.

Mezzo. B. & Gravier. B. (2001). La récidive des délinquants sexuels: une réalité difficile à cerner: Sexual offenders recidivism: The difficulty to define reality. *Medecine et Hygiene, 59*, 2339, 659–666.

Middleton, D. (2003). Assessment of individuals convicted of child pornography offences. *National Probation Service Circular* 14/2003. London: Home Office.

Miller, S. D., Duncan B. L. & Hubble, M. A. (1997). *Escape from Babel: Toward a unifying language for psychotherapy practice.* New York: Norton Press.

Miller, W. R. & Rollnick, S. (2002). *Motivational Interviewing: Preparing people for change* (2nd edition.). New York: Guilford Press.

Mills, J. F. (2005). Advances in the assessment and prediction of interpersonal violence. *Journal of Interpersonal Violence, 2*, 236–241.

Mills, J. F., Kroner, D. G. & Hemmati, T. (2003). Predicting violent behavior through a static-stable variable lens. *Journal of Interpersonal Violence, 8*, 891–904.

Minnesota Department of Corrections (2000). Community Based Sex Offender Program Evaluation Project: 1999. Report to the Legislature. Minnesota Department of Corrections 1450 Energy Park Drive, Suite 200, St. Paul, MN 55108-5219. Available electronically at: http://www.corr.state.mn.us/publications/documents/1999%20CBSOPEP%20Report%20to%20the%20Legislature.PDF

Moore, B. (1996). *Risk Assessment: A practitioner's guide to predicting harmful behaviour.* London: Whiting and Birch.

Monahan, J. (1981). *The Clinical Prediction of Violent Behavior.* Washington, DC: US Government Policing Office.

Monahan, J. (1984). The prediction of violent behavior: Toward a second generation of theory and policy. *American Journal of Psychiatry, 141*, 10–15.

Monahan, J. (1996). Violence prediction: The past twenty and the next twenty years. *Criminal Justice and Behavior, 23*, 107–120.

Morley, R. & Mullender, A. (1994). Preventing domestic violence to women. *Police Research Group – Crime Prevention Series: Paper 48.* London: Home Office.

Mosher, D. L. & Sirkin, M. (1984). Measuring a macho personality constellation. *Journal of Personality, 18*, 150–163.

Mossman, D. (1994). Assessing predictions of violence: Being accurate about accuracy. *Journal of Consulting and Clinical Psychology, 62*, 783–792.

Mossman, D. & Sellke, T. M. (2007). Avoiding errors about 'margins of error'. *British Journal of Psychiatry, 5 July,* 2007. Electronic letters sent to the journal available from: http://bjp.rcpsych.org/cgi/eletters/190/49/s60#5674

Mrazek, P. J. & Haggerty, R. J. (1994). *Reducing Risks for Mental Disorders: Frontiers for preventive intervention.* Washington, DC: National Academy Press.

Mufson, S. & Kranz, R. (1993). *Straight Talk about Date Rape.* NY: Facts on File, Inc.

Mulvey, E. P. & Lidz, C. W. (1998). Clinical prediction of violence as a conditional judgement. *Social Psychiatry and Psychiatric Epidemiology, 33*, S107–S113.

Murphy, F. M. (1996). *The Child Protection Unit.* Aldershot: Avebury Ashgate Publishing Ltd.

Murphy, W. D. (1997). Exhibitionism: Psychopathology and theory. In D. R. Laws & W. O'Donohue (eds.), *Sexual Deviance: Theory, assessment and treatment.* (pp. 22–39). New York: Guilford.

Myhill, A. & Allen, J. (2002). Rape and sexual assault of women: The extent of the problem. *Home Office Study, 237.* London: Home Office. Home Office Publications Unit, 50, Queen Anne's Gate, London, SW1 9AT, England.

National Organisation for the Treatment of Abusers: NOTA (2002). Answers to frequently asked questions about sex offending. *NOTANews, 43*, 13–20.

Nelson, M., Herlihy, B. & Oescher, J. (2002). A survey of counsellor's attitudes towards sex offenders. *Journal of Mental Health Counselling, 24*, 51–67.

Nicholaichuk, T., Gordon, A., Andre, G. & Gu, D. (1995) *Long-term outcome of the Clearwater Sex Offender Treatment Program.* Paper presented to the 14th Annual Conference of the Association for the Treatment of Sexual Abusers, New Orleans, October 1995.

Nicholaichuk, T., Gordon, A., Andre, G., Gu, D. & Wong, S. (2000). Outcome of an institutional sexual offender treatment program: A comparison between treated and untreated offenders. *Sexual Abuse: A Journal of Research and Treatment, 12*, 139–153.

Nichols, H. R. & Molinder, I. (1984). *Manual for the Multiphasic Sex Inventory*. Available from, Nichols and Molinder, 437 Bowes Drive, Tacoma, WA 98466-70747 USA.

Norris, C. (1992, winter). Sex offender treatment: Confronting 'thinking errors' is central to success. *Federal Prisons Journal, 2*, 29–31.

Novaco, R. (1975). *Anger Control: The development and evaluation of an experimental treatment*. Lexington: MA: D.C. Heath.

Nowicki, S. (1976). *Adult Nowicki-Strickland internal-external locus of control scale*. Test Manual available from S. Nowicki, Jr., Department of Psychology, Emory University, Atlanta, GA 30322, USA.

Nufield, J. (1982). *Parole decision-making in Canada: Research towards decision guidelines*. Ottawa, Canada: Ministry of Supply and Services Canada.

Nunes, K. L., Firestone, P., Bradford, J. M., Greenberg, D. M. & Broom, I (2002). A comparison of modified versions of the Static-99 and the Sex Offender Risk Appraisal Guide. *Sex Abuse: A Journal of Research and Treatment, 14*, 253–269.

O'Callaghan, D. (2002). Providing a research informed service for young people who sexually abuse. In M. C. Calder (ed.), *Young People Who Sexually Abuse: Building the evidence base for your practice* (pp. 5–25). Lyme Regis: Russell House Publishing.

Owen, G. & Steele, N. M. (1991). Incest offenders after treatment. In M. Q. Patton (ed.). *Family Sexual Abuse*. London: Sage.

Patterson, G. R., Littman, R. A. & Bricker, W. A. (1967). Assertive behavior in children: A step toward a theory of aggression. *Monographs of the Society for Research in Child Development* (Serial No. 113), *32*, 5.

Pavlov, I. P. (1927). *Conditioned Reflexes*. New York: Oxford University Press.

Piaget, J. (1932). *The Moral Judgement of the Child*. London: Routledge.

Pinheiro P. S. (ed.) (2006). *World Report on Violence Against Children: Secretary General's Study on Violence Against Children*. New York: United Nations.

Pirog-Good, M. (1992). Sexual abuse in dating relationships. In E. C. Viano (ed.), *Intimate Violence: Interdisciplinary Perspectives* (pp. 101–109). Washington, DC: Taylor & Francis.

Pithers, W. D. (1990). Relapse prevention with sexual aggressors: A method for maintaining therapeutic change and enhancing external supervision. In. W. L. Marshall, D. R. Laws & H. E. Barbaree (eds.), *Handbook of Sexual Assault: Issues, theories and treatment of the offender* (pp. 363–385). New York: Plenum.

Pithers, W. D., Kashima, K. M., Cumming, G. F. & Beal, L. S. (1988). Relapse prevention: A method of enhancing maintenance of change in sex offenders. In A. C. Salter (ed.), *Treating Child Sex Offenders and Victims: A practical guide* (pp. 131–170). Newbury Park, CA: Sage.

Pithers, W. D., Marques, J. K., Gibat, C. C. & Marlatt, G. A. (1983). Relapse prevention with sexual aggressors: A self-control model of treatment and maintenance of change. In J. C. Greer & I. R. Stuart (eds.), *The Sexual Aggressor: Current perspectives on treatment* (pp. 214–239). New York: Van Nostrand Reinhold.

Plotnikoff, J. & Woolfson, R. (1995). *Prosecuting Child Abuse: An evaluation of the Government's speedy progress policy*. London: Blackstone Press.

Polizzi, D. M., MacKenzie, D. L. & Hickman, L. J. (1999). What works in adult sex offender treatment? A review of prison and non-prison based treatment programs. *International Journal of Offender Therapy and Comparative Criminology, 43*, 357–374.

Porter, S., Birt, A. R. & Boer, D. P. (2001). Investigation of the criminal and conditional release profiles of Canadian federal offenders as a function of psychopathy and age. *Law and Human Behavior, 25*, 647–661.

Porter, S., Fairweather, D., Drugge, J., Herve, H., Birt, A. & Boer, D. P. (2000). Profiles of psychopathy in incarcerated sexual offenders. *Criminal Justice and Behavior, 27*, 2, 216–233.

Porteus, S. D. (1955). *The Maze Test: Recent advances.* Palo Alto, CA: Pacific Books.

Powell, A. (2007). *Paedophiles, Child Abuse and the Internet.* Oxford: Radcliffe.

Prentky, R. A. & Burgess, A. W. (2000). *Forensic Management of Sexual Offenders: Perspectives in sexuality, behavior, research and therapy.* New York: Kluwer Academic/Plenum Publishers.

Prentky, R. A., Haris, B., Frizzell, K. & Righthand, S. (2000). An actuarial procedure for assessing risk with juveniles sex offenders. *Sexual Abuse: A Journal of Research and Treatment, 12,* 71–93.

Prentky, R. A. & Lee, A. F. S. (2007). Effect of age-at-release on long term sexual re-offence rates in civilly committed sexual offenders. *Sexual Abuse: A Journal of Research and Treatment, 119,* 43–59.

Prentky, R. A. & Knight, R. A. (1991). Identifying critical dimensions for discriminating among rapists. *Journal of Consulting and Clinical Psychology, 59,* 643–661.

Prentky, R. A., Knight, R. A. & Lee, A. F. S. (1997a). Risk factors associated with recidivism among extrafamilial child molesters. *Journal of Consulting and Clinical Psychology, 65,* 141–149.

Prentky, R. A., Lee, A. F. S, Knight, R. A. & Cerce, O. (1997b). Recidivism rates among child molesters and rapists: A methodological analysis. *Law and Human Behavior, 21,* 6, 635–659.

Preston, D. L. (2000). Treatment resistance in corrections. *Forum on Corrections Research, 12,* 24–28.

Print, B., Morrison, M. & Henniker, J. (2001). An inter-agency assessment and framework for young people who sexually abuse: Principles, processes and practicalities. In M. C. Calder (ed.), *Juveniles and Children who Sexually Abuse: Frameworks for assessment.* (pp. 271–281). Lyme Regis. Russell House Publishing.

Prior, V., Glaser, D. & Lynch, M. A. (1997). Responding to child sexual abuse: The criminal justice system. *Child Abuse Review, 6,* 128–140.

Prochaska, J. O. & DiClemente, C. C. (1982). Transtheoretical therapy: Toward a more integrative model of change. *Psychotherapy: Theory, Research, and Practice, 19,* 276–288.

Proulx, J., Pellerin, B., McKibben, A., Aubut, J. & Ouimet, M. (1997). Static and dynamic risk predictors of recidivism in sexual offenders. *Sexual Abuse: A Journal of Research and Treatment, 9,* 7–27.

Proulx, J., Pellerin, B., McKibben, A., Aubut, J. & Ouimet, M. (1999). Recidivism in sexual aggressors: Static and dynamic predictors of recidivism in sexual aggressors. *Sexual Abuse: A Journal of Research and Treatment, 11,* 117–129.

Quackenbush, R. (2000). *The assessment of sex offenders in Ireland and the Irish sex offender risk tool.* Unpublished manuscript, Granada Institute, Dublin, Ireland.

Quinsey, V. L., Chaplin, T. C. & Carrigan, W. F. (1980). Biofeedback and signaled punishment in the modification on appropriate sexual age preferences. *Behavior Therapy, 11,* 567–576.

Quinsey, V. L. & Earls, C. M. (1990). The modification of sexual preferences. In. W. L. Marshall, D. R. Laws & H. E. Barbaree (eds.), *Handbook of Sexual Assault: Issues, theories and treatment of the offender* (pp. 279–295). New York: Plenum Press.

Quinsey, V. L., Harris, G. T., Rice, M. E. & Cormier, C. A. (1998). *Violent Offenders: Appraising and managing risk.* Washington, DC: American Psychological Association.

Quinsey, V. L., Harris, G. T., Rice, M. E. & Cormier, C. A. (2006). *Violent Offenders: Appraising and managing risk (Second Edition).* Washington, DC: American Psychological Association.

Quinsey, V. L., Harris, G. T., Rice, M. E. & Lalumière, M. (1993). Assessing treatment efficacy in outcome studies of sex offenders. *Journal of Interpersonal Violence, 8,* 512–532.

Quinsey, V. L., Khanna, A. & Malcolm, B. (1998). A retrospective evaluation of the regional treatment centre sex offender treatment program. *Journal of Interpersonal Violence, 13,* 621–644.

Quinsey, V. L., Lalumière, M. L., Rice, M. E. & Harris, G. T. (1995). Predicting sexual offenses. In J. C. Campbell (ed.), *Assessing Dangerousness: Violence by sexual offenders, batterers and child abusers* (pp. 114–138). London: Sage.

Quinsey, V. L. & Maguire, A. (1983). Offenders remanded for a psychiatric examination: Perceived treatability and disposition. *International Journal of Law and Psychiatry, 6,* 193–205.

Quinsey, V. L., Maguire, A. & Varney, G. W. (1983). Assertion and over controlled hostility among mentally disordered murderers. *Journal of Consulting and Clinical Psychology, 51,* 550–556.

Quinsey, V. L., Rice, M. E. & Harris, G. T. (1995). Actuarial prediction of sexual recidivism. *Journal of Interpersonal Violence, 10,* 85–105.

Raymond, N. C., Colman, E., Ohlerking, F., Christenson, G. A. & Miner, M. (1999). Psychiatric comorbidity in pedophilic sex offenders. *American Journal of Psychiatry, 156,* 786–788.

Renzetti, C. M. (1992). *Violent Betrayal: Partner abuse in lesbian relationships.* London: Sage.

Rhodes, W. & Brown, W. (1991). *Why Some Children Succeed Despite the Odds.* New York: Praeger.

Rice, M. E. & Harris, G. T. (1997). Cross-validation and extension of the violence risk appraisal guide for child molesters and rapists. *Law and Human Behavior, 21,* 2, 231–241.

Rice, M. E. & Harris, G. T. (1999, October). *A multi-site follow-up study of sex offenders: The predictive accuracy of risk prediction instruments.* Third Annual Research Day of the University of Toronto Forensic Psychiatry Program, Penetanguishene, Canada.

Rice, M. E. & Harris, G. T. (2002). Men who molest their sexually immature daughters: Is a special explanation required? *Journal of Abnormal Psychology, 111,* 329–339.

Rice, M. E. & Harris, G. T. (2003). The size and sign of treatment effects in sex offender therapy. In R. Prentky., E. Janus., M. Seto. & A.W. Burgess (eds.), *Understanding and Managing Sexually Coercive Behavior. Annals of the New York Academy of Science, 989,* 428–440.

Rice, M. E. & Harris, G. T. (2005). Comparing effect sizes in follow-up studies: ROC areas, Cohen's d, and r. *Law and Human Behavior, 29,* 5, 615–620.

Rice, M. E., Harris, G. T. & Cormier, C. (1992). Evaluations of a maximum security therapeutic community for psychopaths and other mentally disordered offenders. *Law and Human Behavior, 16,* 399–412.

Rice, M. E., Harris, G. T. & Quinsey, V. L. (1990). A follow-up of rapists assessed in a maximum-security psychiatric facility. *Journal of Interpersonal Violence, 5,* 435–448.

Rice, M. E., Harris, G. T. & Quinsey, V. L. (1996). Treatment for forensic patients. In B. D. Sales & S. A. Shah (eds.), *Mental Health and Law: Research, policy and services* (pp. 141–189). New York: Academic Press.

Rice, M. E., Quinsey, V. L. & Harris, G. T. (1991). Sexual recidivism among child molesters released from a maximum security psychiatric institution. *Journal of Consulting and Clinical Psychology, 59,* 381–386.

Richards, H. J., Casey, J. O. & Lucente, S. W. (2003). Psychopathy and treatment response in incarcerated female substance abusers. *Criminal Justice and Behavior, 30,* 251–276.

Roberts, C. F., Doren, D. M. & Thornton, D. (2002). Dimensions associated with assessments of sex offender recidivism risk. *Criminal Justice and Behavior, 29,* 596–589.

Robins, L. & Rutter, M. (1990). *Straight and Devious Pathways from Childhood to Adulthood.* Cambridge: Cambridge University Press.

Robinson, D. (1995). The impact of cognitive skills training on post-release recidivism among Canadian federal offenders. *Research Report No. R-41.* Correctional Research and Development, Correctional Service Canada. Available electronically from: http://www.csc-scc.gc.ca/text/rsrch/reports/r41/r41e. shtml

Rogers, C. M. & Terry, T. (1984). Clinical intervention with boy victims of sexual abuse. In I. R. Stuart., & J. G. Greer, (eds.), *Victims of Sexual Aggression: Men, women and children.* (91–103). New York: Van Nostrand Reinhold.

Rogers, C. R. (1961). *On Becoming a Person.* Boston, MA: Houghton-Mifflin.

Rogers, R. (2000). The uncritical acceptance of risk assessment in forensic practice. *Law and Human Behavior, 24,* 5, 595–605.

Rorty, R. (1989). *Contingency, Irony and Solidarity.* Cambridge: Cambridge University Press.

Ross, R. R. & Fabiano, E. A. (1985). *Time to Think: A cognitive model of delinquency prevention and offender rehabilitation.* Johnson City: TN: Institute of Social Sciences and Arts.

Rosenthal, R. (1991). *Meta-analytic Procedures for Social Research.* Newbury Park, CA: Sage.

Russell, D. E. H. (1991). Wife rape. In A. Parrot and L. Bechofer (eds.), *Acquaintance Rape: The hidden crime.* (pp. 129–139). New York: Wiley.

Rutter, M. (1987). Psychosocial resilience and protective mechanisms. *American Journal of Orthopsychiatry, 57,* 316–331.

Rutter, M. (1989). Pathways from child to adult life. *Journal of Child Psychology and Psychiatry, 30,* 23–54.

Salekin, R. T. (2002). Psychopathy and therapeutic pessimism: Clinical lore or clinical reality? *Clinical Psychology Review, 22,* 79–112.

Salekin, R. T., Rogers, R. & Sewell, K. W. (1996). A review and meta-analysis of the Psychopathy Checklist and the Psychopathy Checklist-Revised: Predictive validity of dangerousness. *Clinical Psychology: Science and Practice, 3,* 203–215.

Sarajen, S. (1996) *Women Who Sexually Abuse Children,* Chichester: Wiley.

Schiller, G. & Marques, J. (1999). *California actuarial risk assessment tables for rapists and child molesters (CARAT).* Presented at A. Salter Predicting Sexual Recidivism Conference. Honolulu, Hawaii, 1999.

Seager, J. A., Jellicoe, D. & Dhaliwal, G. K. (2004). Refusers, dropouts, and completers: Measuring sex offender treatment efficacy. *International Journal of Offender Therapy and Comparative Criminology, 48,* 600–612.

Seghorn, T. K., Prentky, R. A. & Boucher, R. J. (1987). Childhood sexual abuse in the lives of sexually aggressive offenders. *Journal of the American Academy of Child and Adolescent Psychiatry, 26,* 262–267.

Seligman, M. E. P. & Csikszentmihalyi, M. (2000). Positive psychology: An introduction. *American Psychologist, 55,* 5–14.

Serin, R. C., Mailloux, D. L. & Malcolm, P. B. (2001). Psychopathy, deviant sexual arousal, and recidivism among sexual offenders. *Journal of Interpersonal Violence, 16,* 234–246.

Seto, M. C. & Barbaree, H. E. (1999). Psychopathy, treatment behavior, and sex offender recidivism. *Journal of Interpersonal Violence, 14,* 1235–1248.

Seto, M. C., Barbaree, H. & Langton, C. (2002). How should we interpret behavior in treatment? Paper presented at the 21st Annual Conference for the Association for the Treatment of Sexual Abusers, Montreal, Canada, October 2002.

Seto, M. C., Cantor, J. M., & Blanchard, R. (2006). Child pornography offenses are a valid diagnostic indicator of pedophilia. *Journal of Abnormal Psychology, 115,* 610–615.

Seto, M. C. & Eke. A.W. (2005). Criminal histories and later offending of child pornography offenders. *Sexual Abuse: A Journal of Research and Treatment, 17,* 2, 201–210.

Seto, M. C., Maric, A. & Barbaree, H. E. (2001). The role of pornography in the etiology of sexual aggression. *Aggression and Violent Behavior, 6,* 35–53.

Shingler, J. & Mann, R. E. (2006). Collaboration in clinical work with sexual offenders: Treatment and risk assessment. In W. L. Marshall, Y. M. Fernandez, L. E. Marshall & G. A. Serran (eds.), *Sexual Offender Treatment: Controversial issues* (pp. 225–240). Chichester: Wiley.

Shover, N. (1996). *Great Pretenders: Pursuits and careers of persistent thieves.* Boulder, CO: Westview Press.

Silver, E. & Miller, L. L. (2002). A cautionary note on the use of actuarial risk assessment tools for social control. *Crime and Delinquency, 48,* 138–161.

Simourd, D. J. & Hoge, R. D. (2000). Criminal psychopathy: A risk and need perspective. *Criminal Justice and Behavior, 27,* 256–272.

Sjöstedt, G. & Långström, N. (2000). *Actuarial assessment of risk for criminal recidivism among sex offenders released from Swedish prisons 1993-1997.* Poster presented at the 19th Annual Conference of the Association for the Treatment of Sexual Abusers, San Diego, California, November 2000.

Sjöstedt, G. & Långström, N. (2002). Assessment of risk for criminal recidivism among rapists: A comparison of four different measures. *Psychology, Crime and Law, 8*, 25–40.

Skeem, J. L., Monahan, J. & Mulvey, E. P. (2002). Psychopathy, treatment involvement, and subsequent violence among civil psychiatric patients. *Law and Human Behavior, 26*, 577–603.

Skinner, B. F. (1938). *The Behavior of Organisms.* New York: Appleton-Century-Crofts.

Skinner, B. F. (1953). *Science and Human Behavior.* New York: Macmillan.

Smallbone, S. W. & Dadds, M. R. (1998). Childhood attachment and adult attachment in incarcerated adult male sex offenders. *Journal of Interpersonal Violence, 13*, 555–573.

Smith, P. & Waterman, M. (2004). Processing bias for sexual material: The Emotional Stroop and sexual offenders. *Sexual Abuse: A Journal of Research and Treatment, 16*, 163–171.

Snyder, C. R. & Lopez, J. S. (2006). *The Handbook of Positive Psychology.* Oxford: Oxford University Press.

Sreenivasan, S., Kirkish, P., Garrick, T., Weinberger, L. E. & Phenix, A. (2000). Actuarial risk assessment: A review of critical issues related to violence and sex-offender recidivism assessments. *The Journal of the American Academy of Psychiatry and the Law, 28*, 438–448.

Stalans, L. J. (2005). Adult sex offenders on community supervision: A review of recent assessment strategies and treatment. *Criminal Justice and Behavior, 31*, 564–608.

Steadman, H. J. (1987). How well can we predict violence in adults? A review of the literature and some commentary. In F. Dutile & C. Foust (eds.), *The Prediction of Criminal Violence* (pp. 5–19). Springflied, IL: Charles C. Thomas.

Stirpe, T. S., Wilson, R. J. & Long, C. (2001). Goal attainment scaling with sexual offenders: A measure of clinical impact at post-treatment and at community follow-up. *Sexual Abuse: A Journal of Research and Treatment, 13*, 65–77.

Sturmey, P. (1996). *Functional Analysis in Clinical Psychology.* Chichester: Wiley.

Sugarman, P., Dumughn, Saad, K., Hinder, S. & Bluglass, R. (1994). Dangerousness in exhibitionists. *Journal of Forensic Psychiatry, 5*, 287–296.

Szmukler, G. (2001). Violence risk prediction in practice. *British Journal of Psychiatry, 178*, 84–85.

Tayler, M. & Quayle, E. (2003). *Child Pornography: An Internet crime.* London: Routledge.

Templeman, T. L. & Wolversheim, J. P. (1979). A cognitive-behavioral approach to the treatment of psychopathy. *Psychotherapy: Theory, Research, and Practice, 16*, 132–139.

Terry, K. J. & Mitchell, E. W. (2001). Motivation and sex offender treatment efficacy: Leading a horse to water and making it drink? *International Journal of Offender Therapy and Comparative Criminology, 45*, 663–672.

Thomas, A. & Chess, S. (1977). *Temperament and Development.* New York: Brunner/Mazel.

Thomas, T. (1994). *The Police and Social Workers: The 2nd edition.* Aldershot, Hampshire: Ashgate Publishing Ltd.

Thomas, T. (2005). *Sex Crime: Sex offending and society (Second Edition).* Cullompton, Devon, UK. Willan Publishing.

Thompson, R. A. (1994). Emotional regulation: A theme in search of definition. In N. A. Fox (ed.), *The Development of Emotion Regulation: Biological and behavioral considerations* (pp. 25–52). Monographs of the Society for Research in Child Development, 59, Serial No. 240.

Thorndike, E. L. (1898). Animal intelligence: An experimental study of the associative processes in animals. *Psychological Review, 2*, 551–553.

Thornhill, R. & Palmer, C.T. (2000). *A Natural History of Rape: Biological bases of sexual coercion.* Boston, MA: MIT Press.

Thornton, D. (1997). *Structured Anchoedr Clinical Judgement Risk Assessment (SACJ):* Proceedings of the NOTA Conference, Brighton; September 1997.

Thornton, D. (1989). *Self-esteem Scale*. Unpublished manuscript. Available from David Thornton, the Sand Ridge Secure Treatment Center, 1111 North Road, PO Box 700, Mauston, WI 53948-0700, USA.

Thornton, D. (2002). Constructing and testing a framework for dynamic risk assessment. *Sexual Abuse: A Journal of Research and Treatment, 14*, 2, 139–153.

Thornton, D. (2006). Age and sexual recidivism: A variable connection. *Sexual Abuse: A Journal of Research and Treatment, 18*, 123–136.

Thornton, D. & Beech, A. R. (2002). *Integrating statistical and psychological factors through the structured risk assessment model*. Paper presented at the 21st Annual Research and Treatment Conference, Association of the Treatment of Sexual Abusers, Montreal, Canada, October 2002.

Thornton, D., Beech, A. R. & Marshall, W. L. (2004). Pre-treatment self-esteem and post-treatment sexual recidivism. *International Journal of Offender Therapy and Comparative Criminology, 48*, 587–599.

Thornton, D. & Doren, D. M. (2002). *How much safer are older offenders?* Presentation at the 21st Annual Conference of the Association for the Treatment of Sexual Abusers, Montreal, Canada, October 2002.

Thornton, D., Mann, R., Webster, S., Blud, L., Travers, R, Friendship, C. & Erikson, M. (2003). Distinguishing and combining risks for sexual and violent recidivism. In R. Prentky, E. Janus, M. Seto & A. W. Burgess (eds.), *Understanding and Managing Sexually Coercive Behavior*. Annals of the New York Academy of Sciences, 989, 225–235.

Thornton, D. & Travers, R. (1991). *A longitudinal study of the criminal behaviour of convicted sexual offenders*. Proceedings of the Prison Psychologists' Conference: HM Prison Service.

Tierney D. W. & McCabe, M. P. (2002). Motivation for behavior change among sex offenders: A review of the literature. *Clinical Psychology Review, 22*, 113–129.

Trecme, N., Fallon, B, MacLaurin, B. Daciuk, J., Felstiner, C. Black, T., Tommyr, L., Blackstock, C., Barter, K., Turcotte, D. & Cloutier, R. (2005). *Canadian Incidence Study of Reported Child Abuse and Neglect – 2003: Major Findings*. Canada: Minister of Public Works and Government Services.

Truesdell, D., McNeil, J. & Deschner, J. (1986). Incidence of wife abuse in incestuous families. *Social Work, 31*, 138–140.

Valentine, E. R. (1992). *Conceptual Issues in Psychology*. London: Routledge.

van der Kolk, B.A., McFarlane, A.C. & Weisaeth, L. (1996). *Traumatic Stress: The effects of overwhelming experience on mind, body, and society*. London: Guilford.

US Department of Justice (2006). *Juvenile offenders and victims: 2006 National Report*. Pittsburgh. National Center for Juvenile Justice, 3700 S, Water Street, Suite 200 Pittsburgh, PA 15203-2363.

Ward, T. (2001). A critique of Hall and Hirschman's Quadripartite Model of child sexual abuse. *Psychology, Crime and Law, 7*, 333–350.

Ward, T. (2002). Marshall and Barbaree's Integrated Theory of child sexual abuse: A critique. *Psychology, Crime and Law, 8*, 209–228.

Ward, T. & Beech, A. R. (2004). The etiology of risk: A preliminary model. *Sexual Abuse: A Journal of Research and Treatment, 16*, 271–284.

Ward, T. & Beech, A. R. (2006). An integrated theory of sex offending. *Aggression and Violent Behavior, 11*, 44–63.

Ward, T. & Gannon, T. (2006). Rehabilitation, etiology, and self-regulation: The comprehensive good lives model of treatment for sexual offenders. *Aggression and Violent Behavior, 11*, 77–94.

Ward, T. & Hudson, S. M. (1998a). The construction and development of theory in the sexual offending area: A meta-theoretical framework. *Sexual Abuse: A Journal of Research and Treatment, 10*, 47–63.

Ward, T. & Hudson, S. M. (1998b). A model of the relapse process in sexual offenders. *Journal of Interpersonal Violence*, *13*, 700–725.

Ward, T. & Hudson, S. M. (2001). Finkelhor's Precondition Model of child sexual abuse: A critique. *Psychology, Crime and Law*, *7*, 291–307.

Ward, T., Hudson, S. M., Johnston, L. & Marshall, W. L. (1997). Cognitive distortions in sex offenders: An integrative review. *Clinical Psychology Review*, *17*, 479–507.

Ward, T., Hudson, S. M. & Keenan, T. (1998). A self-regulation model of the sexual offence process. *Sexual Abuse: A Journal of Research and Treatment*, *10*, 141–157.

Ward, T., Louden, K., Hudson, S. M. & Marshall, W. L. (1995). A descriptive model of the offence chain for child molesters. *Journal of Interpersonal Violence*, *10*, 452–472.

Ward, T. & Mann, R. (2004). Good lives and the rehabilitation of offenders. A positivist approach to sex offender treatment. In P. A. Linley & S. Joseph (eds.), *Positive Psychology in Practice* (pp. 598–616). Chichester: Wiley.

Ward, T., Mann, R. & Gannon, T. A. (2007). The good lives model of rehabilitation: Clinical implications. *Aggression and Violent Behavior*, *12*, 2, 208–228.

Ward, T., Polaschek, D. & Beech, A. (2005). *Theories of Sexual Offending*. Chichester: Wiley.

Ward, T. & Siegert, R. J. (2002). Toward a comprehensive theory of child sexual abuse: A theory knitting perspective. *Psychology, Crime and Law*, *8*, 319–351.

Ward, T. & Stewart, C. A. (2003a). The treatment of sex offenders: Risk management and good lives. *Professional Psychology: Research and Practice*, *34*, 353–360.

Ward, T. & Stewart, C. A. (2003b). Criminogenic needs and human needs: A theoretical model. *Psychological, Crime and Law*, *9*, 125–143.

Ward, T., & Stewart, C. A. (2003c). The relationship between human needs and criminogenic needs. *Psychological, Crime and Law*, *9*, 219–224.

Ward, T., Yates, P. M. & Long, C. A. (2006). *The self-regulation model of the offence and relapse process: Volume 2: Treatment*. Victoria, BC, Canada: Pacific Psychological Associate Corporation.

Waterhouse, L. & Carnie, J. (1990). Investigating child sexual abuse: Towards inter-agency co-operation. *Adoption and Fostering*, *14*, 4, 7–12.

Watkins, B. & Bentovim, A. (1992). The sexual abuse of male children and adolescents: A review of current research, *Journal of Child Psychology and Psychiatry*, *33*, 1, 197–248.

Watson, J. B. & Rayner, R. (1920). Conditioned emotional reactions. *Journal of Experimental Psychology*, *3*, 1–14.

Webster, C. D., Douglas, K. S., Eaves, D. & Hart, S. D. (1997). *HCR-20: Assessing Risk for Violence (Version 2)*. Vancouver: Mental Health, Law and Policy Institute, Simon Fraser University.

Webster, S. D., Mann, R. E., Carter, A. J., Long, J., Milner, R. J., O'Brein, M. D., Wakeling, H. C. & Ray, N. L. (2006). Inter-rater reliability of dynamic risk assessment with sexual offenders. *Psychology, Crime and Law*, *12*, 439–452.

Webster, S. D., Mann, R. E., Thornton, D. & Wakeling, H. C. (2007). Further validation of the short self-esteem scale with sexual offenders. *Legal and Criminological Psychology*, *12*, 2, 207–216.

Weinrott, M. R. & Saylor, M. (1991). Self-report of crimes committed by sex offenders. *Journal of Interpersonal Violence*, *6*, 286–300.

Weiss, P. (1999). Assessment and Treatment of sex offenders in the Czech Republic and in Eastern Europe. *Journal of Interpersonal Violence*, *14*, 411–421.

West Midlands Police (2003). *Keeping Communities Safe: West Midlands Multi-Agency Public Protection Arrangements Annual Report 2002-03*. Birmingham: West Midlands Police.

Wilson, J. Q. & Hernstein, R. J. (1985). *Crime and Human Nature*. New York: Simon and Schuster.

Wilson, R. J., Huculak, B. & McWhinnie, A. (2002). Restorative justice innovations in Canada. *Behavioral Sciences and the Law, 20,* 363–380.

Windelband, W. (1904). *Theories in Logic.* New York: Philosophical Library.

Witt, P. H., DelRusso, J., Oppenheim, J. & Ferguson, G. (1996, Fall). Sex offender risk assessment and the law. *Journal of Psychiatry and Law,* 343–377.

Wood, R. M., Grossman, L. S., & Fichtner, C. G. (2000). Psychological assessment, treatment, and outcome with sex offenders. *Behavioral Sciences and the Law, 18,* 23–41.

Woodworth, M. & Porter, S. (2002). In cold blood: Characteristics of criminal homicides as a function of psychopathy. *Journal of Abnormal Psychology, 111,* 436–445.

World Health Organisation (2002). *World Report on Violence and Health.* Geneva: WHO.

World Health Organisation (2003). *Guidelines for Medico-Legal Care for Victims of Sexual Violence.* Geneva: WHO.

Worling, J. (2001). Personality based typology of adolescent male sexual offenders: Differences in recidivism rates, victim-selection characteristics, and personal victimisation histories. *Sexual Abuse: A Journal or Research and Treatment, 13,* 149–166.

Worling, J. & Curwen, T. (1998). *The Adolescent Sexual Offender project: A 10-years follow-up study.* Report on the SAFE-T Program, Thistletown Regional Centre for Children and Adolescents, Toronto, Canada: Ontario Ministry of Community and Social Services.

Worling, J. & Curwen, T. (2000). Adolescent sexual offender recidivism: Success of specialized treatment and implications for risk prediction. *Child Abuse and Neglect, 24,* 965–982.

Yates, F. J. & Stone, E. R. (1992). *The Risk Construct-risk Taking Behaviour* (pp. 1–25). Chichester: Wiley.

Zettle, R. D. (1990). Rule-governed behavior: A radical behavioral answer to the cognitive challenge. *The Psychological Record, 40,* 41–49.

Index

Lightning Source UK Ltd.
Milton Keynes UK
UKOW04f1940051216

289264UK00001B/15/P